Local Engagement with International Economic Law and Human Rights

Local Engagement with International Economic Law and Human Rights

Edited by

Ljiljana Biukovic

Associate Professor of Law, Peter A. Allard School of Law, University of British Columbia, Canada

Pitman B. Potter

Professor of Law, Peter A. Allard School of Law, University of British Columbia, Canada

Edward Elgar
PUBLISHING

Cheltenham, UK • Northampton, MA, USA

Published by
Edward Elgar Publishing Limited
The Lypiatts
15 Lansdown Road
Cheltenham
Glos GL50 2JA
UK

Edward Elgar Publishing, Inc.
William Pratt House
9 Dewey Court
Northampton
Massachusetts 01060
USA

A catalogue record for this book
is available from the British Library

Library of Congress Control Number: 2016962554

This book is available electronically in the **Elgar**online
Law subject collection
DOI 10.4337/9781785367199

MIX
Paper from
responsible sources
FSC
www.fsc.org
FSC® C013056

ISBN 978 1 78536 718 2 (cased)
ISBN 978 1 78536 719 9 (eBook)

Typeset by Servis Filmsetting Ltd, Stockport, Cheshire
Printed and bound in Great Britain by TJ International Ltd, Padstow

Contents

Contributors

Sarah Biddulph is Australian Research Council Future Fellow, and Director of the China Program at the Asian Law Centre and Professor in Melbourne Law School at University of Melbourne, Australia. Her research focuses on the Chinese legal system with a particular emphasis on legal policy, law making and enforcement as they affect the administration of justice in China. Her particular areas of research are contemporary Chinese administrative law, criminal procedure, labour, comparative law, and the law regulating social and economic rights. Her recent publications include: Sarah Biddulph, *Legal Reform and Administrative Detention Powers in China* (Cambridge: Cambridge University Press, 2007); Sarah Biddulph and Pip Nicholson (eds), *Examining Practice, Interrogating Theory: Comparative Legal Studies in Asia* (Leiden: Brill, 2008); Sarah Biddulph, Sean Cooney and Ying Zhu (eds), *Law and Fair Work in China: Making and Enforcing Labour Standards in the PRC* (Abingdon and New York: Routledge, 2013); Sarah Biddulph, Susan Trevaskes, Elis Nesossi and Flora Sapio (eds), *The Politics of Law and Stability in China* (Cheltenham: Edward Elgar, 2014); and Sarah Biddulph, *The Stability Imperative: Human Rights and Law in China* (Vancouver: UBC Press, 2015).

Ljiljana Biukovic is Associate Dean of Graduate Studies and Professional Programs and Associate Professor, Peter A. Allard School of Law at University of British Columbia, Vancouver, Canada. Her research interests are in the areas of international economic law and European Union integration. She publishes regularly on topics of legal transplantation of international norms and standards by national governments, the impact of regionalism on multilateral trade negotiations, mega-regional trade and investment agreements, and the development of the European Union. Her recent publications include: "Is There Policy Space for Human Rights in China's Trade and Investment Network?" in D. Drache and L. Jacobs, *Linking Global Trade and Human Rights: New Policy Space in Hard Economic Times* (New York: Cambridge University Press, 2014), "Transparency Issues in Negotiations of the Comprehensive Economic and Trade Agreement between Canada and the European Union" (2012) 39(1) *Legal Issues of Economic Integration* 93 and "International Law

Interrupted—A Case of Selective Adaptation" (2010) 60 *University of New Brunswick Law Journal* 161.

Erika Cedillo is a PhD Candidate at Peter A. Allard School of Law at University of British Columbia, Vancouver, Canada. Her research focuses on applying a pluralistic approach to the understanding of public policy in the public policy exception for the recognition and enforcement of international arbitral awards, using Mexico as a case study. Publications include Erika Cedillo (ed.), *Coordination of International Trade and Human Rights: Research Papers* (Institute of Asian Research, The University of British Columbia, 2012) and Erika Cedillo, Pitman B. Potter and Heather Gibb (eds), *Gender Equality Rights and Trade Regimes: Coordinating Compliance* (The North-South Institute and Asia Pacific Dispute Resolution Research, Faculty of Law, The University of British Columbia, 2012).

Thomas Cottier is Emeritus Professor of Law and Senior Research Fellow at World Trade Institute of University of Bern, Switzerland and Adjunct Professor of Law at the Faculty of Law at the University of Ottawa, Canada. His research interests are international and European economic law, intellectual property rights and multilayered governance. He is former Managing Director of the World Trade Institute and the Institute of European and International Economic Law, and former director of the national research programme on trade law and policy (NCCR Trade Regulation: From Fragmentation to Coherence) located at the WTI. He has over 250 publications on a wide range of trade and international law issues. His recent publications include "Addressing climate change under preferential trade agreements: Towards alignment of carbon standards under the Transatlantic Trade and Investment Partnership" (2015) 35 *Global Environmental Change* 514; *Equitable Principles of Maritime Boundary Delimitation: The Quest for Distributive Justice in International Law* (Cambridge: Cambridge University Press, 2015); and "The Common Law of International Trade and the Future of the World Trade Organization" (2015) 18 *Journal of International Economic Law* 3.

Moshe Hirsch is the Maria Von Hofmannsthal Chair in International Law and Professor of Law in the Faculty of Law and Department of International Relations at Hebrew University of Jerusalem, Jerusalem, Israel. He specializes in international economic law and international legal theory. His recent publications include Moshe Hirsch, *Invitation to the Sociology of International Law* (Oxford: Oxford University Press, 2015); Melaku Desta and Moshe Hirsch, "The African Countries in the World Trading System: International Trade, Domestic Institutions and the Role of International Law" (2012) 61 *International & Comparative Law Quarterly* 127; Moshe Hirsch, "Interactions between Investment and Non-Investment Obligations in International Investment Law", in Peter Muchlinski, Federico Ortino and Christoph Schreuer, eds, *Oxford Handbook of International Law on Foreign Investment* (Oxford: Oxford University Press, 2008); Moshe Hirsch, "Developing Countries", in Rüdiger Wolfrum, ed., *Max Planck Encyclopedia of Public International Law* (Oxford: Oxford University Press, 2008); and Moshe Hirsch, "The Sociology of International Economic Law" (2008) 19 *European Journal of International Law* 277.

Mor Mitrani is a Post-Doctoral Fellow in the Berlin-Jerusalem Joint Post-Doctoral Program. She is currently an associate Post-Doctoral Fellow in the KFG "Transformative Power of Europe" at Freie Universtät Berlin, Germany and an associate Post-Doctoral Fellow in the Davis Institute for International Relations at the Hebrew University of Jerusalem, Israel.

Ernst-Ulrich Petersmann is Emeritus Professor and former Head of the Department of Law at the European University Institute, Florence, Italy. He specializes in international and European law, notably economic, environmental, constitutional and human rights law. He is the (co)-author of 30 books and more than 300 articles and book contributions. During 40 years, he has combined academic teaching at numerous universities in Europe, the United States and Asian countries with work as legal advisor in the German Ministry of Economic Affairs, German representative in UN and European institutions, legal advisor/consultant in the GATT and WTO Secretariats, and secretary, member or chairman of numerous GATT/WTO dispute settlement panels. He was chairman of the international trade law committee of the International Law Association (1999–2014) and participates actively in many other academic associations like the European Society of International Law.

Pitman B. Potter is Professor of Law at Peter A. Allard School of Law at University of British Columbia, Vancouver, Canada. His teaching and research focus on PRC and Taiwan law and policy in the areas of foreign trade and investment, dispute resolution, property law, contracts, business regulation, and human rights. Dr Potter has published many books, including most recently *Assessing Treaty Performance in China: Trade and Human Rights* (Vancouver: UBC Press, 2014) and *China's Legal System* (Cambridge: Polity Press, 2013). He has published over one hundred articles and essays. Prior to his retirement from law practice in 2016, Dr Potter practiced law in British Columbia, Washington State and California for more than 30 years and was a consultant to the Canadian national law firm of Borden, Ladner, Gervais LLP. Dr Potter has served on the boards of directors for several public institutions, including the Asia Pacific Foundation of Canada where he also served as a Senior Fellow. He chaired the APFC Taskforce Report, "Advancing Canada's Engagement with Asia on Human Rights: Integrating Business and Human Rights" (2013). Dr Potter is ordained a Deacon in the Anglican Church of Canada (Diocese of New Westminster). He is a Fellow of the Royal Society of Canada.

Naayeli E. Ramírez-Espinosa is a postdoctoral fellow at Universidad Veracruzana in Mexico. She is currently working and collaborating with indigenous communities, non-governmental organizations (NGOs) and the Intercultural University of Veracruz with the support of a Mexican Council of Science and Technology (CONACyT) Fellowship on a project entitled "The adoption of Totonac, Purépecha and Mayan law in the processes of consultation and agreement in Mexico" and her most recent publications are on this topic. Her current teaching and research focuses on intercultural legal education, community participatory research, indigenous peoples' law, the duty to consult, and judicial interpretation of human rights. She has taught and done research on conflict and law in Latin America, transnational law and sociology of law. Aside from her research and academic activities, she has practised law in Mexico since 2001 and is currently also assisting communities, NGOs and collectives as a legal consultant.

Lisa Toohey is Professor of Law and Deputy Dean (Academic) at the University of Newcastle, Australia. She teaches and researches in the fields of international trade law and dispute resolution. She is a member of the Executive Council of the Society of International Economic Law, a member of the Asian WTO Research Network, and a founding member of the University of New South Wales' China International Business and Economic Law (CIBEL) Initiative. Prior to academia, she practised commercial law in Australia at Corrs Chambers Westgarth and in Vietnam at Baker & McKenzie. Her recent publications include *China in the International Economic Order: New Directions and Changing Paradigms* (Cambridge: Cambridge University Press, 2015).

Valentina Vadi is Professor of International Economic Law at Lancaster University, United Kingdom. She was formerly a Reader in International Business Law at the same University (2013–2015), an Emile Noël Fellow at the Jean Monnet Centre for International and Regional Economic Law at New York University (2013–2014), and a Marie Curie Postdoctoral Fellow at Maastricht University (2011–2013). She also lectured at Hasselt

University (Belgium), the University of Rome III (Italy), the China EU School of Law (PRC) and Maastricht University (The Netherlands). She has published more than 80 articles in various areas of public international law in journals, including the *Vanderbilt Journal of Transnational Law*, the *Stanford Journal of International Law*, the *Columbia Human Rights Review*, the *European Journal of International Law*, the *Journal of International Economic Law* and others. Publications include Valentina Vadi and Hildegard Schneider (eds), *Art, Cultural Heritage and the Market: Legal and Ethical Issues* (Springer: Heidelberg 2014), and Valentina Vadi and Bruno De Witte (eds), *Culture and International Economic Law* (Abingdon, Routledge: 2015). She is the author of *Public Health in International Investment Law and Arbitration* (Abingdon: Routledge, 2012), *Cultural Heritage in International Investment Law and Arbitration* (Cambridge: Cambridge University Press, 2014) and *Analogies in International Investment Law and Arbitration* (Cambridge: Cambridge University Press, 2016).

Introduction

Ljiljana Biukovic and Pitman B. Potter

Managing the effects of trade policy on local human rights conditions is a critical challenge for the world today. While there is an emerging recognition of the need to balance international trade policy with human rights protection, empirical research and policy analysis are lacking.[1] In response, this book aims to explore the socio-legal dimension of the interaction between international economic law and human rights, and particularly the relationships between local arrangements and international legal regulations/rules. International economic law and human rights represent two branches of international law that have been rapidly evolving and expanding in the recent decades. This ongoing expansion raises many intriguing questions about the interplay between these two spheres of modern international law. The present study aims to shed light on socio-legal dimensions of the inter-relationships between trade and human rights, and particularly the interaction between international legal rules and the local context in which they are interpreted and implemented.

Coordination of trade and human rights compliance has been hampered by normative and organizational factors. From a normative perspective, the lack of consensus over the meaning and purpose of trade and human rights goals has often undermined local efforts at coordination.[2] As well, compliance with international trade standards tends to privilege consumption,[3] local business models[4] and reliance on financial and

---

[1] John H. Jackson, "Reflections on the Possible Research Agenda for Exploring the Relationship between Human Rights Norms and International Trade Rules" in Frederick M. Abbot, Christian Breining-Kaufmann and Thomas Cottier, eds, *International Trade and Human Rights: Foundations and Conceptual Issues* (Ann Arbor: University of Michigan Press, 2006), pp. 19–28.

[2] Henry J. Steiner, Philip Alston and Ryan Goodman, *International Human Rights in Context: Law, Politics, Morals*, 3rd ed. (Oxford: Oxford University Press, 2008), Sections 3B and 4B, pp. 160–74 and 280–93, respectively.

[3] Jeffrey Barber, "Production, Consumption, and the World Summit on Sustainable Development" (2003) 5 Environment, Development and Sustainability 63.

[4] Ian Barney, "Business, community development and sustainable livelihoods approaches" (2003) 38:3 Community Development Journal 255.

regulatory incentives for private behavior,[5] which frequently are detrimental to enforcement of local human rights standards and policies. International discourses on private property and trade liberalization also work to limit the range of approaches available locally to promote human rights.[6] Conversely, human rights discourses often tend to confront the norms and institutions of international trade as obstacles rather than potential contributors to human rights conditions. Achieving trade goals of efficiency, economic growth and private property rights is seen to conflict with enforcement of human rights standards in areas of both civil and political rights and economic, social and cultural rights.[7] Coordinating local performance of international trade and human rights standards has also been difficult for institutional and operational reasons, as officials and specialists who manage local interpretation and implementation in these discourses often have few opportunities or incentives for collaboration. All of these factors contribute to inhibiting development of alternative approaches that might support coordinated performance of both trade and human rights standards.

In an effort to address these issues and offer policy solutions, a major international research project on "Coordinating Performance with International Trade and Human Rights Standards in Comparative Perspective" was launched in 2009 at the University of British Columbia with the support of the Major Collaborative Research Initiative (MCRI) Program of the Social Sciences and Humanities Research Council (SSHRC) of Canada. Under the direction of Dr Pitman B. Potter, the project involves more than 50 academic and policy specialists from more than a dozen universities and research institutes in North America, Europe, Australia and Asia, working collaboratively to explore the dynamic relationships among global trade and human rights policies and practices.

As part of our Coordinated Performance project, the current volume offers a collection of essays presented at a session on "Mapping the Impact

---

[5] Bob Frame and Rhys Taylor, "Partnerships for Sustainability: Effective Practice?" (2005) 10:3 Local Environment 275; Douglas A. Kysar, "Sustainable Development and Private Global Governance" (2005) 83 Tex L Rev 2109.

[6] Ernst-Ulrich Petersmann, "Human Rights and International Trade Law: Defining and Connecting the Two Fields" in Thomas Cottier, Joost Pauwelyn and Elisabeth Burgi, eds, *Human Rights and International Trade* (Oxford: Oxford University Press, 2005) 29.

[7] See Walter Carlsnaes, Thomas Risse, Beth A. Simmons, eds, *Handbook of International Relations* (London: Sage Publications, 2002), pp. 518–21; Ross E. Burkhart, "The Capitalist Political Economy and Human Rights: Cross-National Evidence" (2002) 39 Soc. Sci. Jour. 155.

of International Trade and Human Rights on Local Practice" (July 2014) at the International Institute for the Sociology of Law in Oñati, Spain. The essays contribute to socio-legal studies by illuminating the role of norms and operational conditions for coordination of international economic law and local human rights performance. The conceptual orientation of the collected essays span two prominent discourses on international law development: (a) fragmentation of diverse rules of international law; and (b) convergence through constitutionalization of international law.[8] The authors examined global regulation and the impacts of international organizations on domestic law of states by focusing on a variety of modes of interaction of global norms and local practice. The resulting collection of essays presented here offers conceptual approaches and operational policy methods for coordinating local performance of international trade and human rights standards in light of the challenges balancing regimes of fragmentation and convergence in international law.

I. THE DILEMMA OF LOCAL PERFORMANCE: NORMS AND OPERATIONS

The fact that states agree to adopt international rules and practices does not mean that they have reached consensus on normative underpinnings of these adopted practices and rules or their practical application. The level of compliance with international rules ultimately depends on an understanding of differences between local and non-local norms, on the

[8] For example, Ernst-Ulrich Petersmann, *State Sovereignty, Popular Sovereignty and Individual Sovereignty: from Constitutional Nationalism to Multilevel Constitutionalism in International Economic Law?* (European University Institute – Law Working Papers, 2006), available at http://hdl.handle.net/1814/6446 (accessed 3 January 2017); Ernst-Ulrich Petersmann, "Multilevel Judicial Governance of International Trade Requires a Common Conception of Rule of Law and Justice" (2007) 10:3 J Int'l Econ L 529; Makau W. Mutua and Robert L. Howse, "Protecting Human Rights in a Global Economy: Challenges for the World Trade Organization" (2000) Human Rights in Development Yearbook 1999/2000 The Millennium Edition 51; Robert Howse and Kalypso Nicolaidis, "Legitimacy through 'Higher Law'? Why Constitutionalizing the WTO is a Step Too Far" in Thomas Cottier and Petros C. Mavroidis, eds, *The Role of the Judge in International Trade Regulation: Experience and Lessons for the WTO* (Ann Arbor: University of Michigan Press, 2003) 307; Cottier, Pauwelyn and Elisabeth Burgi, eds, *Human Rights and International Trade* (Oxford: Oxford University Press, 2006); Harold H. Koh, "Why Do Nations Obey International Law?" (1997) 106:8 Yale LJ 2599; Jutta Brunnee and Stephen J. Toope, *Legitimacy and Legality in International Law* (Cambridge: Cambridge University Press, 2010).

degree of support from local communities and on the extent to which international standards are complementary with local norms.[9] In addition, operational dynamics of local treaty performance involve matters of institutional capacity reflecting the impact of local socio-economic and political conditions on local performance.

By combining normative and operational perspectives, the essays presented in this volume reflect the application of socio-legal scholarship to issues of local treaty compliance and the coordination of trade and human rights performance. When legal forms such as treaties and statutes derive content and legitimacy from socio-cultural norms, legal performance operates at the intersection of law and society. When legal operations involve operational matters of institutional capacity, the interplay between legal and socio-economic and political conditions comes into sharp relief. These normative and operational perspectives in turn support policy solutions on coordination of trade and human rights performance that previously may have been out of reach. The challenge of coordinating performance of trade and human rights standards remains, but can be resolved through attention to the norms and operations of treaty behavior.

Understanding the potential for coordinating local performance of international trade and human rights standards necessarily involves engaging with local conditions, cultures and perspectives – what Clifford Geertz termed "local knowledge".[10] This has particular relevance in Asia, where commitments to trade liberalization have not often been coupled with attention to strengthening human rights protection. By building better understanding of the potential for coordinated performance of international trade and human rights standards in Asia, we hope to lay the foundation for policy responses on trade development and human rights protection in a significant region of the world. Understanding the potential for unifying contending policy and political constituencies associated with trade and human rights in Asia can also help to overcome competition for influence and resources among these constituencies that can be counterproductive to efforts to find common purpose and build cooperation domestically and internationally. Such an approach would strengthen the ability of economies in Asia to respond to different kinds of trade and human rights compliance challenges.

---

[9] Pitman B. Potter, *Assessing Treaty Performance in China: Trade and Human Rights* (Vancouver: UBC Press, 2014).

[10] Clifford Geertz, *Local Knowledge: Further Essays in Interpretive Anthropology* (New York: Basic Books, 1983).

The common thread of the chapters in this volume involves the application of socio-legal paradigms to build knowledge and policy support for coordinating local performance of international trade and human rights standards in ways that are mutually sustaining rather than conflicting. While some work has already been done on the relationships between trade policy and human rights, most of these focus on the relationship between institutions and norms at the international level.[11] By contrast and in an effort to build on existing efforts, this volume focuses on coordinating performance of international trade and human rights standards in light of local normative and operational conditions.

A. Part I: Re-imagining Local Engagement with International Law

Proceeding from an appreciation of the importance of local knowledge, the contributors focus primarily on local conditions for coordinating trade and human rights performance. By combining normative and institutional analysis, the chapters in Part I of the volume identify key challenges in coordinating local performance of international trade and human rights standards while setting a foundation for the discussion that follows. Thus, the volume opens with an institutional overview examining issues of interaction among international legal regimes. These chapters discuss theories and methodologies as frameworks within which many of the dilemmas of coordinating local performance of international standards on trade and human rights were examined.

Thomas Cottier's chapter "International trade, human rights and policy space" explores the implications of a multilevel governance doctrine for the local protection of human rights. Cottier focuses on the concept of public policy as a component of regulatory theory that facilitates the allocation of regulatory powers between different layers of governance, international and domestic included, which share fundamental values, including human rights, non-discrimination and the rule of law. He explains that policy space also facilitates the appropriate allocation of powers among different institutions on the layers of governance that are involved in the interpretation and application of laws at both international and national levels. Cottier concludes that trade regulation and human rights norms need to be interpreted together and suggests how the protection of different rights can be allocated to different levels of governance. In his opinion, the effective protection of human rights does not necessarily

---

[11] Abbot, Breining-Kaufmann and Cottier, eds, (note 1 above); Cottier, Pauwelyn and Burgi, eds, (note 11 above).

need more domestic policy space; on the contrary, it may need stronger international cooperation in enforcing international trade law.

In "Cosmopolitan constitutionalism: linking local engagement with international economic law and human rights" Ernst-Ulrich Petersmann presents a range of normative and operational dilemmas that continue to pose obstacles for coordinated compliance. He discusses the controversies regarding Hobbesian claims for "policy space" in the context of human rights obligations of all United Nations member states. Petersmann focuses on the effects of intergovernmental "management" and power politics in undermining processes of constitutional democracy and points to the need for greater accountability. The chapter emphasizes the importance of further developing "cosmopolitan constitutionalism" empowering citizens and civil society to hold limited "constituted powers" for multilevel governance of international public goods (in the broader sense of *res publica*) in a globalizing world.

B. Part II: Structural Aspects of Trade and Investment

Following discussion of conceptual issues of multilevel governance and constitutionalism, Part II of the volume considers structural dimensions of international standards and policy. It situates modalities of local performance within specific contexts of the interplay between global and local conditions in several policy areas such as anti-dumping, transparency, foreign direct investment and government regulation. These chapters illustrate how the structures and policy dynamics of international trade and investment affect local policy arrangements in the context of existing international laws and standards.

Ljiljana Biukovic's chapter, "Transparency evolution: more than the right to know", examines the ways in which trade norms associated with the General Agreement on Tariffs and Trade have continued to evolve in response to local conditions and interpretation. In particular, Biukovic examines the ways in which the principle of transparency as a fundamental pillar of the rule of law is internalized through local practices of individuals and various interest groups (including local governments) in the process of their performance of international treaty obligations. She argues that adherence to the principle of transparency has a spillover effect on local practice beyond mere compliance with international trade rules and provides opportunities for a broad range of local interest groups to challenge governments' development loan arrangements.

Naayeli Ramírez–Espinosa's chapter, "Challenging an investment agreement in Canada: Hupacasath First Nation's application for judicial review against the CCFIPPA", focuses even more closely on the interaction between the global and the local through her paper on the Hupacasath First Nation's legal challenge to the 2012 China-Canada Foreign Investment Promotion and Protection Agreement (CCFIPPA). The chapter examines questions around indigenous peoples' self-government and their right to be consulted and accommodated under the constitutional framework in Canada, and the impacts on local compliance with the CCFIPPA treaty. The chapter concludes that due to the current lack of channels for communication and negotiation with federal and provincial governments, indigenous peoples are often the last to learn of the interests of investors to exploit resources in their territories.

Finally, Erika Cedillo's chapter, "The impact of Mexico's 2011 human rights constitutional amendment on arbitral practice: a view from local actors", focuses specifically on human rights standards as a factor in Mexico's policy responses to enforcement of arbitral awards. The chapter focuses on the legal framework and the structural changes that Mexico has set up for the protection of human rights and how local actors perceived its potential effects on arbitration practice and Mexico's status as a pro-arbitration jurisdiction. Cedillo analyzes responses as indicators of legal practitioners' understanding of the concept of public policy. She suggests that the 2011 human rights-related constitutional amendments could affect the way in which judges decide on the enforcement of foreign arbitral awards in Mexico.

C. Part III: The Impact of Communities and Local Culture

The chapters in Part III examine the effects of local normative conditions on coordination of international trade and human rights performance – suggesting that culture generally and legal culture in particular play an important role. Reflecting on social construction of international trade and human rights law, the chapters in this part provide a close examination of the contingencies of local culture and perspective in the implementation of international standards. For, with all its hegemonic features, the international system must still confront the challenges of local performance.

Mor Mitrani argues that the attempt to explain the intersection between local and international practices requires depicting what is the realm of international practices. Her chapter, "Demarcating the international community: where do international practices come from?", examines the historical, legal and political factors affecting the potential for international community. Despite the fact that scholars, practitioners and international political leaders have been regularly using the term "international community", it is not clear how each of these interpretative groups are perceiving the concept and how the concept is constructed by states. The chapter therefore looks through four possible ontologies for the international community: historical, legal, political and discursive, and argues that it is appropriate to use the epistemological method to determine the meaning of the concept as "constructed by states and through inter-state discourse".

Valentina Vadi's chapter examines how economic globalization interacts with cultural diversity. In "Local communities, cultural heritage and international economic law", the author argues that economic globalization can promote as well as jeopardize cultural diversity. She suggests that economic globalization has stimulated an intense global debate among states regarding the promotion of cultural diversity. The chapter first investigates how international economic law governs cultural diversity. Finally, it proposes legal methods to reconcile different values promoted by international trade and investment regimes, on the one hand, and the international human rights regime, on the other, and proposes the adoption of amendments to the existing body of international economic law.

Moshe Hirsch looks at trade and human rights policies as indicators of the EU's identity. In his chapter, "Identity matters: the enforcement of global human rights treaties by European Union's trade instruments", Hirsch argues that there is a correlation between social identity of a nation/state and the enforcement and compliance with international law. He focuses on the EU's use of human rights conditionality, included in its trade agreements with third countries, as an external trade instrument for the promotion of human rights worldwide. This EU policy is significantly motivated by the EU identity, and it is expected to affect the identity of states targeted. The chapter argues that the use of a social identity analysis of the EU trade and human rights policies offers important practical recommendations that may enhance the prospects of compliance with the EU measures with international law.

Lisa Toohey's chapter, "Observing the small gestures: human rights vectors in the Vietnamese trade law environment", looks at the nexus between trade law and human rights through the case study of human rights lawyers in Vietnam. Since international integration under its open door (*đổimới*) policy of the 1980s, Vietnam has remained a subject of substantial and broad-ranging human rights criticism. Toohey suggests that the Asian region provides an interesting context for a study of interpretative communities because of the fact that regional integration has been driven by local economic imperatives that often lead to disregard of human rights dimensions of international trade law. Yet, the chapter argues that international economic integration can be responsive to human rights standards if human rights lawyers conceive and operationalize international economic law in ways that combine human rights discourse with the trade practice.

D. Part IV: Dilemmas of Local Performance: The Case of China

The final section of the volume presents two chapters on the People's Republic of China (PRC), as case studies on coordination of local performance of trade and human rights standards. China offers a compelling case study for understanding local treaty performance and suggests intriguing possibilities for coordinating local performance of international trade and human rights standards. Moving from the "what" and the "how" of treaty performance in China – much of which is well known – to the "why" is an essential step. Thus, although the circumstances of China's accession to international trade and human rights treaties are widely discussed, our understanding of the reasons affecting China's performance of international trade and human rights standards remains imperfect. The two chapters in this section offer important insights in this regard.

In "Coordinating human rights and trade policy in China: the case of environmental protection", Pitman Potter examines the relationships between China's environmental protection regime and performance of international trade standards, and suggests possibilities for improvement. Noting that China's longstanding environmental challenges and the legal regime established to resolve them have affected trade policy performance in areas of subsidies, discriminatory enforcement and food safety, Potter suggests that coordinating normative and operational dimensions of environmental performance locally may improve trade policy performance internationally. Drawing on paradigms of "Selective Adaptation" and "Institutional Capacity" from previous work,[12] Potter explores possibilities for coordinating China's performance of international trade and environmental standards through mechanisms of corporate social responsibility.

In "Structuring China's engagement with international human rights: the case of wage protection law and practice", Sarah Biddulph examines labor rights and the PRC government's policy imperative of maintaining stability as a precondition for export-led economic growth, and highlights contradictions between trade liberalization and protection of human rights at the local level. Enjoyment of social and economic rights is a core promise of the Chinese Party-state to its people that follows principles of the right to development. But beyond the rhetoric, what policies and

---

12 Potter, (note 15 above).

attributes of governance affect the definition and implementation of social and economic rights? The chapter advances the argument that the definition, modes of implementation and responses to citizen demands to respect these rights in domestic law and policy are all shaped by the Chinese Party-state's preoccupation with social stability. Biddulph explores the multiple and shifting ways in which stability imperatives affect the definition and implementation of social and economic rights, with particular attention to labor rights. She considers the ways in which the maintenance of social stability produces distinctive modes of governance of rights and rights claims.

Through conceptual and structural analysis coupled with local analysis and a China-focused case study, this volume aims to provide insights on the dilemma of local performance of international standards on trade and human rights. Through the perspective of "Coordinated Performance", the volume suggests new approaches to government policies on trade development and human rights protection. We hope that readers of this volume will appreciate both the substantive excellence of the research presented and the complexity and acute challenges that face policy efforts to coordinate compliance with international trade and human rights standards.

The research upon which this volume is based was made possible by support from the Major Collaborative Research Initiatives (MCRI) program of the Social Sciences and Humanities Research Council (SSHRC) of Canada, for which the editors are deeply grateful. We would also like to thank the Oñati International Institute for Sociology and Law for their support. The papers herein contain original research inspired by the theme of "Coordinating Performance of International Trade and Human Rights Standards" that informs our broader multi-year SSHRC/MCRI research project and was developed prior to the presentations at the Oñati Institute. Many students at Peter A. Allard School of Law contributed significantly to the success of this project. We would like to thank in particular Erika Cedillo, Matthew Neckelmann, Amy Lai, Liu Yue and Naayeli Ramírez-Espinosa for their research support. We would also like to thank MCRI Project Manager, Rozalia Mate, for her invaluable assistance throughout the course of this project.

Ljiljana Biukovic and Pitman B. Potter
Vancouver, BC
21 February 2017

PART I

Re-imagining local engagement with international law

1. International trade, human rights and policy space

Thomas Cottier

I. THE CALL FOR POLICY SPACE

The call for domestic policy space characterises recent debates on trade and investment in international economic law. In the wake of globalization, the creation of the World Trade Organization (WTO) and a number of new agreements, critics deplore the loss of policy space in domestic law and on national levels, in particular in developing countries.[1] Governments, it is argued, are no longer able to pursue appropriate policies and are unduly restrained by international economic law in the pursuit of development and welfare and the realization of human rights. Trade liberalization is felt to be at the expense of jobs, a major cause of unemployment at home and an ever-increasing disparity of incomes. Moreover, governments are felt to be restrained from implementing appropriate food standards, and consumers are obliged to accept products, which domestically they do not allow, such as GMOs. Investment protection is felt to unduly restrict options to protect the livelihood of people affected. Intellectual property

---

[1] See for example: Kevin P. Gallagher, ed., *Putting Development First: The Importance of Policy Space in the WTO and International Financial Institutions* (Chicago: The University of Chicago Press, 2005); P. Sai-wing Ho, "Arguing for Policy Space to Promote Development: Prebisch, Myrdal, and Singer" (2008) 42:2 Journal of Economic Issues 509; Shahrukh Rafi Khan, "WTO, IMF and the Closing of Development Policy Space for Low-Income Countries: A Call for Neo-Developmentalism" (2007) 28:6 Third World Quarterly 1073; Paul Alexander Haslam, "The Firm Rules: Multinational Corporations, Policy Space and Neoliberalism" (2007) 28:6 Third World Quarterly 1167; on trade regulation in particular see Bernard Hoekman, "Operationalizing the Concept of Policy Space in the WTO: Beyond Special and Differential Treatment" (2005) 8:2 Journal of International Economic Law 405; Kevin P. Gallagher, "Understanding Developing Country Resistance to the Doha Round" (2008) 15:1 Review of International Political Economy 62; Steven Bernstein and Erin Hannah, "Non-State Global Standard Setting and the WTO: Legitimacy and the Need for Regulatory Space" (2008) 11:3 Journal of International Economic Law 575.

standards are considered to be excessively imposing restrictions on regulation by international economic law, hindering development and access to essential goods. These arguments not only exist in relations between developing countries, emerging economies and industrialised countries; they equally dominate current debates among industrialised countries having social safety nets. The Comprehensive Economic and Trade Agreement (CETA) between Canada and the European Union is the subject of criticism as much as the currently negotiated Transatlantic Trade and Investment Partnership Agreement (TTIP) between the European Union (EU) and the United States.[2]

It would seem that trade liberalization as such has reached an end, facing the call for more domestic policy space and a less intrusive framework of international law than those based upon the WTO and the plus elements in the newer generation of preferential trade and investment agreements currently dominating international treaty making in the field. Conceptually, the motives for more domestic policy space are manifold and are voiced from different quarters of the political spectrum. They are nurtured by concern for protecting human rights. They are motivated by self-determination and democracy. They are motivated by cultural diversity, which globalization and its legal framework threaten to undermine. They are motivated by environmental concerns and the call for sustainable development, and less dependence on global markets and globalization. They are also motivated by national conservative agendas, populism exploiting fears of mass immigration, loss of national identity and partly by rent-seeking protectionism. A very mixed composition of motives adds up and may bring traditional modes of trade liberalization to a halt in coming years. This may show in cancelling existing agreements or refraining from entering into new ones.[3] It may show in renegotiating existing agreements and provisions. It may show in refraining from policies of mutual recognition and harmonization of product and process standards.

While these efforts play out in political debates and decision-making, the pursuit of policy space also takes more nuanced forms by means of reinterpreting existing provisions in the process of case law-making. Interpretation of existing law amounts to the main function of human

---

[2] Tereza Novotná, Mario Telò and Jean-Frédéric Morin, eds, *The Politics of Transatlantic Trade Negotiations: TTIP in a Globalized World* (Farnham: Ashgate, 2015).

[3] This chapter is written in times witnessing ardent debates over whether Britain should leave the EU or whether Europe and the EU should enter the Transatlantic Trade and Investment Partnership Agreement (TTIP).

rights courts, investment arbitration and WTO panels and the Appellate Body. Whether or not, these bodies infringe upon domestic prerogatives is a constant theme in the political discourse. All these developments can be analysed in terms of efforts to increase domestic policy space and to restrain the impact of public international law.

Policy space thus is mainly employed with the understanding of a lack of or insufficient levels of policy space granted to domestic law. It is expressed in terms of seeking enhanced exceptions, special and differential treatment or the development of what I called graduation, that is linking legal obligations incurred to economic indicators and thresholds.[4]

The issue whether there is too much policy space allocated to domestic law has hardly ever been raised and addressed in such terms. This is true for human rights, labour standards, investment and trade regulations alike. In political discourse, policy space is a one-way street. It campaigns for less international law and lower levels of intrusiveness. Policy space, however, looks somewhat different if we look at it from the point of view of regulatory theory and the doctrine of multilevel governance.

II. MULTILEVEL GOVERNANCE AND POLICY SPACE

The relationship between international law and domestic law is increasingly perceived as a matter of multilevel governance.[5] This is the case both in analytical terms, looking at existing interdependencies, as well as in normative terms, developing a new constitutional framework to harness the process of globalization and enhanced interdependence. Building upon the traditions of federalism and the interplay of federal, sub-federal and local levels, regional law (EU law or, to a lesser extent, the North American Free Trade Agreement (NAFTA)) and global international law add additional layers of governance, which supplement existing and traditional structures of domestic law. While the formal distinction of domestic and international law remains, these additional layers share characteristics with domestic layers of constitutionalism, liberalism and

4 Thomas Cottier, "From Progressive Liberalization to Progressive Regulation in WTO Law" (2006) 9:4 Journal of International Economic Law 779.

5 See generally Simona Piattoni, *The Theory of Multi-level Governance: Conceptual, Empirical, and Normative Challenges* (Oxford: Oxford University Press, 2010). From a trade policy angle see Christian Joerges and Ernst-Ulrich Petersmann, eds, *Constitutionalism, Multilevel Trade Governance and International Economic Law* (Oxford: Hart Publishing, 2011).

the welfare state. They share fundamental values, in particular human rights, non-discrimination and general principles of law.[6] In the case of the EU as a new layer, a legal system, *sui generis*, emerged that also aspires to respond to the precepts of democratic governance. On the global level, especially the United Nations (UN) and other international organizations, in particular the Bretton Woods Institutions and the WTO, instruments mainly controlled by domestic executive powers draw their legitimacy from outputs and directions defined by democratically elected governments. Multilevel governance, for federalist countries in the tradition of democratic constitutionalism, amounts to what I called a "Five Storey House".[7] Vertical checks and balances of power operate among the different levels of governance, offsetting state failures and allocating regulatory powers ideally suitable to produce appropriate public goods at appropriate levels of governance – local, sub-federal, federal, regional or global. It is the essence of what the late John Jackson called "Sovereignty-modern".[8] It is essentially about allocation of regulatory and interpretive powers in the operation of the law.

In this framework, policy space amounts to an inherent and necessary component of regulatory theory. Ever since, it has been a feature of regulatory powers, defining autonomous areas or delegated powers by means of defining the density of legal norms, from legal principles to detailed regulation. Policy space is defined by the breadth of a norm and the level of detailed regulation. Open-textured norms, including general principles of law and human rights, inherently entail policy space, while detailed regulations do not. Likewise, authorities and courts of law enjoy policy space in applying and interpreting norms commensurate with the open or detailed structure of the norm at hand.[9]

But policy space is also inherent to all law as it defines allocation of

---

[6] Thomas Cottier, "Multilayered Governance, Pluralism, and Moral Conflict" (2009) 16 Indiana Journal of Global Legal Studies 647.

[7] Thomas Cottier, "Towards a Five Storey House" in Joerges and Petersmann (note 5 above) at 495; Thomas Cottier and Maya Hertig, "The Prospects of 21st Century Constitutionalism" in Armin von Bogdandy and Rüdiger Wolfrum, eds, *Max Planck Yearbook of United Nations Law*, vol. 7 (Max Planck Institute, 2003) 261.

[8] John H. Jackson, *Sovereignty, the WTO, and Changing Fundamentals of International Law* (Cambridge: Cambridge University Press, 2006).

[9] See Thomas Cottier and Lucia Satragno, "The Potential of Law and Legal Methodology in Monetary Affairs" in Thomas Cottier, Rosa M. Lastra, Christian Tietje and Lucia Satragno (eds), *The Rule of Law in Monetary Affairs* (Cambridge: Cambridge University Press, 2014) 411 at 421–6 discussing the essence of regulatory theory.

powers between different levels of government. The principles of non-discrimination in global law (national treatment and most favoured nation (MFN)) deploy comparable effects to interstate commerce clauses in the US Constitution and functionally equivalent norms in other constitutions; they all serve the purpose of creating level playing fields and fair conditions of competition and market access on and to subsequent levels of governance.[10] The same is true for human rights guarantees protecting individuals within subsequent jurisdictions from violations by the authorities acting on that level of governance.

Finally, policy space indirectly shapes the relationship among parallel levels of governance, which in federacy and international law find themselves competing in regulatory terms. Policy space granted to subsequent jurisdictions allows for diverging and localised regulations, which in terms define the competitive relationship between subsequent jurisdictions on the same level. For example, autonomous powers to tax will be used differently and define competitive relations among different jurisdictions.

From this point of view, and other than in the political and economic discourse described above, policy space is a perfectly neutral term. It describes and defines the scope and degree of regulatory power assigned to a particular level of government within the overall regulatory system of the Five Storey House. The term does not define appropriate levels as such. It does not per se privilege domestic levels vis-à-vis international or regional law. It does not per se favour regulation over judicial law-making. It applies to all levels of governance alike as it encompasses configurations of discretion and decision-making powers granted to subsequent levels within the law. It entails configuration of full policy space in the absence of preceding norms up to zero policy space in configurations where a matter is exclusively regulated and shaped by a different, often superior layer of government.

Within these constellations, we find the normal configuration of shared policy space where a matter is partly addressed by one layer, but leaves room for differing regulations on a different layer of government. Normally, regulation is a matter of degree. The quest for appropriate policy space and allocation of powers and policy mixes is informed by overarching values and principles which seek to produce appropriate public goods, such as market access and level playing fields, while taking into account the need for differential treatment commensurate with the

---

10 See George Anderson, ed., *Internal Markets and Multi-level Governance: The Experience of the European Union, Australia, Canada, Switzerland, and the United States* (Don Mills: Oxford University Press, 2012).

needs of subsequent levels of government as they may vary in accordance with different societal and economic structures and levels of development. The allocation is informed by the principle of subsidiarity, that is building governance from below and allocating powers on subsequent levels only to the extent necessary to produce agreed public goods, such as security, enjoyment of human rights, welfare systems, market access and equal conditions of competition. Regulatory powers assigned to superior levels mainly serve the purpose of realizing such goals while otherwise respecting cultural diversity and diverging needs. Such policy space, importantly, is not limited to domestic law but may also be needed on the regional or global level, depending on the public goods to be produced. The fundamentals operating in federacy equally operate within the realm of public international law. There is no fundamental difference in terms of underlying interests and values at stake. On all levels of human governance within the Five Storey House, it is a matter of properly defining policy space for each of the layers of governance alike.

Policy space, in other words, is not a one-way street but depicts the interaction of different layers of governance. Sometimes, there will be a need to strengthen local and domestic powers. Sometimes, it will be necessary to reinforce policy space in public international law and limit local and domestic powers to achieve a particular good and realize a particular value, fairness and justice. Sometimes, it is important to strengthen the role of legislators and sometimes the powers of courts in developing the law. This is true alike in trade and human rights, the subjects of prime interest in this chapter.

Allocation of powers on appropriate levels of governance requires careful consideration of the factual and normative environment within which they operate. The proper allocation of policy space is a fact-intensive exercise. It does not allow for simple answers. It operates within a pluralist environment and outcomes or is influenced by different political views in the traditions of federalism or unionism. In reality, allocation of policy space often is driven by interests and does not produce optimal results. Such distortions, however, do not alter the basic and neutral functions of policy space in law and regulation.

Indeed, most political debates in federacies and also within the EU are about diverging perceptions on proper allocation of powers in one or the other way. Most configurations allow for different views and are mixed in nature. Allocation of powers is normally a matter of degree, except for clear-cut configurations, such as the prohibition of torture, which does not allow for any policy space for exceptions on the local or national level. The ban expounded on federal and international law levels is absolute. Vice versa, it would seem that there is no room for centralized policy space on the regional or international level when it comes to regulate a purely local matter; but absolute powers are difficult to find here because the matter may be partly influenced by overriding concerns and interest, such as the principles of non-discrimination and the protection of minorities. Most configurations therefore are mixed, and it is a matter of defining an appropriate policy mixture in support of best possible results and outcomes.

Policy space not only influences the allocation of powers between domestic and international law, but also affects allocations within these layers. The precepts of regulatory theory indicated above fully apply in regional and international law. Recourse to broadly textured norms and principles of international law increases the policy space of those applying and interpreting the law. Principles of law and human rights entail a broader scope of interpretation than detailed, technical and administrative rules. The former entails delegations of interpretative powers by negotiators and legislators, while the latter seeks to limit policy space by enacting detailed regulation. In WTO law, recourse to broad principles inherently expands powers of panels and the Appellate Body within their mandate in accordance with Article 3(2) of the Dispute Settlement Understanding (DSU) without exceeding the limits imposed by the provision.[11] The norm is further specified by means of precedents. Principles and provisions entailing policy space inherently comprise an element of activist interpretation within the bounds delegated to the interpreter and those applying the provisions both on the international and national levels. Or, recourse to equity and equitable principles as a normative concept inherently grants policy space to adjudicators. They are called upon to identify appropriate principles, relevant circumstances and factors, and balance those after fact-intensive assessments with a view to produce an equitable solution. Maritime boundary delimitation is the area most advanced in using this methodology.[12] It is also suitable to apply to other fact-intensive domains, both in international and domestic laws. Policy space is granted to bring about fairness and equity in inherently differing configurations, not suitable to be addressed in terms of rigid rules and exceptions.

Finally, it is important to reiterate that the impact of policy space also affects horizontal relations among states. Granting policy space to

---

[11] World Trade Organization (WTO), *Understanding on Rules and Procedures Governing the Settlement of Disputes* (Geneva: World Trade Organization), available at https://www.wto.org/english/docs_e/legal_e/28-dsu_e.htm (accessed 3 January 2017).

[12] Thomas Cottier, *Equitable Principles of Maritime Boundary Delimitation: The Quest for Distributive Justice in International Law* (Cambridge: Cambridge University Press, 2015).

domestic law also allows members to adopt measures which may affect other countries. Countries with large market powers, to which others need to adapt in order to secure market access, will need to adopt measures imposed using policy space granted by international law. Wide policy space thus may be in the interest of large and dominant countries. It is not necessarily in the interest of median and smaller countries depending upon access to large markets. They often benefit from restrictions of policy space by international law, limiting the scope of autonomous action of large jurisdictions. Competition law and policy is an example in point. The lack of disciplines in international law leaves large jurisdictions with the possibility to unilaterally define extraterritorial effects of competition law commensurate to the effects principle. Countries and industries affected are without remedies in international law and exposed to extensive policy space, which is used to protect domestic interests. In trade policy, the limit imposed by international law, for example in the field of trade remedies, protects other nations from overly intrusive measures. It allows them to defend their interests before panels and the Appellate Body of the WTO. Calls for more policy space in domestic law, in particular on the part of smaller nations and developing countries, need to keep this in mind.

III. TRADE REGULATION

International trade law is a prime example of the need for carefully protecting policy space on the level of international law to limit pre-existing domestic policy space. The history of the interwar period comes to mind and offers a remarkable example of the implications of leaving all policy space on the domestic and national levels.[13] While trade, in particular tariffs, were historically a matter of exclusive domestic taxation and law, international law increasingly limited domestic policy space in serving market access rights abroad. The process of developing rules on anti-dumping, subsidies and countervailing duties are good examples in point. It was a matter of limiting domestic policy space in order to avoid

---

[13] Charles P. Kindleberger, "Commercial Policy between the Wars" in Peter Mathias and Sidney Pollard, eds, *The Cambridge Economic History of Europe from the Decline of the Roman Empire*, vol. 8 (Cambridge: Cambridge University Press, 1989) 161; Barry Eichengreen and Douglas A. Irwin, *The Slide to Protectionism in the Great Depression: Who Succumbed and Why?* National Bureau of Economic Research (NBER) Working Paper 15142 (July 2009), available at http://www.nber.org/papers/w15142 (accessed 3 January 2017).

protectionist and rent-seeking policies often preferred by constituencies dominated by domestic producer interests.[14] Domestic policy space was eventually reduced to enhance the interests of consumer welfare and growth of economies. Subsequent generations of agreements refined these boundaries, seeking a proper balance between the interests of competing political entities and economic interests. From early trade agreements to the General Agreements on Tariffs and Trade (GATT) and the WTO, the process can be observed of offsetting protectionist policies exploiting previously existing policy space due to the absence of an international system while recognizing legitimate policy goals and thus appropriate domestic policy space.

More recent periods after the advent of the WTO in 1995 again emphasize the need for domestic policy space in what could be termed a dialectical and historical process of seeking appropriate and balanced relations between international and domestic policy space, commensurate with the needs of the times. Modern areas of law show complex and intertwined structures and interaction of domestic and international law. For example, rules on subsidies in the field of energy need to be redefined in terms of domestic and international policy space.[15] Financial regulation and capital controls are yet another example in point discussing appropriate policy space on the domestic and international law levels.[16]

The same process of reform can also be observed in refining the law by means of interpretation. The evolution of the case law in GATT and the WTO can be characterized as a process of constitutionalizing the operation of fundamental principles, in particular of national treatment. Under GATT 1947, interpreted in a narrow and functionalist manner in support of trade liberalization,[17] other public policy goals, mainly in the field of the environment, were neglected and called for larger domestic policy space.

---

14 See John H. Jackson, *World Trade and the Law of GATT* (Indianapolis: Bobbs-Merill, 1969) 780.

15 Luca Rubini, "Ain't Wastin' Time No More: Subsidies for Renewable Energy, The SCM Agreement, Policy Space, and Law Reform" (2013) 15:2 Journal of International Economic Law 525; Aaron Cosbey and Petros C. Mavroidis, "A Turquoise Mess: Green Subsidies, Blue Industrial Policy and Renewable Energy: The Case for Redrafting the Subsidies Agreement of the WTO" (2014) 17:1 Journal of International Economic Law 11.

16 Federico Lupo Pasini, "Movement of Capital and Trade in Services: Distinguishing Myth from Reality Regarding the GATS and the Liberalization of the Capital Account" (2012) 15:2 Journal of International Economic Law 581.

17 GATT Panel Report, US – Tuna (Mexico) DS21/R, Circulation Date: 3 September 1991 (not adopted); GATT Panel Report, US – Tuna (EEC) DS29/R, Circulation Date: 16 June 1994 (not adopted).

The quest for defining "like products" is a process of trial and error and is an example in point. The doctrine of aims and effects, or the doctrine of Processes and Production Methods (PPMs) allowing distinguishing like products as such, was an attempt to increase policy space of Members of the GATT and the WTO.[18] Likewise the interpretation of the exceptions of Article XX GATT shows a process of enlarging policy space of members, in particular in the field of environmental protection and animal welfare.[19] Interpreting the Technical Barriers to Trade (TBT) Agreement in a manner to allow for implied exceptions commensurate with the regulatory purposes of the measure is another example in point.[20] WTO law has come a long way in balancing different interests as equally legitimate interests.[21] It no longer places market access and liberalization as its sole and main purpose. Trade liberalization has made way for trade regula-

---

[18] This doctrine and jurisprudence, later rejected by the Appellate Body of the WTO, identified violations of national treatment only when like domestic products were intentionally privileged for protectionist purposes or the regulation deployed such effects. For a discussion see Thomas Cottier, Matthias Oesch and Thomas M. Fischer, *International Trade Regulation: Law and Policy of the WTO, the European Union and Switzerland: Cases, Materials and Comments* (Bern and London: Staempfli Publishers and Cameron May, 2005) 403; US – Taxes on Automobiles, Report of the Panel, 11 October 1994 (not adopted) DS31/R, 33 ILM 1397 (1994).

[19] US – Gasoline Appellate Body Report, United States – Standards for Reformulated and Conventional Gasoline, WT/DS2/AB/R, adopted 20 May 1996, DSR 1996:I, p. 3; US – Gasoline Panel Report, United States – Standards for Reformulated and Conventional Gasoline, WT/DS2/R, adopted 20 May 1996, as modified by Appellate Body; US – Shrimp Appellate Body Report, United States – Import Prohibition of Certain Shrimp and Shrimp Products, WT/DS58/AB/R, adopted 6 November 1998, DSR 1998:VII, p. 2755; US – Shrimp (Article 21.5 – Malaysia) Appellate Body Report, United States – Import Prohibition of Certain Shrimp and Shrimp Products – Recourse to Article 21.5 of the DSU by Malaysia, WT/DS58/AB/RW, adopted 21 November 2001, DSR 2001:XIII, p. 6481 Report WT/DS2/AB/R, DSR 1996:I, p. 29; EC – Measures Prohibiting the Importation and Marketing of Seal Products, WT/DS400/AB/RWT/DS401/AB/R (22 May 2014); EC – Seal Products Panel Reports, European Communities – Measures Prohibiting the Importation and Marketing of Seal Products, WT/DS400/R, WT/DS401/R and Add.1 (25 November 2013).

[20] US – Tuna II (Mexico) Appellate Body Report, United States – Measures Concerning the Importation, Marketing and Sale of Tuna and Tuna Products, WT/DS381/AB/R, adopted 13 June 2012; US – Tuna II (Mexico) Panel Report, United States – Measures Concerning the Importation, Marketing and Sale of Tuna and Tuna Products, WT/DS381/R, adopted 13 June 2012, as modified by Appellate Body Report WT/DS381/AB/R.

[21] This is the essence of a constitutional approach to treaty interpretation, cf. Thomas Cottier, "Limits to International Trade: The Constitutional Challenge" in The American Society of International Law, ed., *International Law in Ferment: A*

tion, not as a matter of undue interventionism but of mainly addressing non-tariff barriers and the legal framework of international trade and investment, both domestically and on the level of international law.[22] This essentially is a matter of allocating policy space and powers on appropriate levels of governance.

While the principle defines policy space on the international level, the exceptions do so for the national level. Importantly, however, the level is defined by international law, albeit granting deference to national interpretations. This is not a matter of discarding international principles, giving up treaty obligations and returning to unfettered domestic policy space. Calibration of policy space takes place within the existing agreements, and may be further developed by additional provisions and disciplines in the process of international negotiations.

Calling for policy space in domestic law must keep this in mind. Calling for clean and unfettered space beyond international or regional law would turn back to configurations and risks of the interwar period and does not make sense to any rational mind. The abolishment of international trade law disciplines or of regional law advocated for in the political process may produce results opposite to what proponents of a national conservative agenda hostile to multilevel governance, regional and international law promise to their constituencies. Defining domestic policy space inherently remains a matter of shaping and interpreting international law. This implies reviewing existing allocations and making necessary changes. We examine to what extent such changes should be made in light of protecting human rights and local cultural practices in particular.

IV. HUMAN RIGHTS

The relationship between trade and human rights is a complex one. Historically sharing the same roots, human rights and trade policy developed in completely separate fora and constituencies.[23] For many years

New Vision for Theory and Practice. Proceedings of the 94th Annual Meeting, 5–8 April 2000. Washington, DC, 2000, pp. 220–2.

[22] Thomas Cottier, "International Economic Law in Transition from Trade Liberalization to Trade Regulation" (2014) 17:3 Journal of International Economic Law 671.

[23] Ernst-Ulrich Petersmann, "Human Rights and International Economic Law in the 21st Century: The Need to Clarify their Interrelationships" (2001) 4:1 Journal of International Economic Law 3; Thomas Cottier, "Trade and Human Rights: A Relationship to Discover" (2002) 5:1 Journal of International Economic Law 111.

they have remained mutually disinterested, if not hostile. Efforts were made to overcome dichotomies and to lead to a more coherent interaction and legal relationship. The gradual recognition of legitimate policy goals in the field of the environment also prepared the way for redefining the relationship between trade and human rights. While academic writing and doctrine worked towards greater coherence of trade, investment and human rights,[24] the fields were increasingly linked in regional and preferential trade agreements.[25] State practice, however, has hardly developed the relationship so far in trade policy within the WTO. Nor do human rights clauses in preferential trade agreement show much impact. Human rights have played a role in adopting economic sanctions under the umbrella of the United Nations and thus justified by Article XXI GATT. But no single case has yet been brought challenging measures taken to protect human rights under Article XX of the GATT or Article XIV General Agreement on Trade in Services (GATS). Likewise, no case has been brought restricting market access rights due to human rights violations abroad, including labour standards, in particular child labour or even prison labour explicitly provided for in Article XX GATT or Article XIV GATS. In addition, little or no experience to this effect exists in implementing and enforcing preferential trade agreements and labour standards. The jury is still out.

Yet, today, it is safe to say that, building upon existing case law, a WTO member is entitled to restrict trade for the purpose of protecting human rights and labour standards in particular. The same is likely under pref-

---

[24] Ernst-Ulrich Petersmann, *International Economic Law in the 21st Century: Constitutional Pluralism and Multilevel Governance of Interdependent Public Goods* (Oxford: Hart Publishing, 2012); Frederick M. Abbott, Thomas Cottier and Christine Breining-Kaufmann, eds, *International Trade and Human Rights: Foundations and Conceptual Issues* (Ann Arbor: University of Michigan Press, 2006); Thomas Cottier, Joost Pauwelyn and Elisabeth Bürgi Bonanomi, eds, *Human Rights and International Trade* (Oxford: Oxford University Press, 2005); Lorand Bartels, "Trade and Human Rights" in Daniel Bethlehem, Isabelle Van Damme, Donald McRae and Rodney Neufeld (eds), *The Oxford Handbook of International Trade Law* (Oxford: Oxford University Press, 2009) 571; Gabrielle Marceau, "Trade and Labour" in Bethlehem et al. (ibid.) 539; Drusilla K. Brown, "Labour Standards and Human Rights" in Amrita Narlikar, Martin Daunton and Robert M Stern, eds, *The Oxford Handbook on the World Trade Organization* (Oxford: Oxford University Press, 2012) 697; Pierre-Marie Dupuy, Francesco Francioni and Ernst-Ulrich Petersmann, eds, *Human Rights in International Investment Law and Arbitration* (Oxford: Oxford University Press, 2009).

[25] See Emilie Hafner-Burton, "Trading Human Rights: How Preferential Trade Agreements Influence Government Repression" (2005) 59 International Organization 593.

erential trade agreements, to the extent that they refer to relevant WTO disciplines in terms of policy space. The way panels and the Appellate Body construed and interpreted the concept of public morals in particular allowed taking into account human rights concerns in shaping trade policy today.

Recent case law in 2014 relating to the ban of seal products in the EU essentially relied upon the power of Member States to invoke public morals to essentially justify the import and marketing restrictions under Article XX(a) GATT.[26] While the notion is one of public international law, panels and the Appellate Body had adopted deferential standards of interpretation before, essentially accepting unilaterally defined perceptions of public morals within a particular constituency.[27] It has largely and essentially become a matter of domestic policy space with some strings attached in international law. The test applied essentially relies upon a coherent recourse and argumentation based upon public morals and the protection of animal welfare in the political process developing and adopting legislation. Thus, it is not possible to have recourse to public morals in defence of a measure that was introduced upon other grounds in the first place. Recourse to public morals calls for a deliberate decision to invoke the policy space offered on its grounds. The approach was essentially confirmed in 2016 by the Appellate Body in a matter related to money laundering.[28] The same test can be applied in defence of measures related to labour standards and to human rights standards broadly speaking. Different configurations can be distinguished:

---

[26] EC – Measures Prohibiting the Importation and Marketing of Seal Products (note 19 above).

[27] US – United States – Measures affecting the Cross-Border Supply of Gambling and Betting Services, WT/D285/AB/R (7 April 2005). For a discussion see Mark Wu, "Free Trade and the Protection of Public Morals: An Analysis of the Newly Emerging Public Morals Clause Doctrine" (2008) 33 Yale Journal of International Law 215; Eric H. Leroux, "From Periodicals to Gambling: A review of systematic issues addressed by WTO adjudicatory bodies under GATS" in Marion Panizzon, Nicole Pohl and Pierre Sauvé, eds, *GATS and the Regulation of International Trade in Services* (Cambridge: Cambridge University Press, 2008) 236. For an early assessment of Article XX(a) GATT see Steve Charnovitz, "The Moral Exception in Trade Policy" (1998) 38 Virginia Journal of International Law 689; Nicolas F. Diebold, "The Morals and Order Exceptions in WTO Law: Balancing the Toothless Tiger and the Undermining Mole" (2008) 11:1 Journal of International Economic Law 43.

[28] Colombia – Measures Relating to the Importation of Textiles, Apparel and Footwear, WT/DS461/AB/R (7 June 2016).

(a) A country is in a position to restrict imports of products with a view to defend domestically applied labour and human rights standards. Such measures may take recourse to import restrictions beyond bound tariffs, for example by means of quantitative restrictions or price controls in support of minimal wages imposed on the production of domestic and exported products (goods and services). All measures take effect within the territory of the Member imposing the restriction.
(b) A country is in a position to restrict import products with a view to defend labour standards and human rights not only applied at home, but also sought after in exporting markets. Trade restrictions – quantitative restrictions – can be applied, including a total ban on the product with a view to combat practices abroad. The measures deliberately target production practices abroad and are not limited to ancillary effects. It is conceivable to restrict imports the production of which violated labour or human rights standards in the wake of making and processing the products. Public morals, in other words, deploy not only effects within the territory of the Member, but also within the territory of the exporting country.

European Communities – Seal Products did not rule on the contentious issue as to whether WTO allows for recourse to so-called PPMs. The parties did not address the issue, and the Appellate Body left the issue open.[29] Yet, the ruling in effect does rely upon PPMs – banning methods of killing considered inhuman and thus contrary to public morals. The same configuration also applies to labour standards and human rights based upon the assessment of the domestic regulation adopted generally banning certain practices.

Whether or not such measures are compatible with WTO law will depend on the specific measures taken, assessing whether they are necessary and cannot be replaced by less intrusive instruments achieving the goals of the regulation. Secondly, they need to comply with the requirements of the chapeau of Article XX GATT. This provision essentially protects good faith, preventing abuse of rights and examining whether all parties, where the same conditions prevail, enjoy equal or comparable treatment. The provision also requires that prior to the adoption of measures a negotiated settlement of the issue has been sought with Member States affected by the measure. So far, all measures examined under the umbrella of Article XX GATT have failed to pass the test of the chapeau and have been sent back

---

[29] EC – Measures Prohibiting the Importation and Marketing of Seal Products, (note 19 above) at para. 5.173.

to the drawing board for improvement, yet without rejecting the lawfulness of such measures in principle.[30]

Policy space for the protection of public morals at home and abroad thus essentially exists. Main problems in terms of policy space and human rights in fact have not arisen under the exception clauses, but in relation to other provisions of WTO law. The right to food was invoked to justify export restrictions under Article XI GATT and the Agreement on Agriculture by India. It led to stalemate and last-minute informal settlement at the Bali Ministerial Conference in 2013, but no changes to WTO law have taken place subsequently. The policy space related to export restrictions of agricultural commodities remains controversial and still awaits a more principled approach.[31] The second main issue related to policy space is procuring essential drugs, a well-known issue. The rules adopted under the Agreement on Trade-Related Aspects of Intellectual Property Rights (TRIPS), obliging developing countries to adopt patent protection for pharmaceuticals by 2005, limited the export of generic drugs to the world market and to developing countries in particular. Compulsory licensing was not available for exports under Article 31(f) of the TRIPS Agreement, which states that compulsory licensing of patent products shall be authorized predominantly for the supply of the domestic market. The policy space available was too narrow to serve the interests of exporting and importing developing countries. Subsequent negotiations following the adoption of the 2001 Declaration on Public Health led to the adoption of a waiver and eventual revision of the provision. Compulsory licensing was made available under narrowly defined conditions to serve export markets in developing countries. While the waiver of compulsory licensing has not been used often, its very existence contributed to reducing price levels of original HIV products and thus contributed to enhancing affordable supplies to people in need.[32]

---

[30] For the case law see note 19 above; for procedural requirements in particular, see US – Shrimp (Article 21.5 – Malaysia).

[31] Irene Musselli Moretti, *Agricultural Price Stabilization and Trade Rules: A Principled Approach*, doctoral thesis adopted by the Faculty of Law of the University of Bern 2016 (on file with author, forthcoming Leiden, Bosten: Brill Nijhoff 2017).

[32] See WTO, "TRIPS and public health", available at https://www.wto.org/english/tratop_e/trips_e/pharmpatent_e.htm (accessed 3 January 2017); WTO, "The separate Doha Declaration explained", available at http://www.wto.org/english/tratop_e/trips_e/healthdeclexpln_e.htm (accessed 3 January 2017); WTO, "Decision removes final patent obstacle to cheap drug imports" (30 August 2003), available at http://www.wto.org/english/news_e/pres03_e/pr350_e.htm (accessed 3 January 2017); Frederick M. Abbott, "The Doha Declaration on the TRIPS

There may be other areas of WTO law where policy space of developing countries or Members in general is needed to protect human rights and labour standards. The main area under discussion is investment protection. Do existing standards of fair and equitable treatment sufficiently respond to human rights concerns of local populations? Recent developments in doctrine and jurisprudence point towards enhanced policy space for domestic government and law.[33]

The main problem, however, lies elsewhere. Labour standards and human rights protection often suffer from lack of support from domestic law and government. Human rights and the protection of minorities and of labour standards all too often fail to be protected at home under domestic laws and practices. Those dependent on such rights often are not well represented within the domestic political system, and courts of law are not able to protect them on their own. All states risk such failures, and the record of the European Court of Human Rights shows that this also applies to democracies and is not limited to authoritarian governments prevailing in many parts of the world. Governments often are not primarily interested in creating policy space for local communities and practices but in controlling and deterring local autonomy and self-determination. Alternatively, local practices clearly violating human dignity and integrity, in particular the practices of female genital mutilation, remain without legal disciplines and remedies, both in domestic and international law.[34]

Efforts to comply with labour standards and human rights thus depend upon external pressures. Such pressures include, but are not limited to, international trade. Incentives granted may be financial, development assistance or defined in terms of trade measures, and a combination and appropriate policy mixture. Here, it is not a matter of defining policy space of exporting and importing countries or the international community at large in relation to the country concerned with a view to address labour standards and human rights concerns abroad. Such policy space inherently needs to be defined by international law.

It is submitted that additional disciplines in international law are

---

Agreement and Public Health: Lighting a Dark Corner at the WTO" (2002) 5 Journal of International Economic Law 469.

[33] Suzanne A. Spears, "The Quest for Policy Space in a New Generation of International Investment Agreements" (2010) 13:4 Journal of International Economic Law 1037.

[34] "Female genital mutilation: An agonising choice" *The Economist* (18 June 2016), available at http://www.economist.com/news/leaders/21700658-after-30-years-attempts-eradicate-barbaric-practice-it-continues-time-try-new (accessed 3 January 2017).

required and, thus, enhancing policy space of international law and international institutions. As indicated, main efforts have been made in preferential trade and investment protection agreements, defining the policy space to exert influence and pressure on compliance with human rights standards in exporting countries.[35] Additional efforts need to be made within the multilateral trading system to this effect. But foremost, the political will to use such policy space needs to be developed.

The first example relates to the protection of labour standards in international trade. While the GATT and GATS rules specifically apply to the treatment of particular products, modern preferential trade agreements allow for trade sanctions for failing respect for labour and human rights standards not specifically related to a product, in particular freedom of association. More recent agreements concluded by the United States contain such clauses. For example, the Regional Trade Agreement (RTA) between the United States and Vietnam allows the United States to withdraw trade concessions to Vietnam upon failure to respect labour standards and freedom of association. Similar provisions form part of the Trans-Pacific Partnership Agreement (TPP) concluded among 12 Pacific countries. The record of such clauses, including withdrawal of the General System of Preferences (GSP) shows some impact on labour conditions, but political will to take recourse to such measures has been limited.[36] For example, restricting labour practices and the detention of activists in Vietnam are not a matter of the past.[37] It is thus as much a matter of political will, paying for the costs, for using policy space to foster human rights protection abroad. In light of weak enforcement mechanisms within the International Labour Organization (ILO), enhanced and effective protection of labour standards calls for additional disciplines in international law, reducing domestic policy space and also obliging importing countries to act in case of violations. The approach developed in preferential trade agreements is a first step but does not adequately define policy space in international law.

Another example relates to intellectual property rights (IPRs) and the protection of traditional knowledge (TK). Developing countries seeking to protect economic rights of communities holding traditional

---

[35] Hafner-Burton (note 25 above).

[36] For an empirical account of US measures see Brown (note 24 above), at 710–14.

[37] "Cash for questions: Can freer trade soften Vietnam's thuggish ways?" *The Economist* (21 May 2016) at 43, available at http://www.economist.com/news/asia/21699162-can-freer-trade-soften-vietnams-thuggish-ways-cash-questions (accessed 3 January 2017).

knowledge, potentially important in bioprospecting and genetic engineering, are impaired from doing so due to minimal standards on patenting new products under the TRIPs Agreement. Members of the WTO and of the World Intellectual Property Organization (WIPO) are discussing the introduction of a transparency obligation to indicate the source and origin of an invention to be protected by patent. Such disclosure will facilitate the identification of prior art potentially denying the novelty of the invention. It will also assist in finding an appropriate agreement between communities and right holders in terms of compensation under rules developed by the Convention on Biodiversity in implementing instruments, most recently the Nagoya Protocol.[38] Yet, unless international law contains an obligation to recognize traditional knowledge in terms of what I called traditional intellectual property rights (TIPRs) a proper balance on use of, and compensation for, such knowledge is difficult to achieve.[39] Again, human rights concerns depend, in other words, on more stringent disciplines in international law itself, restricting both users and holders of traditional knowledge.

A third and trade-related example relates to freedom of information. The free flow of information is a prerequisite for the operation of markets and avoidance of distorting asymmetries of information and thus market power. International trade law should make the recognition of freedom of information (perhaps other than freedom of expression) a prerequisite for full market economy status in WTO law.

These examples show that labour standards, human rights protection, economic interests in TK and freedom of information do not depend upon policy space granted to countries, but on appropriate disciplines in public international law itself and the possibility of implementing and enforcing these disciplines by means of international economic law. It is a fallacy to believe that labour standards and human rights are best protected by domestic law and thus by reducing the impact and scope of public international law. To the contrary, effective protection is mainly secured by appropriate disciplines within public international law and its institutions. Such space may need to be wider, or more narrowly construed, depending upon the appropriate allocation of regulatory powers

---

38 The Nagoya Protocol on Access to Genetic Resources and the Fair and Equitable Sharing of Benefits Arising from their Utilization (ABS) to the Convention on Biological Diversity, available at https://www.cbd.int/abs/about/default.shtml (accessed 3 January 2017).

39 Thomas Cottier and Marion Panizzon, "Legal Perspectives on Traditional Knowledge: The Case for Intellectual Property Protection" (2004) 7:2 Journal of International Economic Law 371.

and the possibility of correcting failures produced by particular levels of government.

The finding corresponds to the theory of multi-level governance, which has its foundation in international protection of human rights with a view to correct failings of domestic law and courts to adequately protect individuals and minorities in light of newly emerging challenges. More policy space allocated to national law often results in lower levels of protection of local practices and minorities. Less domestic policy space increases the potential of effective protection, in particular when combined with trade and economic measures linked to the failure to comply with minimal standards set out in public international law.

The same also applies to policy space in the field of international trade. Enhanced domestic policy space may be necessary in particular constellations to support human rights, especially the right to health and the right to food; in other instances, however, it may increase rent-seeking protectionism and lower levels of competition to the detriment of consumers and their interests. It is a matter of correcting such failures by means of recourse to higher-ranking levels of governance within the framework of the Five Storey House. Realization and implementation of human rights in local practices will benefit from such protection by international law.

V. INTERNATIONAL POLICY SPACE IN HUMAN RIGHTS PROTECTION: A COMMON CONCERN OF HUMANKIND

The insight that policy space is a neutral concept, equally applying to domestic law and to the realm of international law, and within the different layers, begs the question whether there are configurations where domestic policy space should be excluded or severely limited by international law. Areas may exist not allowing for domestic exemptions.

Likewise, questions of enforcing policy space on the level of international law arise. Responsibilities to realize, specify and implement human rights guarantees primarily lie with domestic law and institutions. This is clearly true for domestic policy space, but also for policy space assumed by levels of regional and international law. Unless these levels develop programmes of their own, such as the EU, regional and international law supports and enforces human rights guarantees within the Five Storey House. While states are supposed to have the power and resources to realize policy space, human rights implementation and enforcement has been notoriously weak on the level of international law. The responsibilities of the international community and other states for domestic practices are unsettled and unclear. What are the obligations of states to enforce, and to support, such rights in international law? Can we focus on areas with exclusive policy space in international law? It is submitted that exclusive policy spaces in international law exist, and that realization and enforcement of such spaces is a matter of shared responsibility of the international community under the emerging principle of Common Concerns of Humankind.

In search of exclusive allocations of policy space to international law, disciplines of *jus cogens* or peremptory norms first come to mind. Fundamental precepts of justice, in particular the prohibition of torture, of apartheid, of refoulement of refugees, and arguably the ban on child labour without providing education, the principle of non-aggression and prohibition of use of force are not only peremptory; they do not leave states and governments policy space as a matter of prohibitions. Being norms *ergo omnes*, however, they leave policy space and discretion to other subjects of international law in reacting to violations of *jus cogens*. I argued elsewhere that these fundamental norms of *jus cogens* form part of Common Concerns of Humankind, and obligations in response to violations should be framed accordingly.[40]

Climate change and biological and cultural diversity have been recognized as a Common Concern of Humankind in treaty law, yet without specifying normative contents and implications. It is submitted that an emerging doctrine and principle of Common Concern of Humankind is also relevant in the present context. We elsewhere defined common concern as a problem affecting more than two states and which cannot be solved alone and in isolation. Climate change is the classical example in point, but by no means limited to it.[41] Other challenges in international environmental law, such as the depletion and pollution of oceans or keeping international peace and security, come to mind. Common concern relates to the creation of public goods, but is not a public good in itself, but as said before a concern and unresolved issue and problem, which need attention by more than two jurisdictions. Importantly, common concern is not limited to global relations, but applies on all layers of government; common concerns may be limited to a problem shared by two or more local communes in a particular region.

As a normative concept, it is submitted that it entails three types of

---

[40] Thomas Cottier, "Improving Compliance: Jus Cogens and International Economic Law" (2015) 46 Netherlands Yearbook of International Law 329.

[41] Thomas Cottier, Philipp Aerni, Baris Karapinar, Sofya Matteotti, Joëlle de Sépibus and Anirudh Shingal, "The Principle of Common Concern and Climate Change" (2014) 52:3 Archiv des Völkerrechts 293.

obligations: first, to take necessary action at home and within domestic jurisdiction; second, to engage in international cooperation jointly addressing the problem; third, failing action at home or international cooperation, or insufficient efforts made, it allows for unilateral action deploying extraterritorial effect. Again, climate change mitigation is the prime example in point. Due to existing collective action problems and free-riding, unilateral action in the absence of adequate domestic measures, such as carbon taxes, and international cooperation, such as funding and transfer of technology, may eventually take place and impose trade restrictions on products exported from otherwise free-riding jurisdictions. International law thus prescribes obligations to act, but also defines the scope and limits of policy space allocated to states in responding to the problem at hand.

The same approach, it is submitted, can also apply to fundamental human rights and core labour standards. We need to determine to what extent violations of human rights amount to a common concern as described above. First, peremptory norms leaving no policy space to domestic jurisdictions are matters of common concern. Common concern as a concept is more suitable to address the importance of fundamental precepts of justice than the doctrine of *jus cogens v. jus dispositivum* – a distinction which no longer corresponds to modern legal theory and fails to improve the enforcement of basic rights.[42]

Beyond rights traditionally recognized as *jus cogens*, the question arises to what extent violations of human rights amount to a common concern. As human rights in general offer domestic policy space in terms of exceptions and the pursuit of compelling legitimate public policy interests, the doctrine of common concern cannot apply across the board. States remain free to lawfully restrict the exercise of human rights within the bounds defined by international law and should be protected from intervention. However, violations of what in constitutional law doctrine is termed the core or inalienable content of human rights is suitable to amount to a common concern. It is here that no domestic policy space exists. Violations of the core of rights therefore amount to common concern in terms of threat to international security and the rule of law. This should also comprise protection of children from female genital mutilation.

Rights and obligations of states vis-à-vis violations of *jus cogens* and the inalienable core of human rights can and should thus be defined by the three categories defined above under the doctrine and principle of common concern. First, states are obliged to honour the rights

[42] Cottier (note 40 above).

domestically and refrain from violating *jus cogens* and core contents of human rights. They are obliged to cooperate internationally with other states with a view to realizing and implementing such rights. Other states are obliged to take action failing such efforts. The emerging doctrine of Responsibility to Protect (R2P) obliges governments to react in appropriate circumstances.[43] Policy space is limited to assess appropriate action but no longer leaves room to stay away idly in full discretion.

Common Concern of Humankind, depicting basic and unresolved problems, therefore, stands for the proposition of limiting domestic policy space in the field of human rights protection. Again, it is a matter of addressing state failures and shortcomings with a framework of multilevel governance and appropriate institutions. Trade law and policy thus can play an important role in realizing and enforcing human rights.[44] As a corollary, it is a matter of limiting policy space for national governments in the field of *jus cogens* and the core of human rights, rather than expanding it by taking recourse to local practices of human rights and the need for pluralism and variably adapted measures. Obligations to do the homework, to cooperate internationally and to take appropriate unilateral measures are all defined by international law and policy space. Beyond *jus cogens* and the inalienable core of human rights, states remain free to limit the exercise of human rights for public policy purposes and enjoy domestic policy space – the limits of which should be subject to judicial review by courts of law of preceding levels of governance within the Five Storey House.

VI. CONCLUSION

While policy space is mainly invoked as a means to increase the scope for domestic action and to limit the impact of international law, regulatory theory suggests using the concept in a neutral manner realizing appropriate allocation of powers to domestic law, international law and among different bodies on layers of governance. Trade and human rights do not unequivocally call for increasing the scope of domestic law, but may also impose the opposite of limiting policy space and leave basic decisions and interpretation of norms within the realm of public international law.

---

[43] Krista Nadakavukaren Schefer and Thomas Cottier, "Responsibility to Protect (R2P) and the Emerging Principle of Common Concern" in Peter Hilpold, ed., *Responsibility to Protect (R2P). A New Paradigm of International Law?* (Leiden: Brill Nijhoff, 2015) 123.

[44] Cottier (note 40 above).

Violations of rights pertaining to *jus cogens* and the inalienable core of human rights are a common concern of humankind which triggers obligations to comply, to cooperate and to take unilateral action vis-à-vis failing states. There are others where more policy space is required to operate on the level of public international law within an overall system of vertical checks and balances and the quest of allocating powers to the level and body most suitable to bring about fairness and justice to humans affected. But clearly, human rights do not inherently call for more domestic space. Generally, effective protection of human rights calls for less domestic policy space and stronger guarantees and procedures in international law, taking into account international trade regulation in cooperation and enforcing such disciplines. Trade, human rights and policy space are thus inherently intertwined and need to be dealt with accordingly.

2. Cosmopolitan constitutionalism: linking local engagement with international economic law and human rights*

Ernst-Ulrich Petersmann

I. INTRODUCTION AND OVERVIEW

Local markets, commerce and their transnational linkage through trade and law have existed since the beginnings of written history. As explained by economists, linking the rational pursuit of self-interests (for example, in producing and selling food in local markets) to the collective production of public goods (PGs) (for example, PGs like food security) offers strong incentives for improving the efficiency between *means* and *ends*. As long ago as 2500 years, the democratic constitutionalism in ancient Athens and republican constitutionalism in ancient Rome emphasized the need for 'linking local engagement with law' on systemic grounds, for instance by linking democratic and republican rights of citizens to collective supply of PGs in order to hold governments accountable and promote 'public reason'. Modern human rights law (HRL), European economic integration law, international labour, investment, health, intellectual property and criminal laws increasingly link cosmopolitan rights to collective supply of transnational PGs so as to limit 'market failures' as well as 'governance failures' by 'countervailing rights' of citizens. This contribution explains why – the more globalization transforms *national* into *transnational PGs* whose multilevel regulation must remain embedded in constitutional democracies establishing 'communities of rights' – the necessary constitution, limitation, regulation and justification of multilevel governance of PGs must remain legally constrained by rights of citizens

* This chapter is based on a paper presented to the workshop on 'Mapping the Impact of International Trade and Human Rights on Local Practice', held in July 2014 at the International Institute for the Sociology of Law in Oñati, Spain.

so as to limit abuses of public and private powers and enable citizens as 'constitutive powers', 'agents of justice', democratic principals and main economic actors to hold all multilevel governance powers accountable.

Moral cosmopolitanism linking local engagement with global humanity emerged in ancient Greek philosophy and continues to influence modern human rights constitutionalism (section II). *Legal cosmopolitanism* was part of Roman contract and commercial law (*lex mercatoria*) and continued to influence merchant trade throughout the 'holy Roman empire' (for example, Baltic maritime trade in the Hanseatic League of city republics); it progressively expanded all over the world since the 'human rights revolutions' of the eighteenth and twentieth centuries (section III). *Economic* and *political cosmopolitanism* offer additional justifications of basing the international division of labour on new kinds of cosmopolitan cooperation law and '*cosmopolitics*' aimed at protecting 'republican peace' (section IV). Modern constitutional democracies integrate the diverse traditions of democratic, republican and cosmopolitan constitutionalism at national and regional levels of governance, for instance through transnational civil society cooperation and private-public partnerships in multilevel governance of global PGs and in newly emerging 'global public spheres' (section V). The universal recognition of human rights by all United Nations (UN) member states constitutionally limits the power-oriented, state-centered foundations of the 'international law of coexistence' (notably since 1648) and the 'international law of cooperation' (notably since 1945) through citizen-oriented 'integration law' based on respect for human dignity and equal rights of all human beings in local and transnational jurisdictions as primary sources of the legitimacy of legal systems and democratic governance in the twenty-first century (section VI). Section VII concludes that rights-based 'cosmopolitan international law' linking the rational self-interests of individuals to multilevel governance of PGs has empirically proven to protect PGs more effectively than 'disconnected' UN/WTO governance dominated by diplomats and rulers that negotiate and ratify – but subsequently often violate – international treaty obligations without effective legal, democratic and judicial accountability vis-à-vis adversely affected citizens. Reducing the 'disconnect' between 'inter-governmental power politics' (for example, in UN and World Trade Organization (WTO) institutions) and domestic laws and governance requires legally designed multilevel governance of transnational PGs in conformity with democratic, republican, cosmopolitan and 'economic constitutionalism' by recognizing citizens as 'democratic principals' regarding governance agents with limited, delegated powers, whose legitimate exercise requires democratic inclusion of all citizens and of other 'stakeholders' affected by multilevel regulation. Constitutional rights and limitations of public and private powers, and respect for the constitutional principles of subsidiarity, proportionality and economic efficiency of multilevel regulation, offer the most legitimate and most effective framework for transforming the 'international law in the books' into 'law in action' that effectively protects citizens, their human and constitutional rights and reasonable, human needs.

II. MORAL COSMOPOLITANISM AS FOUNDATION OF HUMAN RIGHTS

The idea of dual citizenship – in local communities as well as 'citizens of the world' in a 'cosmopolitan community' based on a shared morality of mutual respect for strangers – is traced back to Diogenes (ca 412 BC), the founder of the Cynic movement in ancient Greece; when asked where he came from, he answered: 'I am a citizen of the world' (*kosmopolitês*).[1] Ancient and modern cosmopolitanism (for example, based on Kantian moral theory) emphasize that human beings – as they 'are born free and equal in dignity and rights' and are endowed with 'reason and conscience' (cf. Article 1 of the Universal Declaration of Human Rights (UDHR)) – must justify their conduct by 'universalizable' principles that respect human dignity (for example, in the sense of equal autonomy rights) and reconcile individual, legitimate self-interests with those of all others.[2] Peaceful cooperation for protecting PGs demanded by citizens across national borders must be based on 'cosmopolitan rights' of individuals and peoples as proclaimed in the 1776 US Declaration of Independence, the 1789 French Declaration of the Rights of Man and the Citizen, and in the UDHR of 1948. Just as individuals must reasonably limit the exercise of their individual freedoms by respecting the equal freedoms of all others, so must democracies, states and international organizations respect the equal democratic rights of foreign peoples and jurisdictions as emphasized

---

1 Diogenes Laertius, *Lives of the Eminent Philosophers* (translated by R.D. Hicks), Vol. 2 (Cambridge: Harvard University Press, 1925) 63.

2 Cf. Pauline Kleingeld, *Kant and Cosmopolitanism: The Philosophical Ideal of World Citizenship* (Cambridge: Cambridge University Press, 2012); James Bohman and Matthias Lutz-Bachmann, eds, *Perpetual Peace. Essays on Kant's Cosmopolitan Ideal* (Cambridge: MIT Press, 1997). On the 'social contract question' of which principles of justice a group of reasonable individuals would choose in an 'original position' where they would be deprived of any information about themselves that could bias their individual choices, see Timothy Hinton, ed., *The Original Position* (Cambridge: Cambridge University Press, 2016).

in UN human rights conventions, for instance in the UN legal guarantees of the rights of all *peoples* to self-determination (cf. the common Article 1:1 of the 1966 UN Covenants on civil, political, economic, social and cultural rights).

National (big C) Constitutions and HRL recognize citizens as 'constituent powers' and '*democratic principals*' who delegate only limited 'constituted powers' to *government agents* subject to constitutional restraints like 'inalienable' human rights, including rights of access to justice and judicial remedies. Citizens agree on national Constitutions as the supreme law of the land and are responsible for 'constitutionalizing' legal systems by transforming the constitutional 'law in the books' into democratic legislation, administration, adjudication and institutionalized 'public reason' in order to protect PGs like human rights, rule of law and democratic governance by free and equal citizens. The UN Charter was concluded on behalf of 'We the peoples of the United Nations' (Preamble). European Union (EU) law recognizes that the 'peoples of Europe, in creating an ever closer Union among them', founded this Union 'on the indivisible, universal values of human dignity, freedom, equality and solidarity', 'the principles of democracy and the rule of law' (Preamble EU Charter of Fundamental Rights (EUCFR)). Cosmopolitan rights may be justified not only by 'primary allegiance to the world community of human beings'.[3] The derivative nature of EU citizenship from EU member state citizenship (cf. Article 20 Treaty on the Functioning of the EU (TFEU)) reflects additional interrelationships between local, national and regional polities, for instance in individual and democratic, multilevel governance of transnational 'aggregate PGs' inside, between and across diverse political communities that accept moral principles of protecting all citizens whose interests are affected, who are subjected to law and governance, or who have a legitimate stake in membership in political communities.[4]

State-centered international lawyers often neglect that the 'international legal community' consists today also of citizens, peoples and non-governmental and international organizations rather than only of states.

---

[3] Cf. Martha Nussbaum, 'Patriotism and Cosmopolitanism' in Martha Nussbaum and Joshua Cohen, eds, *For Love of Country: Debating the Limits of Patriotism* (Boston: Beacon Press, 1996) 4.

[4] On these three spheres of domestic, transnational and international justice and diverse 'inclusion principles' justifying inclusive citizenship rights see, for example: Seyla Benhabib, *The Rights of Others* (Cambridge: Cambridge University Press, 2004); Rainer Bauböck, 'Global Justice, Freedom of Movement and Democratic Citizenship' (2009) 50 European Journal of Sociology 1.

The legitimacy of modern international law derives 'bottom-up' from the mutual recognition among citizens of human rights and from the consent by citizens, peoples and representative governments to international rules and governance institutions. 'Constitutional contract' justifications of democratic legal systems are preceded by mutual recognition of human rights and other 'principles of justice' among citizens as preconditions for inclusive, democratic discourse and lawmaking.[5] The constitutional principles of limited delegation of powers, subsidiarity and proportionality (cf. Article 5 Treaty of the European Union (TEU)) reflect the human rights requirements of limiting restrictions and of 'balancing' of human rights to what is necessary for protection of other human rights (cf. Article 29:2 UDHR); they confirm that the limited authority of international law and institutions must remain justifiable in terms of constitutional rights of citizens and related principles of justice. As already explained by Kantian legal theory, the moral principles and universal legal recognition of respect for human dignity, responsibility and 'hospitality' vis-à-vis strangers in social interactions 'finally bring the human race ever closer to a cosmopolitan constitution'.[6] They are of foundational importance for transnational PGs like human rights, rule of law and other 'general principles of law recognized by civilized nations' (Article 38 International Court of Justice (ICJ) Statute) as justifications of modern international law. Modern theories of justice – for instance, by grounding the legitimacy of national and international legal systems in the human right to justification[7] – emphasize that, regardless of liberal or communitarian conceptions of law and governance, the legitimacy and effectiveness of modern, national and international legal systems derives from democratic consent and support by citizens.

---

[5] On discourse theory, and the implicit, moral respect of discourse partners as having reasonable autonomy and dignity, as justification of human rights 'without metaphysics' see: Robert Alexy, 'Menschenrechte ohne Metaphysik?' (2004) 52 Deutsche Zeitschrift für Philosophie 15.

[6] Immanuel Kant, 'Perpetual Peace' in H.S. Reiss, ed., *Kant Political Writings* (Cambridge: Cambridge University Press, 1991) 106.

[7] On the human right to justification see Rainer Forst, *The Right to Justification. Elements of a Constructivist Theory of Justice* (New York: Columbia University Press, 2012).

III. COSMOPOLITAN PRINCIPLES AS INTEGRAL PARTS OF MODERN CONSTITUTIONAL AND INTERNATIONAL LAW

Many of the *moral principles* underlying cosmopolitanism have become universally recognized as integral parts of modern *positive law* in hundreds of human rights treaties, international economic law (IEL) treaties, environmental, criminal, humanitarian, consular law and other treaties ratified by UN member states and incorporated into domestic law. The more globalization transforms *national* into *transnational PGs* that no single state can unilaterally protect without international law and institutions, the more national Constitutions reveal themselves as 'partial Constitutions' that increasingly depend on multilevel governance of transnational PGs through international law and institutions that protect human rights across national frontiers, including the cosmopolitan right of 'everybody . . . to a social and international order in which the rights and freedoms set forth in this Declaration can be fully realized' (Article 28 UDHR). The universal recognition of human rights in constitutional law and HRL in the twenty-first century goes far beyond the Kantian claims of cosmopolitan 'rights to hospitality' and recognition as 'citizens of the world'. Hundreds of UN and GATT/WTO agreements protect individual access to foreign goods and services, international communications, prevention of 'crimes against humanity' and of other international PGs. As human rights also protect individual and democratic diversity, modern 'cosmopolitan international law' – for example, international commercial, trade, investment and intellectual property law and arbitration, international consular, criminal and humanitarian law, HRL, internet law, air and maritime transportation law – protects governmental as well as individual rights, respect for diverse states, cultures, minorities and 'indigenous peoples', and national sovereignty to decide autonomously which international agreements a country wishes to ratify. Sociological evidence confirms the increasing importance of non-governmental 'global citizen movements' in mobilizing civil society support for international 'PGs treaties' like the Rome Statute for the International Criminal Court, international trade and environmental treaties.[8]

---

[8] Cf. Ronald Pierik and Wouter Werner, eds, *Cosmopolitanism in Context. Perspectives from International Law and Political Theory* (Cambridge: Cambridge University Press, 2010).

A. From 'Human Rights Constitutionalism' to Transnational Citizenship Rights

The term 'constitutionalism' tends to be used for:

(1) the *normative proposition* that law and governance – in order to be accepted by citizens as legitimate and voluntarily complied with – need to be justified in relation to citizens through agreed 'principles of justice' and rules of a higher legal rank that must be transformed into constitutional and democratic legislation, administration, adjudication, international 'PGs treaties' and 'public reason' so as to induce citizens to peacefully cooperate in collective supply of PGs; as well as for
(2) the *sociological 'six-stage constitutionalization processes'* of law and governance by transformation of (a) agreed 'principles of justice' (for example, in the US Declaration of Independence of 1776, the UDHR of 1948) into (b) constitutional, (c) legislative, (d) administrative, (e) judicial and (f) international rules and institutions that protect equal rights of citizens and promote 'constitutional mind-sets' limiting rational egoism and 'constitutionalizing' law and governance; and
(3) the *empirical claim* that constitutional democracies have a historical record of protecting PGs for the benefit of their citizens more effectively than non-democracies.

The universal recognition of human and constitutional rights (including also freedom of contract, private property and private arbitration as foundations of international commercial law) in modern 'positive law' protects 'local engagement' and requires 'normative bottom-up review' of state-centered rules and institutions from the point of view of reasonable citizens and their individual and democratic rights, for instance as 'agents of justice', 'constituent powers' and 'democratic principals' of governance agents with limited 'constituted powers' that must protect and promote equal rights of citizens as the main economic and 'republican actors' in the global division of labour. Human rights, rule of law, democracy, sovereignty and other 'principles of justice' referred to in UN law and EU law (like non-discrimination, equality, necessity, proportionality, 'fair and equitable treatment') remain indeterminate concepts. Their legal clarification may legitimately differ depending on democratic value preferences, legal methodologies and local contexts for implementing international rules in domestic legal systems. Compared with path-dependent top-down governance and specialized 'legal fragmentation regimes', HRL and constitutional democracies provide for more comprehensive frameworks of individual and democratic self-governance and constitutional 'checks and balances' for clarifying indeterminate rules and reconciling civil, political, economic, social and cultural rights of all citizens.

The multilevel protection of human rights through national, regional and worldwide legal guarantees and judicial remedies has limited governance powers by 'human rights constitutionalism' and increasing 'judicial comity' among national, regional and worldwide courts in interpreting, clarifying and protecting human rights for the benefit of citizens. For instance, in the 2010 and 2012 judgments in the *Diallo Case (Guinea v Congo)*, the ICJ assessed breaches of human rights treaty obligations by referring to the jurisprudence of UN and regional human rights bodies.[9] The European Court of Justice (CJEU) and the European Court of Human Rights (ECtHR) interpret EU law and the European Convention on Human Rights (ECHR) as 'constitutional instruments'. The protection by worldwide, regional and national courts of local, transnational and international rule of law contributes to the 'constitutionalization' of multilevel governance of PGs for the benefit of citizens. HRL requires legal and judicial respect for national and local 'margins of appreciation' and 'policy space' in implementing international treaty obligations in diverse local contexts with different democratic preferences and resources. Following the legal protection of 'EU citizenship' rights (cf. Article 18 TFEU) aimed at promoting collective supply of transnational PGs, diverse forms of 'cosmopolitan citizenship' (for example, based on common passports, free movement rights, transnational labour rights) are promoted also in a number of regional economic unions beyond the EU, notably in Latin America (like MERCOSUR, the Andean Common Market, the Central American Common Market) and Africa (like the West, East and Southern African Economic Unions).

B. Access to Justice, Constitutional Treaty Interpretations and Local Remedies

In constitutional democracies, the human rights guarantees of individual access to justice and to democratic and judicial justification of governmental restrictions of equal freedoms of citizens justify 'constitutional interpretations' of law that progressively extend democratic, republican

---

[9] For a discussion of these ICJ judgments (awarding damages as reparation for the violation of the human rights of *Diallo*), see Annemarieke Vermeer-Künzli, 'Diallo: Between Diplomatic Protection and Human Rights' (2013) 4:3 Journal of Int'l Dispute Settlement 487.

and cosmopolitan rights so as to protect PGs more effectively. Equal rights and judicial remedies empower citizens to assume responsibility not only for their private spheres of individual autonomy, but also for their democratic autonomy and 'republican responsibility' for collective protection of PGs. The jurisprudence of international courts confirms the task of 'constitutionalizing' multilevel governance of *transnational PGs* by justifying 'constitutional interpretations' of international treaties as constituting not only rights of governments, but also of citizens (for example, to consular protection, investment protection, 'consistent interpretations' of national and international obligations of governments to protect PGs). Justifications of national legal systems as deriving their democratic legitimacy from 'constitutional contracts' among citizens increasingly challenge 'Westphalian claims' by government executives to be 'masters of international treaties'; the *Kadi*-jurisprudence of the CJEU, for instance, insisted on 'constitutional interpretations' of international agreements 'in conformity with principles of justice' and the 'human rights and fundamental freedoms for all', as prescribed by the customary rules of treaty interpretation and codified in the Vienna Convention on the Law of Treaties (VCLT) (cf. Preamble and Article 31 VCLT).[10] As democratic parliaments enact international treaties for the benefit of their citizens, courts of justice – in interpreting the 'principles of justice' underlying international agreements and the human rights obligations of UN member states – increasingly construe treaties no longer only in terms of reciprocal rights and obligations among states and their governments; treaties should also protect rights of citizens vis-à-vis multilevel governance institutions that must remain constitutionally restrained by corresponding legal obligations to protect equal rights of citizens.

Such 'constitutional interpretations' are particularly warranted for international agreements that are 'founded on the values of respect for human dignity, freedom, democracy, equality, the rule of law and respect for human rights' (Article 2 TEU), including 'strict observance of international law' (Article 3 TEU), without conferring powers on international institutions (like the EU) to violate international treaties approved by par-

---

[10] The CJEU declared EU regulations implementing 'smart sanctions' by the UN Security Council to be inconsistent with human rights and illegal; cf. Joined Cases C-402/05P and 415/05 P *Kadi* ECLI:EU:C:2008:461, [2008] ECR I-6351, for example para. 284: 'It is also clear from the case-law that respect for human rights is a condition of the lawfulness of Community acts (Opinion 2/94, paragraph 34) and that measures incompatible with respect for human rights are not acceptable in the Community (Case C-112/00, *Schmidberger* [2003] ECR I-5659, paragraph 73 and case-law cited)'.

liaments for the benefit of citizens. 'Constitutional interpretation' of international agreements – as constituting multiple legal layers of reciprocal obligations among states, governments, peoples and citizens – recognize citizens and their equal human rights and constitutional rights – rather than states – as ultimate sources of legal legitimacy in modern international law. They limit 'Hegelian prioritization' of the state as having moral, communitarian autonomy and organic unity, as well as purely utilitarian justifications of state power (for example, as being necessary for protecting collective security). Respect for legitimate 'constitutional pluralism' and national 'margins of appreciation' protect 'reasonable disagreements' among diverse peoples, for instance on whether constitutional contracts should be justified by Kantian ideals of morality as protecting equal freedoms under the rule of law, or whether citizens and democratic people justify their national Constitutions on communitarian grounds that may be less tolerant regarding foreigners with different beliefs. Due to the transformation of *national* into *transnational PGs*, republican governance requires that 'state citizenship' be complemented by 'cosmopolitan citizenship rights' in order to hold multilevel governance institutions more accountable for protecting *transnational PGs* demanded by citizens. Just as national citizenship laws differ among countries, the scope and justification of EU citizenship rights and of similar rights in other regional integration systems remain contested. Neither in democratic national Constitutions nor in EU law and UN law are human rights and other cosmopolitan rights conferred top-down by the rulers, even if cosmopolitan rights are reciprocally recognized in international commercial, investment, intellectual property, labour and human rights treaties among states. From the constitutional perspective of citizens with 'inalienable human rights', including their democratic rights as holders of constituent power, such treaties must be interpreted as being concluded on behalf of citizens mutually recognizing and protecting individual rights vis-à-vis abuses of public and private power. If citizens do not confer on international institutions (like the EU) powers to violate treaties that were approved by parliaments for the benefit of citizens, then constitutional guarantees of individual rights to effective remedies and to a fair trial – as in Article 47 EUCFR – must include individual 'access to justice' for those adversely affected by arbitrary treaty violations (for example, in the case of persistent EU violations of WTO dispute-settlement rulings to the detriment of EU citizens).[11] Recognition of additional 'cosmopolitan rights' (for

---

[11] On the unjustified denial by EU courts of such remedies, see Anne Thies, *International Trade Disputes and EU Liability* (Oxford: Oxford University Press, 2013).

example, in international trade, investment, environmental, criminal and human rights law) tends to strengthen the constitutional foundations of multilevel governance of transnational PGs for the benefit of citizens and the legal accountability and constitutional duties of multilevel governance institutions. Even if 'states' are valued (for example, by 'realist theories' of 'international law among states' and Rawls' 'society of peoples' approach to international law) independently from ideals of 'cosmopolitan justice', cosmopolitan rights *strengthen* rights of citizens, democratic peoples and multilevel governance of global PGs in relation to abuses of public and private power with adverse 'external effects'.

IV. ECONOMIC AND POLITICAL COSMOPOLITANISM AS 'DRIVERS' FOR COSMOPOLITAN INTERNATIONAL LAW

In contrast to *private goods*, *PGs* are not provided spontaneously in commercial markets; they must be produced collectively because their consumption is open to all ('non-excludable') and/or does not reduce their availability to others ('non-rival'). Moral and legal cosmopolitanism say little about how multilevel governance institutions must be legally designed in order to protect more effectively PGs demanded by citizens. Yet, since their emergence in ancient Greece and Italy, democratic and republican constitutionalism emphasize the need for limiting abuses of government powers and for collectively supplying PGs through rules, institutions and 'principles of justice' rather than merely by power politics.

A. Cosmopolitan Economic Constitutionalism Protects Local Empowerment and Competition

Based on multilevel legal protection of freedom of contract, private property and peaceful dispute settlement (for example, through arbitration), international commercial law has promoted peaceful, transnational cooperation among producers, investors, traders and consumers from diverse jurisdictions since ancient times. Since the eighteenth century, economists and political philosophers have argued that – following the example of the progressive creation of common markets among confederated states (for example, in North-America in the eighteenth century, in Europe during the nineteenth century) and their later transformation into federal states (for example, the United States, Swiss and German Federations) – mutually beneficial international trade and *economic cooperation* among citizens across national frontiers can also reinforce mutually beneficial *political* and *legal integration*. The 1919 Constitution establishing the International Labour Organization (ILO) and the more than 180 ILO conventions are based on cosmopolitan principles protecting labour rights and social justice. Following World War II, multilevel judicial protection of individual rights and transnational rule of law has contributed to 'civilizing', de-politicizing and 'constitutionalizing' ever more fields of international law for the benefit of citizens, for instance through:

- cooperation between national courts and arbitral tribunals in the recognition, surveillance and enforcement of arbitral awards (for example, deciding on contractual commercial rights, property rights and judicial remedies) pursuant to the 1958 New York Convention on the Recognition and Enforcement of Foreign Arbitral Awards;
- cooperation among national and regional economic and human rights courts that protect individual rights and transnational rule of law for the benefit of citizens in free trade areas (FTAs) and customs unions, for instance by enlarging individual rights beyond national frontiers through EU law, the law of the European Economic Area (EEA), the ECHR and by multilevel judicial protection of such rights in domestic and regional courts;
- the arbitration, annulment and enforcement procedures of the International Centre for the Settlement of Investment Disputes (ICSID) in cooperation with national courts that enforce ICSID awards on protection of investor rights and obligations under bilateral and multilateral investment treaties; or
- the more than half a dozen international criminal courts complementing national criminal jurisdictions and protecting individual rights and legal accountability through multilevel judicial cooperation.

The constitutional principles of limited delegation of powers, subsidiarity and proportionality underlying federal democracies and European integration law (cf. Article 5 TEU) protect local and national communities against abuses of federal and supranational powers; they also underlie the arguments against a world state and 'global governance' that risk becoming despotic without multilevel 'constitutional checks and balances'. International trade law (for example, Article XXIV General Agreement on Tariffs and Trade (GATT); Article V General Agreement on Trade in Services (GATS)) promotes hundreds of FTAs and customs unions (like the EU) that often protect not only rights of governments, but also rights of citizens (for example, to transnational movements of goods, services, persons, capital and related payments). Similarly, international investment law dynamically evolves through more than 3000 bilateral investment treaties (BITs) that protect investor rights and complement regional and worldwide investment rules (for example, in the 1965 World Bank Convention establishing the ICSID). EU and EEA law illustrate how multilevel legal and judicial protection of common market freedoms, social rights and other constitutional rights can contribute to progressive 'constitutionalization' of IEL by empowering citizens to enforce their equal rights against abuses of public and private powers. The increasing local engagement with IEL and human rights is also illustrated by the 'UN Global Compact' (UNGC), which was launched in 1999 as a joint initiative of five UN agencies (the UN Development Program, ILO, the UN Industrial Development Organization, the UN Environmental Program and the UN Office on Drugs and Crimes) and the UN High Commissioner of Human Rights, in cooperation with now more than 6000 companies, 2000 non-business non-governmental organizations (NGOs) (like the International Federation of Football Associations) and local UNGC networks based in more than 135 countries. Its ten principles concerning the protection of human rights, core labour standards, the fight against corruption, the protection of the environment and of sustainable development aim at 'local mainstreaming' of 'cosmopolitan principles of justice' into global business activities that may 'catalyze' business support of UN goals through private-public partnerships between business and UN agencies, civil society and governments, and other 'corporate social responsibility' activities.[12] The recognition of individuals, peoples, non-governmental and supra-national organizations as legal subjects of modern international law and the increasing 'private-public partnerships' in multilevel governance of transnational PGs (like the internet) constitute 'new global public domains'; by promoting competition and open markets as decentralized information and coordination mechanisms, economic cosmopolitanism contributes to using more, decentralized information than any central government authority can process.

B. Cosmopolitan Political Constitutionalism Protects Local Diversity and Social Justice

In contrast to the *nationalist mercantilism* and *laissez-faire liberalism* preceding World War I, the economic liberalism since World War II

---

[12] Cf. Ernst-Ulrich Petersmann, *International Economic Law in the 21st Century. Constitutional Pluralism and Multilevel Governance of Interdependent Public Goods* (Oxford: Hart Publishing, 2012) 226 ff.

remains embedded in multilevel protection of human and constitutional rights that – especially in the common market among 31 EEA member states in Europe – are 'founded on the values of respect for human dignity, freedom, democracy, equality, the rule of law and respect for human rights' (Article 2 TEU) and codified in regional law (like the EUCFR). IEL rules increasingly connect individual rights and local economic activities (for example, production, investments, demand for goods and services in different jurisdictions) with multilevel legal regulation and dispute-settlement procedures so as to provide 'security and predictability to the multilateral trading system' (Article 3 Dispute Settlement Understanding, DSU) and to 'global supply chains' enabling 'international production' of goods based on components produced in many supplier countries. Hundreds of multilevel governance institutions regulate national 'policy externalities' such as:

- coordination problems calling for coordinated policy responses in order to enhance 'positive externalities' (for example, by internationally agreed product and production standards reducing transaction costs in the international division of labour); and
- cooperation problems calling for limitation of harmful 'negative externalities' (for example, caused by inadequate national regulation of bankruptcies in the financial sector, harmful tax competition, environmental pollution, or international terrorism).

International regulation (for example, of protection of cultural heritage, biodiversity and social justice) increasingly requires private-public partnerships for protecting transnational PGs. As illustrated by the civil society opposition against secretive negotiations of transatlantic FTAs disregarding rights of citizens, modern information technologies have contributed to the emergence of transnational 'public spheres' and civil society pressures on governments to meet their moral and legal 'duties of justice' to establish just governance institutions for transnational legal systems. Cosmopolitan legal principles (like normative individualism, equal respect for all human beings, *erga omnes* obligations to all) increasingly challenge and legally limit 'Hobbesian claims' for authoritarian 'policy space' and power politics. Yet, they say little about the necessary legal design of multilevel governance institutions. 'Cosmopolitan justice' is further impeded by 'reasonable disagreements' among citizens, public and private power politics (for example, due to the lack of effective WTO competition rules), and unequal concern for the basic needs of peoples in many countries.

V. FROM DEMOCRATIC AND REPUBLICAN TO COSMOPOLITAN CONSTITUTIONALISM IN GOVERNANCE OF PUBLIC GOODS

According to the moral and legal cosmopolitanism underlying HRL and constitutional democracies, democratic consent and human and constitutional rights of citizens constitute the legitimacy of national and international legal systems. As rights of states and their foreign policy powers have only derivative, instrumental value for protecting the human and constitutional rights of citizens:

- How must UN, WTO and regional law be interpreted, designed and developed in order to protect human rights and other PGs demanded by citizens more effectively? How tolerant must 'liberal peoples' be vis-à-vis non-liberal states?[13]
- Which legal and institutional governance structures at local, national, regional and worldwide levels of governance of transnational PGs offer the most effective and legitimate 'checks and balances' so as to limit abuses of power and protect human and other cosmopolitan rights of citizens? Are democratic and judicial clarifications of indeterminate human rights principles equally legitimate?
- How should international law and institutions reconcile the unity of cosmopolitan values (for example, arguing for egalitarian liberalism so as to promote distributive justice) with the need for protecting individual, democratic and legal diversity of local, national and transnational governance institutions (for example, respect for national immigration restrictions on communitarian and democratic grounds)?
- Has the incorporation of human rights and other 'principles of justice' into the law of some UN Specialized Agencies (like the ILO, WHO, UNESCO) made their multilevel governance of transnational PGs more effective than that of GATT/WTO law, which does not mention human rights? Do 'law and economics' also reflect human rights values?
- Is it legitimate if legal and judicial UN and WTO institutions reconcile their 'state-centered' and 'person-centered principles of justice' in different and potentially conflicting ways (for example, in case of conflicts between intellectual property rights and human rights)?

---

[13] Cf. John Rawls, *The Law of Peoples* (Cambridge: Harvard University Press, 1999) 3–4.

- Why are some international investment tribunals, criminal courts and economic courts balancing public and private interests in terms of human rights and other 'principles of justice' that are hardly ever mentioned by WTO dispute-settlement bodies in spite of the cosmopolitan objectives of liberal trade regimes?
- Why have national and international commercial, investment and criminal courts, like regional economic and human rights courts, engaged in more coherent judicial cooperation (for example, in terms of mutually 'consistent interpretations' and 'judicial comity') than national, regional and WTO dispute-settlement bodies adjudicating trade disputes?
- How can nationalist and 'realist approaches' to IEL be reconciled with competing constitutional, cosmopolitan or 'global administrative law' (GAL) approaches?[14]

A. Treaty Interpretation and Adjudication 'in Conformity with Principles of Justice'

Due to different democratic preferences, local people often apply the customary law requirement of treaty interpretation and adjudication 'in conformity with principles of justice' in diverse ways. For instance, European courts have interpreted FTA and common market rules of the EU Treaty as conferring fundamental rights on individuals. Governmental limitations of such 'market freedoms' – for example, in case of imported laser games that simulate killing of peoples and were prohibited in the German town of Bonn as offending 'human dignity' and public order – were accepted by the CJEU as legally justifiable and 'proportionate' even if other towns in Germany and other EU member states did not adopt similar prohibitions due to their different conceptions of 'human dignity'.[15] The four '*Kadi* judgments' of the General Court and CJEU since 2005 can be understood in conformity with the '*solange*-jurisprudence' of the German Constitutional Court and of the ECtHR to the effect that 'as long as' (which means *solange* in German language) the higher level of law (that is, UN law in the *Kadi* cases, EU law in the *solange*-jurisprudence of the German Constitutional Court) does not guarantee equivalent protection of fundamental rights, the courts at lower levels of multilevel legal and judicial systems must guarantee such fundamental rights in domestic jurisdictions. The German Constitutional Court and the ECtHR refrain from

---

14 Cf. Petersmann (note 12 above) at 78 ff.

15 Cf. Case C-36/02 *Omega* ECLI:EU:C:2004:614, [2004] ECR I-9609.

exercising their jurisdiction 'as long as' the CJEU protects fundamental rights in ways equivalent to the constitutional protection under German constitutional law and the ECHR respectively. The CJEU may, similarly, limit its judicial review of EU measures implementing UN Security Council sanctions once UN law offers equivalent procedural and substantive legal protection of individual rights of the defence, property rights and effective judicial protection.

Both the *Kadi* and the '*solange-jurisprudence*' suggest that – as UN and regional human rights conventions leave states 'margins of appreciation' for implementing and protecting human rights in their national legal systems – multilevel regulation and judicial protection of civil, political, economic, social and cultural rights must be based on mutually consistent interpretations and 'judicial comity', 'subsidiarity' and 'loyal cooperation' among the different levels of governance, with due respect for the sovereign rights of states to guarantee higher levels of constitutional protection in domestic and local jurisdictions than at international levels of governance.[16] Yet, UN and WTO governance institutions remain dominated by government executives who prioritize rights of governments over rights of citizens and pursue self-interests in limiting their legal, democratic and judicial accountability regarding adversely affected citizens. For instance, as government executives prefer to construe the WTO rules on state responsibility and judicial remedies in domestic courts narrowly, local governments often disregard WTO legal obligations.

B. Learning from Comparative Institutional Analyses

Moral, legal, political and economic cosmopolitanism have neglected the task of designing multilevel governance institutions to protect international PGs for the benefit of citizens and their constitutional rights rather than for the benefit of rulers. Comparative constitutional and institutional analyses emphasize that the respective advantages of economic markets, political decision-making, constitutional, legislative, administrative, judicial and intergovernmental processes depend on which institution is in a better position to protect the constitutional values inherent in the relevant rules and arbitrate competing legal claims.[17] For instance, due to

---

16 As neither Canada nor the United States have ratified the Inter-American Convention on Human Rights, international HRL seems to have less influenced the interpretation of North American Free Trade Agreement (NAFTA) law (for example, investment arbitration referring to the rights of indigenous peoples).

17 Cf. the interdisciplinary constitutional, legal, economic and 'public choice' analyses of multilevel economic regulation in: Meinhard Hilf and Ernst-Ulrich

the collective action problems (like 'free-riding') in the collective supply of transnational 'pure PGs' whose consumption benefits are non-excludable and non-rival, transformation of 'pure PGs' (like an open, undistorted global trading system) into 'club goods' (like the WTO and FTAs) can set incentives for cooperation and avoid free-riding (for example, by making membership conditional on reciprocal trade liberalization). Democratic governance of such 'club goods' can be strengthened by linking the treaty rules concerned to corresponding cosmopolitan rights that enable decentralized enforcement of rules by self-interested citizens.

Arguably, 'globalization' and its transformation of many *national* into *transnational PGs* require embedding 'democratic constitutionalism' into multilevel republican and 'cosmopolitan constitutionalism' in order to constitute, limit, regulate and justify multilevel governance institutions more effectively for the benefit of citizens, their human and constitutional rights and transnational rule of law.[18] Historically, democratic constitutionalism (since the ancient Constitution of Athens), republican constitutionalism (since the ancient Roman, Florentine and Venetian republics), and cosmopolitanism prioritized different values (for example, democratic participation of male property owners in the ancient Athenian democracy, aristocratic protection of public goods for the benefit of Roman citizens, protection of 'inalienable human rights'). Each of these different approaches to 'constitutionalism' entailed different forms of regulating private and public goods (for example, through the unique system of Roman private law and its progressive transformation into a *jus commune* in Europe). Following the return to humanism in the *renaissance* and in 'enlightenment philosophies' of man (as illustrated by the focus on the dignity of man founded on man's freedom and reasonableness in the renaissance philosophy of Pico della Mirandola and the enlightenment philosophy of I. Kant), the recognition of human rights helped to establish ever more 'constitutional democracies' that protect human and constitutional rights, rule of law and other PGs in more integrated and effective ways than in non-democratic governance regimes. Yet, extending

---

Petersmann, eds, *National Constitutions and International Economic Law* (The Hague: Kluwer, 1993). On participation-oriented 'comparative institutional analysis' of alternative decision-making processes like markets, political processes and judicial procedures, see Neil K. Komesar, *Imperfect Alternatives: Choosing Institutions in Law, Economics and Public Choice* (Chicago: Chicago University Press, 1994).

[18] Cf. Ernst-Ulrich Petersmann, *Multilevel Constitutionalism for Multilevel Governance of Public Goods – Methodology Problems in International Law* (Oxford: Hart Publishing, 2016).

'constitutional democracy' beyond states to multilevel governance of transnational PGs has proven difficult, for instance in view of the lack of a 'transnational *demos*', the inadequate constitutional restraints of many multilevel governance institutions, and the reality of intergovernmental power politics in UN and WTO institutions that resist citizen-oriented proposals for multilevel *demoi-cracy*. Also the multilevel 'human rights constitutionalism' based on national, regional and UN human rights conventions and on functionally limited, international 'treaty constitutions' – like the 1919 Constitution establishing the ILO – has failed to effectively protect human and labour rights in many countries, notably in Africa and Asia. Can the 'implementation deficits' in power-oriented and 'dis-connected' UN/WTO governance be reduced for the benefit of citizens?

C. Lessons from Democratic Constitutionalism

The more *parliamentary democracies* fail to effectively guide and control UN/WTO governance of global PGs in an antagonistic world without 'global democracy' and without a single *demos*, the more must *constitutional, participatory* and *deliberative democracy* be extended 'bottom-up' beyond state borders in order to hold intergovernmental power politics more accountable. Empirical evidence confirms that *multilevel constitutionalism* – by empowering citizens through civil, political, economic, social and cultural rights and remedies to hold multilevel governance institutions legally, democratically and judicially accountable – has protected PGs more effectively (for example, in European law, international commercial, investment and criminal law) than path-dependent forms of intergovernmental power politics.

'Global democracy' is likely to remain a utopia for a long time. As HRL protects individual and democratic diversity, the diverse social preferences for prioritizing and reconciling human, constitutional and economic rights of citizens in legitimately different ways must be accepted as a permanent fact. Most national and international parliamentary assemblies fail effectively to participate in – and control – multilevel UN, WTO and regional governance of transnational PGs. Such 'parliamentary democracy deficits' need to be compensated by stronger multilevel rights and remedies of citizens aimed at promoting more inclusive and more representative governance of PGs through transnational rights of citizens and stronger legal, democratic and judicial accountability of multilevel governance institutions, for instance based on cosmopolitan principles of protecting all affected interests and all stakeholders subject to legal coercion. History confirms that functionally limited transnational communities can develop (for example inside the EU) also without a 'single demos'. Multilevel *deliberative democracy* requires multilevel duties to promote transparency of intergovernmental decision-making and of its public justification regarding all affected citizens. Also the constitutional principles of conferral, subsidiarity and proportionality (cf. Article 5 TEU) serve 'democratic functions' aimed at limiting delegation of powers and abuses of the 'constituted powers' by multilevel governance institutions so as to protect individual and democratic freedoms of citizens. Democracy has become an indispensable source of legitimacy also of *international law*; yet, it does not require constituting, limiting, regulating and justifying *international institutions* in the same way as *national democratic institutions*. The supranational EU constitutionalism – and the more deferential forms of transnational cooperation in the EU external relations with democracies – illustrate how multilevel governance of transnational PGs can be 'constitutionalized' in legitimately diverse forms.

D. Lessons from Republican Constitutionalism

The provision of PGs (*res publica*) remains the main justification of states and of international organizations. Legal and political republicanism is much older than the economic distinction between *private* and *public goods* in Adam Smith's *The Wealth of Nations* (1776). The 'ancient liberties' in the Greek and Roman republics protected democratic participation in the rule of the public sphere rather than individual rights and freedoms in the private and social sphere.[19] The ancient Greeks emphasized democratic rights and the need for justifying law and governance (for example, based on Aristotelian 'principles of justice' and 'virtue politics'). The Roman republican tradition focused more on PGs (like the Roman legal system) that were perceived (for example, by Cicero) as the 'common property' of Roman citizens and protected by complex 'constitutional checks and balances'. Modern economic and political PGs theories emphasize that – apart from '*intermediate PGs*' like human rights and rule of law – non-excludable and non-rival 'pure PGs' remain rare. Most PGs are 'impure' in the sense that their consumption is either non-rival but exclusive (for example, patented knowledge whose industrial use is limited to patent holders) or non-exclusive but rival (for example, common pool

---

[19] Cf. Philip Pettit, *Republicanism: A Theory of Freedom and Government* (Oxford: Clarendon Press, 1997) 18. Pettit argues for a 'communitarian character of freedom as non-domination' recognizing that 'the freedom of a community is as basic a notion as the freedom of individuals' (at 275).

resources like fish in the High Seas). Transformation of 'pure PGs' (like the world trading system) into 'club goods' (like the WTO and regional trading, legal and dispute-settlement systems with limited membership) reduces collective action problems (like free riding). Similarly, states often exclude foreigners from *national PGs* (for example, national market freedoms, democracy, social security systems) and agree to *transnational PGs regimes* only on condition of reciprocity (for example, common markets among EU and EEA member states). Democratic and republican constitutionalism focuses on democratic and republican rights and communitarian cooperation of citizens as the most important incentives for collective supply of PGs and for holding governments accountable through 'principal-agent relationships'. Economic theories explain why linking rational self-interests of citizens to their collective supply of PGs can render governance more efficient than naïve reliance on benevolent rulers.

The diverse structures of the UN Specialized Agencies for collective supply of international PGs confirm that – depending on their diverse contexts and 'collective action problems' – different PGs regimes may require different legal structures and 'production strategies'. For instance:

- Some 'single best efforts PGs' may be supplied locally through private-public partnerships and the support by a single state (for example, development of polio vaccines in the United States).
- The collective production of 'weakest link PGs' may focus on the local problems in a few 'risk states' even if the latter contribute the least (like eradication of smallpox through WHO-sponsored programs in poor African countries such as Somalia).
- Collective supply of global 'aggregate PGs' can be facilitated through mutually beneficial, burden-sharing arrangements financed by international institutions and the most developed countries.[20]

The ILO's tripartite membership structures (governments, employers, employees) were justified by the nature of labour rights and by the political power of trade unions following World War I. The treaty 'constitutions' establishing the World Health Organization (WHO), the Food and Agriculture Organization (FAO) and UNESCO likewise define their republican tasks of protecting public health, food security and public

[20] On the different kinds of PGs and their diverse 'production technologies', see Scott Barret, *Why Cooperate? The Incentive to Supply Global Public Goods* (Oxford: Oxford University Press, 2007).

education by references to corresponding rights of citizens. Yet, as WHO law, FAO law and UNESCO law remain dominated by government executives without effective legal and judicial protection of individual rights and remedies in UN governance practices, they often fail to build on the 'intermediate PGs' that must constitute transnational 'aggregate PGs' as legal foundations at local, national and regional levels of governance and regulation.

Why is it that human rights, rule of law, democracy, monetary stability and open markets – even though they are 'pure PGs' whose supply offers non-excludable and non-exhaustible benefits to all citizens protected by such rules and institutions – remain under-supplied in so many UN member countries? Arguably, the lack of local and national 'component PGs' inside so many UN member states (notably in Africa and Asia) undermine multilevel governance of transnational 'aggregate PGs'. Democratic, republican and cosmopolitan constitutionalism explain such policy challenges in terms of lack of inadequate insistence by citizens on constituting, limiting, regulating and justifying governance powers coherently through constitutional rights and legal, democratic and judicial accountability mechanisms. History offers numerous examples of 'republican Constitutions' (like the German 'Weimar Constitution' of 1919) that failed to prevent arbitrary abuses of power due to inadequate 'democratic struggles for justice' by citizens. Globalization and its transformation of national into transnational 'aggregate PGs' call for multilevel 'republican conceptions' of international law that – by empowering citizens, democratic institutions and courts of justice to constitute, limit and regulate multilevel governance powers in terms of democratic, republican and cosmopolitan rights and remedies of citizens – can limit the existing 'implementation deficits' of 'disconnected' UN and WTO law in many UN member states. Even in the transatlantic FTA negotiations between constitutional democracies, the Comprehensive Economic and Trade Agreement (CETA) between Canada and the EU – by excluding private rights and judicial remedies in domestic courts to invoke CETA rules (cf. Article 30.6) and by privileging *foreign investors* to challenge government regulations through international arbitration (cf. Article 8.23 CETA) – disempowers and discriminates domestic citizens and limits governmental accountability for violations of FTAs.[21]

---

[21] Cf. Ernst-Ulrich Petersmann, 'Transformative Transatlantic Free Trade Agreements without Rights and Remedies of Citizens?' (2015) 18 J Int Economic Law 579.

VI. LESSONS FROM COSMOPOLITAN CONSTITUTIONALISM FOR MULTILEVEL GOVERNANCE OF PUBLIC GOODS

Cosmopolitan constitutionalism – as illustrated by the multilevel legal and judicial protection of fundamental rights and of corresponding governance duties in European law – limits the flaws of national, single-polity perspectives by protecting transnational PGs and common, reasonable interests of transnational legal communities. *Cosmopolitan citizenship* should include 'membership rights' in self-governing local, national and transnational polities responsible for multilevel protection of transnational PGs, based on distinctions between the national *demos* (composed of citizens having the franchise) and a broader '*cosmopolitan citizenry*' including all who have a stake in being members of transnational polities responsible for protecting transnational PGs. Democratic, republican and cosmopolitan constitutionalism complement each other by synergies that – as in the story of the blind men describing an elephant depending on the different body parts they touched – enable a more coherent understanding and regulation of the collective action problems in multilevel governance of transnational 'aggregate PGs', for instance based on inclusive representation of all interests that are actually affected by democratic regulation, and of the rights of all who are subject to the jurisdiction of government decisions affecting their individual autonomy. The 'public consultation' by the EU Commission on CETA's investment rules in 2014 illustrates how 'participatory demoi-cracy' by transnational legal communities can successfully resist intergovernmental power politics and insist on changing intergovernmental rules that circumvent domestic constitutional guarantees.

A. Cosmopolitan Rights Render International Law More Effective

The more national Constitutions depend on international law and multilevel governance institutions for protecting human rights and other transnational PGs, the stronger becomes the need for recognizing economic, social and other cosmopolitan rights of citizens and promoting decentralized enforcement of international rules, as it is successfully done in:

- HRL and international criminal law;
- international contract, commercial and corporate law and related agreements on the recognition and enforcement of arbitral awards;
- international investment law and arbitration;
- international intellectual property law and arbitration;

- international labour rights and other social rights (for example, regarding free movement of workers and protection of their families under EU and EEA law);
- international trading rights and related judicial remedies (for example, under some WTO rules and regional FTAs in Europe); and
- internet regulations and related human rights guarantees (for example, on privacy rights).

UN human rights bodies and Specialized Agencies increasingly cooperate with international economic organizations (like the World Bank and the WTO) in clarifying and coordinating interrelationships between HRL (for example, health rights and 'corporate social responsibilities') and IEL, for instance by adopting:

- the 2003 WHO Framework Convention on Tobacco Control (FCTC) which has been ratified by 180 states and regulates the interrelationships between health rights, trading rights (for example, to sell toxic tobacco products) and intellectual property rights (like trade marks of tobacco companies);
- the UN 'Respect, Protect and Remedy' Framework and Guiding Principles for business and human rights, adopted by the UN Human Rights Council in 2008; and
- the additional 'Guiding Principles on Business and Human Rights: Implementing the UN Respect, Protect and Remedy Framework' that were endorsed by the UN Human Rights Council in June 2011 and increasingly influence human rights, business and arbitration practices.

Civil society support for international 'PGs treaties' becomes ever more important for conclusion and parliamentary approval of international economic, environmental, criminal law and human rights agreements. Legal practice confirms that – in conformity with the constitutional premise that the effectiveness of constitutional rules and 'principles of justice' depends on their transformation into democratic legislation, administration and judicial protection of individual rights – multilevel judicial protection of cosmopolitan rights enhances the effectiveness of international agreements, for instance if regional economic and human rights courts, investment and commercial tribunals protect human, economic and social rights that can be subsequently enforced through national courts. Also the 'dispute settlement system of the WTO' (Article 3 DSU) prescribes and protects judicial remedies for individuals and non-governmental actors in domestic legal systems, for instance in the field of GATT (Article X), the WTO Antidumping Agreement (Article 13), the WTO Agreement on Customs Valuation (Article 11), the Agreement on Pre-shipment Inspection (Article 4), the Agreement on Subsidies and Countervailing Measures (Article 23), the GATS (Article VI), the Agreement on Trade-Related Intellectual Property Rights (Articles 41–50, 59 TRIPS) and the Agreement on Government Procurement (Article XX). Yet, as many WTO member governments prevent domestic citizens from invoking GATT/WTO rules in domestic jurisdictions, GATT/WTO legal obligations continue to be frequently disregarded by governments in domestic legal practices of WTO members.

B. Cosmopolitan Rights Strengthen Republican and Economic Constitutionalism

Commercial law has long promoted – for example, through multilevel legal protection of freedom of contract, private property and arbitration – the PG of transnational division of labour. 'Law and economics' also justifies individual rights (like common market freedoms, private property and investor rights, corporate and tort law, labour and social rights) as legal incentives for pursuing reasonable self-interests in multilevel protection of PGs. If the democratic legitimacy of governments and states depends on protecting *national PGs* and corresponding rights of citizens, efficient governance of *transnational PGs* must likewise be justified, limited and regulated in terms of rights of citizens, as increasingly recognized in regional economic integration law and other commercial, investment, intellectual property, environmental, labour and human rights treaties. Also authoritarian governments in non-democratic (for example, communist) countries – which often present themselves as 'peoples republics' without protecting citizens through 'republican constitutionalism' against abuses of power – increasingly accept the need for reforming their domestic economies through membership in the Bretton Woods and WTO institutions and domestic legal reforms based on the IEL of the International Monetary Fund, the World Bank and WTO law. China, for instance, uses WTO law and FTAs for recreating a common market among the four Chinese WTO memberships (China, Hong Kong, Macao, Taiwan) and for reforming its domestic legal and judicial system in conformity with WTO legal obligations.

In constitutional democracies, national legal and economic systems derive their democratic and republican legitimacy from 'constitutional contracts' among citizens and from republican rights of citizens to governmental protection of PGs. Also in multilevel governance of *transnational PGs*, 'Westphalian claims' by government executives to be 'masters of international treaties' are increasingly challenged by civil society and democratic institutions. Article 3 TEU explicitly requires the EU to contribute in its external relations 'to the protection of its citizens', 'human rights and . . . strict observance of international law', without granting powers to the EU to violate international agreements concluded by the EU and approved by parliaments for the benefit of citizens. Courts of justice must construe treaties no longer only in terms of reciprocal rights and obligations among states and their governments, but also as protecting rights of free and equal citizens vis-à-vis multilevel governance institutions that must remain constitutionally restrained by corresponding legal obligations to protect civil, political, economic, social and cultural rights of citizens, as universally recognized in UN HRL. The task of 'constitutionalizing' multilevel governance of *transnational PGs* justifies 'constitutional interpretations' of many international treaties as protecting rights of citizens, for instance to consular protection, investment protection, and 'consistent interpretations' of national and international obligations of governments to protect rule of law and other PGs.

VII. CONCLUSION: COSMOPOLITAN CONSTITUTIONALISM IS NECESSARY FOR PROTECTING GLOBAL PUBLIC GOODS

Modern HRL refutes Hobbesian claims that international anarchy and unreasonableness of human beings justify unlimited policy powers of states and their rulers. Modern constitutional democracies increasingly integrate the diverse traditions of democratic, republican and cosmopolitan constitutionalism at national and regional levels of governance of PGs, for instance by cooperating with transnational civil society (for example, 'stakeholder consultations' in FTA negotiations) and empowering citizens and non-governmental actors to legally challenge abuses of power in multilevel governance of global PGs (for example, through judicial remedies). *Democratic constitutionalism* emphasizes the need for participatory and deliberative 'democratic input-legitimacy', accountability of 'representative democracy', and 'output-legitimacy' of multilevel governance institutions. *Republican* and *cosmopolitan constitutionalism* explain more specifically the need for justifying, limiting and regulating multilevel governance of transnational PGs in terms of republican and cosmopolitan rights of citizens and related constitutional 'checks and balances' limiting abuses of public and private power. The path-dependent 'constitutional nationalism' inside UN member states needs to be reconciled with the human rights requirements of protecting transnational PGs through functionally limited 'cosmopolitan constitutionalism' so that citizens can hold multilevel governance institutions accountable for transnational protection of PGs.

As illustrated by the opportunities and risks of modern information technologies, globalization entails new governance challenges that affect existential interests of citizens all over the world. They can be evaluated more appropriately in the comprehensive context of HRL rather than only in the interest-driven context of fragmented treaty regimes focusing on 'piecemeal engineering' (for example, of modern information societies). Multilevel recognition of civil, political, economic, social and cultural rights of citizens promotes 'constitutionalization' of international law and requires reviewing the 'primary rules of conduct' and 'secondary rules of recognition, change and adjudication' of international legal systems. This contribution has argued for limiting 'disconnected UN/WTO governance' by stronger legal, democratic and judicial rights and remedies of citizens to insist on transnational rule of law. Unless multilevel governance institutions cooperate in conformity with international agreements that were approved by democratic institutions for the benefit of citizens, transnational rule of law and equal rights of citizens cannot be protected. IEL illustrates how legal empowerment of citizens and the linkage of their rational self-interests to collective supply of PGs (like undistorted market competition as enforced by competition rules and citizen-driven adjudication) can promote stronger cooperation among national and international jurisdictions in protecting transnational rule of law and rights of citizens in international cooperation.

The increasing references to HRL in the jurisprudence of national and regional tribunals can assist in reconciling fragmented legal regimes by 'constitutionalizing social piecemeal engineering'. In worldwide dispute-settlement systems (for example, of the WTO), the deliberate avoidance of references to HRL may be justified in view of the 'reasonable disagreement' among the contracting parties on many indeterminate (for example, economic and social) human rights obligations. Cosmopolitan constitutionalism will remain contested as long as UN and WTO governance institutions remain dominated by government executives that prioritize rights of governments over rights of citizens and pursue self-interests in limiting their legal, democratic and judicial 'duties to protect' and accountability regarding adversely affected citizens. As instruments of social change, constitutionalism and law depend on institutionalizing citizen-driven, legal cultures and 'public reason' in order to progressively limit the ubiquity of abuses of public and private powers. This contribution has argued, inter alia, as follows:

- Democratic, republican and cosmopolitan constitutionalism call for 'constitutionalizing' multilevel governance of transnational PGs so as to integrate the competing conceptions of IEL and better protect civil, political, economic, social and cultural rights of citizens.
- Even if most citizens remain 'rationally ignorant' of complex UN/WTO negotiations among governments, political pressures for the needed 'constitutional reforms' of IEL are more likely to come from civil society, democratic parliaments and courts of justice than from UN and WTO diplomats.
- The task of constituting, limiting, regulating and justifying multilevel governance of the international economy in terms of equal rights of citizens must take into account the lessons from comparative institutional analyses of multilevel governance of transnational PGs as well as the historical lessons from democratic, republican and cosmopolitan constitutionalism for limiting abuses of power.
- The 'constitutional functions' of republican and cosmopolitan rights for constituting, limiting, regulating and justifying multilevel governance of transnational 'aggregate PGs' for the benefit of citizens require empowering citizens to invoke and enforce precise and unconditional 'PGs treaties' in domestic jurisdictions through stronger judicial protection of their rights.
- As IEL remains embedded in the reality of diverse national and international institutions, GAL conceptions of IEL (for example, promoting transparency, accountability, rule of law) require more coherent constitutional justifications and legal methodologies (for example, clarifying the 'legal sources' of GAL principles).
- Private law conceptions of IEL must remain consistent with the reality of 'constitutional pluralism' and of legitimately diverse approaches in constitutional democracies for regulation of 'market failures' (for example, in self-regulation of the financial sector and of information technologies), 'governance failures' and 'constitutional failures'.
- 'Economic approaches' to IEL continue to be distorted by power politics (for example, trade protectionism, exchange rate manipulation, disempowerment of citizens and judicial privileges for foreign investors in many FTAs) and suffer from justice-deficits (for example, inconsistencies of 'Kaldor-Hicks efficiency' with 'justice as human rights').

From the perspective of the universal recognition of human rights and cosmopolitan constitutionalism, 'market citizens', 'state citizens' and 'cosmopolitan citizens' should be the legitimate 'drivers' of individual and democratic self-government through market economies and 'principal-agent governance'. The political reality of multilevel economic regulation remains dominated by private and public power politics (for example, VW engineers manipulating car emissions so as to circumvent multilevel environmental regulations). The history of constitutionalism suggests that abuses of public and private regulation can be successfully limited by transforming fundamental rights, rule of law and democracy into legislation, administration, adjudication and international law – provided the latter institutionalize 'public reason' and 'constitutionalize' law and the economy. EU and EEA law confirm that also *multilevel governance* of *transnational PGs* can be effectively 'constitutionalized' for the benefit of citizens, for instance by constitutional and judicial protection of 'countervailing rights' of foreign market participants if they are adversely affected by national regulations. The persistent violations of the EU's 'monetary constitution', (for example, the EU rules on budget and debt disciplines), 'area of freedom, security and justice' (for example, the Schengen and Dublin rules for immigration) and 'foreign policy constitution' (for example, Articles 3, 21 TEU) illustrate the need for permanent 'Sisyphean struggles' and 'republican virtues'[22] to 'constitutionalize' IEL and the global division of labour. 'UN/WTO governance' of the global economy remains dominated by power politics and 'disconnected' from citizens as 'democratic principals' of multilevel governance agents. The 'principles of justice' underlying modern international law (like human rights, democratic self-determination, rule of law) require citizens to struggle for stronger protection of their human and constitutional rights in multilevel regulation of the global economy so that IEL and multilevel governance of PGs also protect rights of citizens in local jurisdictions where citizens live, work and die.

---

[22] According to Aristotle's *Nicomachean Ethic*, among the four 'cardinal virtues' (prudence, justice, courage and temperance), only prudence requires intelligence rather than willpower. The three 'theological virtues' (faith, love and hope) likewise do not require particular intelligence; they support humanistic 'cosmopolitics' rather than state-based power politics.

PART II

Structural aspects of trade and investment

3. Transparency evolution: more than the right to know*

Ljiljana Biukovic

I. INTRODUCTION

The interaction between international trade and human rights in the context of economic globalization often raises questions as to whether international trade and investment treaties are a good mechanism to protect human rights and, if so, what human rights should be protected and how. In the absence of explicit legal linkages between the two areas of international law, answers to these questions tend to focus on political dialogue between various international actors and institutions obliged to comply with both international trade and human rights laws in specific factual situations.[1] Two such situations, related to the investment of Chinese companies in Peru's extractive industry projects, are examined in this chapter: Shougang's operation of the Macrona mine and Chinalo's operation of the Toromocho mine.

Some scholars argue that trade obligations are constitutionalized in international trade treaties as human rights and that international trade treaties could therefore evolve to develop mechanisms for the protection of human rights other than economic rights.[2] Building on the twenty-first-century concepts of the constitutionalism of international trade law

---

* This chapter is based on a paper presented to the workshop on "Mapping the Impact of International Trade and Human Rights on Local Practice", held in July 2014 at the International Institute for the Sociology of Law in Oñati, Spain. I am grateful to Sarah Biddulph, Moshe Hirsch and Pitman Potter for their comments on the earlier drafts of this chapter. Erica Zacharias, Peter A. Allard School of Law second year JD student, provided valuable research assistance.

[1] For further discussions, see Frederick M. Abbott, Christine Breining-Kaufmann and Thomas Cottier, eds, *International Trade and Human Rights; Foundations and Conceptual Issues* (Ann Arbor: The University of Michigan Press, 2006) and Thomas Cottier, Joost Pauwelyn and Elisabeth Bürgi, eds, *Human Rights and International Trade* (Oxford: Oxford University Press, 2005).

[2] Ernst-Ulrich Petersmann, this volume, Chapter 2.

and the evolution of human rights protection, some scholars believe that the doctrine of multilevel governance is the most suitable framework to systematically address the problems of fragmentation and coherence in different areas of international law, especially those problems arising out of the relationship between human rights and international trade law.[3] That doctrine asserts that states, having already conceded some of their regulatory powers to international organizations, should act as intermediaries between different layers of governance, such as international, transnational and national.[4] States should build the framework of interaction of governance institutions on the basis of a clearly defined constitutional process including the allocation of powers and the communication among the different layers of governance. Others argue that the two areas of law – international trade and human rights – should be kept separate because the use of international trade institutions to protect human rights is legitimizing a neoliberal and market-focused dimension of human rights that does not adequately address the obligations of states to protect individual non-economic rights under international human rights law and United Nations rules.[5] Scholars also argue that the requirement for states to respect human rights, as a condition for the membership in international trade organizations and in order to be able to access international financial aid, raises for developing countries sensitive issues such as the scope of their remaining regulatory sovereignty and the relevance of human rights treaties in the light of developing countries' commitment to the WTO regime.[6]

International trade and investment treaties are agreed upon primarily for the purpose of advancing trade in goods and services and for the promotion and protection of foreign investments. The treaties do not directly address the issue of the protection of human rights although they indirectly address human rights by creating their own rules of gov-

---

[3] Thomas Cottier and Maya Hertig, "The Prospects of 21st Century Constitutionalism" (2003) 7:1 Max Planck YB UN L. 299. See also Michael Zürn, "Global Governance as Multi-Level Governance" in Henrik Ederlein, Sonja Wälti and Michael Zürn, eds, *Handbook on Multi-level Governance* (Cheltenham and Northampton: Edward Elgar, 2010) 80.

[4] Cottier and Hertig (note 3 above) at 313–17.

[5] Philip Alston, "Resisting Merger and Acquisition of Human Rights by Trade Law: A Reply to Petersmann" (2002) 13:4 EJIL 815. But see Emilie M. Hafner-Burton, *Forced to Be Good; Why Trade Agreements Boost Human Rights* (Ithaca: Cornell University Press, 2009).

[6] See, for example, Sisule Frederich Musungy, "International Trade and Human Rights in Africa: A Comment on Conceptual Linkages" in Abbott, Breining-Kaufmann and Cottier, eds (note 1 above) 321 at 322.

ernance or by referring to rules of international human rights treaties.[7] Moreover, they create legal rules and institutions that form an integral part of a rule-based system of world trade built on principles of non-discrimination and transparency. Human rights law, too, is based on these principles. Therefore, international trade law and human rights law seem to interact through the principles of governance and the rule of law.[8] The transparency rules in those agreements are often cited as evidence of possible incorporation of human rights provisions into the international trade regime.[9] Hence, transparency is linked to the human right to information,[10] and to the corresponding correlated duty of states to facilitate individuals' access to information and to participation in public affairs.[11] In that context, transparency and the right to access information as captured in international treaties, including trade treaties, are seen as the basis for the enjoyment of all other human rights.

This chapter considers two aspects of the advancement of transparency rules in international law and national laws. The first aspect is referred to as the "transparency turn,"[12] and it concerns the proliferation of transparency rules in many areas of international law, including international economic law and human rights law. The second aspect relates to the evolution of transparency policy from the right to know to the duty imposed by government on private and public actors to disclose information to the public or targeted transparency, and, finally, towards the right of private

---

[7] See Thomas Cottier, "Governance, Trade and Human Rights" in Abbott, Breining-Kaufmann and Cottier (note 1 above) 93 at 104, and Susan Ariel Aaronson and Jean Pierre Chauffour, *The Wedding of Trade and Human Rights: Marriage of Convenience or Permanent Match?*, WTO Research and Analysis, available at https://www.wto.org/english/res_e/publications_e/wtr11_forum_e/wtr11_15feb11_e.htm (accessed 4 January 2017).

[8] See Thomas Cottier, "Governance, Trade and Human Rights" in Abbott, Breining-Kaufmann and Cottier (note 1 above) 93 at 95. The World Bank Institute broadly defines governance as "the traditions and institutions by which authority in a country is exercised". See World Bank Institute, *Governance Matters 2009: Release of Worldwide Governance Indicators 1996–2008*, available at http://www.worldbank.org/en/news/press-release/2009/06/29/governance-matters-2009-release-of-worldwide-governance-indicators-1996-2008 (accessed 4 January 2017).

[9] Aaronson and Chauffour (note 7 above).

[10] Maeve McDonagh, "The Right to Information in International Human Rights Law" (2013) 13:1 HRL Rev 25 at 29.

[11] Mark Festner, "Seeing the State: Transparency as Metaphor" (2010) 62 Admin L Rev 617.

[12] Anne Peters, "The Transparency Turn of International Law" (2015) 1 CJGG 3.

parties to participate in designing transparency policies or collaborative transparency.[13] This evolution indicates that transparency as a human right is a part of the democratic principle in modern administrative states and that the right to access information is the precondition for citizens' getting an opportunity to not only learn about government policies but also to participate in government's decision-making related to government policies.

This chapter examines domestic transparency rules of China and Peru and related domestic laws in the context of the countries' implementation and enforcement of international transparency laws. Free trade agreements (FTAs) and bilateral investment treaties (BITs) are cornerstones of economic development of the two countries; in each they are important tools for the countries' integration into the global market.[14] Not only has the mining industry been at the core of said economic cooperation[15] but it has also been the subject of global public scrutiny due to its long history of poor resource management, including a lack of transparency, corruption, and violation of the human rights of miners and members of local communities affected by the extractions ("resource curse"[16]). In response to

---

[13] Archon Fung, Mary Graham and David Weil, *Full Disclosure: The Perils and Promises of Transparency* (New York: Cambridge University Press, 2007) 25–8.

[14] China has 13 FTAs in force and has been negotiating eight new FTAs. China started entering into FTAs with other countries only after its accession to the WTO in 2001: see http://fta.mofcom.gov.cn/english/. China has been actively negotiating bilateral investment treaties since the 1980s and has signed 145 BITs, 34 of which are either terminated or not yet in force: see http://investmentpolicyhub.unctad.org/IIA/CountryBits/42. Peru has 16 FTAs in force and is a member of a regional economic bloc (Andean Community). About 95 percent of all the country's export is regulated by those agreements. Peru is also a part of the Trans Pacific Partnership (TPP) negotiations: see http://www.limaeasy.com/business-guide/free-trade-agreements-ftas-with-peru#signed-agreements. In addition, Peru has signed 32 BITs, four of which are terminated: see http://investmentpolicyhub.unctad.org/IIA/CountryBits/165 (all websites accessed 4 January 2017).

[15] More than 30 percent of all Peruvian mining investment portfolios is held by Chinese companies. See Cynthia Sanborn and Victoria Chann, "Chinese Investment in Peru's Mining Industry: Blessing or Curse?" (2015) Boston University Global Economic Governance Initiative Discussion Paper No. 2015/8 at 2. See also Rebecca Ray, Kevin Gallagher, Andres Lopez and Cynthia Sanborn, "China in Latin America: Lessons for South-South Cooperation and Sustainable Development" (2015) Boston University Global Economic Initiative, Working Group Final Report 04/2015, 5, available at http://www.bu.edu/pardeeschool/files/2014/12/Working-Group-Final-Report.pdf (accessed 4 January 2017).

[16] Moises Arce, *Resource Extraction and Protest in Peru* (Pittsburgh: University of Pittsburgh Press, 2014) 45–65.

external and internal requests for increased transparency in the activities of their governments and for the broader participation of private actors in the governments' decisions about economic development and the distribution of economic wealth, China and Peru have engaged in domestic governance reforms. The case studies investigate whether international transparency rules, in particular those embedded in international trade and investment agreements, have contributed to the two countries' protection of human rights.

II. BACKGROUND

Transparency is a term frequently used by lawyers, politicians and civil society engaged in globalization-fuelled debates about the overarching impact of international trade laws on the domestic laws of states, and about good governance, the relationships between citizens and state institutions, and the problem of corruption. Transparency is viewed as a necessary component in the proper functioning of any democratic state or organization,[17] as the principle that underpins the rule of law, and as the key element of good governance as embedded in Western ideas of modern statehood founded on the concepts of democratic accountability and legitimacy of governance.[18] It has national and international dimensions, but it lacks a universally accepted definition.

In its national dimension, transparency transcends the realm of legal standards and embodies the fundamental moral values of society. It is "a standard of judgment of people's conduct".[19] In modern states transparency is accepted as an indispensable condition of democratic governance and as the primary tool employed in holding policy makers accountable

---

[17] On theoretical foundations of transparency, see Carl-Sebastian Zoellner, "Transparency; An Analysis of an Evolving Fundamental Principle in International Economic Law" (2005–2006) 27 Mich. J. Int'l L. 579; and Stephan Schill, "Transparency as a Global Norm in International Public Law" (15 September 2014), Kluwer Arbitration Blog, available at http://kluwerarbitrationblog.com/2014/09/15/transparency-as-a-global-norm-in-international-investment-law/ (accessed 4 January 2017). Schill argues that "transparency promises more accountable more democratic and much more legitimate system of global governance".

[18] Francis Fukuyama, *State-Building: Governance and World Order in the 21st Century* (Ithaca: Cornell University Press, 2004).

[19] Andrea Bianchi, "Introduction" in Andrea Bianchi and Anne Peters, eds, *Transparency in International Law* (Cambridge: Cambridge University Press, 2013) 2.

to society.[20] Consequently, whenever states or their agencies are involved in economic activity, including entering into international trade and investment agreements, citizens call for transparency and "publicity"[21] with respect to the government process and for information about the states' goals and about the outcome. Such requests for more information are associated in the literature on democratic governance with the "right to know" transparency policies, which guarantee public access to government information, and with "targeted transparency" policies, which ensure that governments establish information services for their citizens and provide them with information otherwise unavailable.[22] These two generations of transparency policies in democratic states facilitate development of what is called "collaborative transparency" policies, the third generation of transparency policy. Collaborative transparency has been made by an unprecedented development in information and communications technology, which allows members of the public to be both users of information and initiators of transparency systems, transforming them into actors who share and monitor information.[23] According to Archon Fung, Mary Graham and David Weil, governments operate in the most efficient and democratic manner when all three generations of transparency policies are working together.[24]

The international dimension of transparency, often related to the legitimacy and quality of governance in global institutions,[25] is equally

---

[20] Anne Peters, "The Transparency of Global Governance" in Photini Pazartzis and Maria Gavouneli, *Reconceptualising the Rule of Law in Global Governance, Resources, Investment & Trade* (Oxford: Hart Publishing, 2015) 3 at 6.

[21] Peters, ibid. Peters argues that transparency is often used as a synonym for "publicity", a traditional political theory term whose origins could be found in the ancient Greek philosophy that linked "publicness" and democracy.

[22] Archon Fung, Mary Graham and David Weil, *Full Disclosure: The Perils and Promises of Transparency* (New York: Cambridge University Press, 2007) 24–8.

[23] Ibid.

[24] Ibid.

[25] Peters (note 20 above). The term "quality of governance" is broadly determined as "the process by which governments are selected, monitored and replaced, the capacity of the government to effectively formulate and implement sound policies, and the respect of citizens and the state for the institutions that govern economic and social interactions among them". See Daniel Kaufmann, Aart Kraay and Massimo Mastruzzi, "Governance Matters III: Governance Indicators for 1996–2002" (2004) World Bank Policy Research Working Paper No. 3106 at 3. According to the authors, determination of the quality of governance involves examination of activities of governments and institutions with respect to their adherence to the rule of law, their accountability, efficiency and transparency.

complex and it is controversial. On the one hand, transparency plays an instrumental role in the proper functioning of international organizations by increasing their effectiveness, their accountability, and the legitimacy of their rules and procedures.[26] On the other hand, international transparency has an impact on the domestic laws of a state by influencing the transparency of these laws, the administrative decisions, and procedures that facilitate competition, trade and foreign investment. Thus, the transparency principle is central to the full functioning of the world trade system.[27] Despite the positive impact of the principle on the functioning of the global trade regime, there is considerable criticism of the impact that the international rules of transparency have on the regulatory governance of individual states when they are imposed as a condition of membership in international organizations.[28] Such criticism is frequently made of the WTO and other systems of international economic law, such as international investment law and the law governing international finance.

Recently, it has been argued that there is a genuine "transparency turn" in international law and governance as all major areas of international law, particularly human rights laws and international economic law, impose numerous transparency-related requirements on the functioning of

---

[26] See for example, Robert Wolfe, "Letting the Sun Shine in at the WTO: How Transparency Brings the Trading System to Life" (2013) Staff Working Paper ERSD-2013/03; Gregory Shaffer, "How the World Trade Organization Shapes Regulatory Governance" (2015) 9 Regulation & Governance 1; Megan Donaldson and Benedict Kingsbury, "The Adoption of Transparency Policies in International Governance Institutions: Justifications, Effects and Implications" (2013) 9 Annual Review of Law and Social Science 119; Allen Buchanan and Robert O. Keohane, "The Legitimacy of Global Governance Institutions" (2006) 20 Ethics & International Affairs 405; Aarti Gupta, "Transparency under Scrutiny: Information Disclosure in Global Environmental Governance" (2008) 8 Global Environmental Politics 1.

[27] Article X of the GATT 1994 is the central transparency-related provision that imposes an obligation on all members of the WTO to publish all applicable laws and regulations and to administer them properly. The Asia Pacific Economic Cooperation (APEC) in the *2002 Statement to Implement APEC Transparency Standards* states: "[Transparency] is a basic principle underlying trade liberalization and facilitation, where the removal of barriers to trade is in large part only meaningful to the extent that the members of the public know what laws, regulations, procedures and administrative rulings affect their interests, can participate in their development, can participate in administrative proceedings applying them and can request review of their application under domestic law". See http://unctad.org/en/PublicationsLibrary/unctaddiaeia2011d6_en.pdf (accessed 4 January 2017).

[28] Shaffer (note 26 above).

international institutions (the so-called transparency OF governance) and states (the so-called transparency FOR governance).[29]

A. International Trade and Investment Treaties

The transparency turn in international law suggests that multiple international treaties impose a variety of transparency obligations on the states that entered into these treaties. For example, at the multilateral level, the General Agreement on Tariffs and Trade (GATT),[30] without defining transparency, imposed on states mandatory transparency-related obligations.[31] Those GATT obligations required the contracting states to publish domestic trade-related laws and regulations, to administer their laws and regulations in an impartial manner, and to publish the agreements affecting international trade policy that were in force between their government or government agencies and the governments or government agencies of any other contracting parties (GATT Article X). GATT also imposed several transparency-related obligations in order to eliminate or reduce non-tariff barriers to trade (GATT Articles XI:1 and XVII:1). The World Trade Organization (WTO) agreements that succeeded the GATT trade regime imposed additional transparency-related provisions but, like GATT, did not include a definition of transparency. The WTO agreements provided institutional support for monitoring the compliance of states with their WTO obligations and for the enforcement mechanism and remedies available to states in case of other states' violation of the obligations.

Both the GATT and WTO transparency rules apply to trade-related issues and do not directly relate to individual human rights. Binding WTO transparency rules address states as both obligors and obligees but they are only enforceable through claims brought by one state against another and before the WTO Dispute Settlement Body. Remedies for violations are available to states in the form of retaliatory trade sanctions until the measure violating the WTO rule is repealed or amended. These binding

---

[29] Peters (note 12 above) at 4–5. See also Anne Peters, "Towards Transparency as a Global Norm" in Bianchi and Peters (note 19 above) at 534. See also Megan Donaldson and Benedict Kingsbury, "The Adoption of Transparency Policies in Global Governance Institutions: Justifications, Effects, and Implications" (2013) 9 Annual Review of Law and Social Science 119; and Rachel M. Gisselquist, "Good Governance as a Concept, and Why This Matters for Development Policy" (2012) United Nations University WIDER Working Paper No. 2012/30.

[30] General Agreement on Tariffs and Trade, 30 October 1947, 55 UNTS 194.

[31] Zoellner (note 17 above) at 591.

rules affect the WTO members' domestic regulatory quality, particularly their transparency laws and policies, benefiting private parties (foreign and domestic) – suppliers of goods and services, consumers and investors. Thus, the WTO transparency rules do have a cascading or spillover effect on individual rights enabling them to make better-informed decisions not only about their economic but also about political, social and cultural rights.

The Trade Policy Review Mechanism (TPRM) provides a form of assessment of each WTO member's trade policies and practices through periodical WTO Secretariat reports and the review meetings of the Trade Policy Review Body (TPRB). The assessments thus provided are not utilized in the enforcement of specific transparency-related WTO obligations nor do they impose any additional obligations on non-complying member states. Therefore, the assessment process is not a substitute for domestic governance institutions and domestic transparency reforms. What it does do is provide a collective evaluation of members' trade policies and practices and valuable feedback to the reviewed members as to the impact of their policies on the functioning of the multilateral trade system. The greater a member's weight in the multilateral trading system, the more frequent is its TPRB review. China's trade policies and practices have been reviewed once every four years [32] while Peru's have been reviewed every six years.[33] There have been five TPRM reports on China since that country's accession to the WTO in 2001. These reports have revealed increased transparency in the country's trade policies and practices, but they have highlighted areas of concern, such as insufficient transparency in government procurement, in competition policy, and in government support for state owned enterprises.[34] There have been four reviews of Peru's trade polices and practices, the most recent in 2013, indicating that Peru has improved transparency in government trade policies and practices.[35]

FTAs often extend the WTO transparency rules by requiring their signatories to comply with more comprehensive transparency provisions, especially if they address regulatory cooperation of the parties.[36]

---

[32] The other three major trading powers reviewed every two years are the European Union, the United States and Japan.

[33] Most of the member states, that is, developing countries and economies in transition, are reviewed every six years.

[34] See China's TPR 2014, WT/TPR/S300/China.

[35] See Peru's TPR 2013, WT/TPR/S/289.

[36] See Bernard Hoekman and Petros C. Mavroidis, "Regulatory Spillovers and the Trading System: From Coherence to Cooperation" (2015) E15 Task Force on Regulatory Systems Coherence, ICTSD, World Economic Forum & the EUI, Overview Paper, available at http://e15initiative.org/wp-content/uploads/2015/04/E15-Regulatory-OP-Hoekman-and-Mavroidis-FINAL.pdf (accessed 5 January

Research conducted for the Organization for Economic Cooperation and Development (OECD) found that countries with good governance and institutions firmly based on democratic ideals include provisions requiring greater transparency in their trade agreements with developing countries.[37] Consequently, North-South agreements are "more transparency-intensive than North-North or South-South agreements".[38] China, in particular, states that it does not include good governance provisions and promotes economic cooperation with other developing countries with no interference in their domestic politics ("no-strings-attached"[39]). The agreements between OECD countries and non-OECD countries are particularly strict in their transparency requirements[40] because OECD countries use FTAs as "a vehicle for disseminating best practices in transparency, particularly to countries where administrative systems may be less mature".[41]

Transparency rules in international investment law tend to develop on the basis of models and practices of those states that are strongest economically and thus have more clout in negotiating the BITs.[42] Since the late

---

2017). See also Jacues Bourgeois, Kamala Dawar and Simon J. Evenett, "A Comparative Analysis of Selected Provisions in Free Trade Agreements" (October 2007), The Study Commissioned by the DG Trade of the European Commission, available at http://trade.ec.europa.eu/doclib/docs/2008/march/tradoc_138103.pdf (accessed 5 January 2017). The FTAs negotiated by the EU and the US with developing countries often impose requirements for a higher level of transparency with respect to policy areas such as intellectual property (IP) protection and competition policy. See Henrik Horn, Petros Mavroidis and André Sapir, "Beyond the WTO? An Anatomy of EU and US Preferential Trade Agreements" (2009) Breugel Blueprint Series, Vol. II, available at http://bruegel.org/wp-content/uploads/imported/publications/bp_trade_jan09.pdf (accessed 5 January 2017).

[37] Iza Lejarraga and Ben Shepherd, *Quantitative Evidence on Transparency in Regional Trade Agreements* (2013) OECD Trade Policy Papers No. 153, TAD/TC/WP (2012) 20/FINAL, at 4.

[38] Ibid.

[39] Chinese President Xi Jinping's speech during a plenary session at the Asian African Summit in Jakarta, Indonesia on 22 April 2015 emphasized that China supports South-South Cooperation based on "mutual respect and equality" and that it will "continue to offer assistance to developing countries with no political strings attached", available at http://www.voanews.com/content/xi-rich-nations-should-offer-aid-with-no-strings-attached/2729832.html (accessed 5 January 2017). That means that China will not link economic cooperation with human rights protection.

[40] Ibid.

[41] Ibid.

[42] UNCTAD, *Series on Issues in International Investment Agreements II: Transparency*, New York and Geneva, 2012, UNCTAD/DIAE/IA/2011/6 ('2012 Transparency Sequel').

1980s and the formulation of the Washington Consensus, international investment agreements (IIAs), including BITs, have contained provisions for good governance and transparency-related duties for the regulatory agencies of the developing countries that are hosting investments from developed countries.[43] BITs often provide for the establishment of international arbitration tribunals as dispute-settlement institutions in lieu of the host state's administrative or judicial institution. Foreign investors benefit directly from BITs by being able to make claims related to state violations of treaty obligations, including transparency, directly before these arbitral tribunals, circumventing the state's domestic judicial and administrative tribunals. The investors can seek monetary compensation from these tribunals for state violations of transparency. In that context, BITs seem to serve as substitutes, rather than as incentives, for governance reform in developing countries.

B. International Guidelines and Best Practices

There are many international treaties that stipulate transparency – the "hard law" on governance. Similarly, there are many international guidelines promoting and regulating transparency – the "soft law" on governance that regulates the obligations of private economic actors, namely multinational corporations and foreign investors, vis-à-vis host governments and local communities.[44]

---

[43] On the Washington Consensus and the World Bank macroeconomic policies, see John Williamson, *A Short History of the Washington Consensus*, a paper commissioned by Fundación CIDOB for a conference "From the Washington Consensus towards a new Global Governance", Barcelona, 24–25 September 2004, available at https://piie.com/publications/papers/williamson0904-2.pdf (accessed 5 January 2017). See also Jose Alvarez, "What are Investment Treaties For?" in Jose Alvarez, *The Public International Law Regime Governing International Investment* (The Hague: All-Pocket, 2011) 95–177. The US BIT model of 1987 is an example of the US practice of using the investment treaty provisions to impose a minimum standard of protection of US foreign direct investment by promoting the "fair and equitable treatment" of investments and to ensure a stable, predicable and secure legal framework for investments. Ibid. at 100.

[44] See Kenneth W. Abbot and Duncan Snidal, "Hard and Soft Law in International Governance" (2000) 54:3 International Organization 421. The authors define hard law as "legally binding obligations that are precise . . . and that delegate authority for interpreting and implementing law": ibid. at 421. They define soft law as an obligation or agreement not formally binding, or which is vague with respect to the discretion of implementation, or does not delegate authority for interpreting and implementing law to the third party. See ibid. at 422. See also Gregory Shaffer and Mark Pollack, "Hard vs. Soft Law: Alternatives,

The 2004 OECD Principles of Corporate Governance and the 2005 OECD Guidelines on Corporate Governance of State Owned Enterprises[45] included the principle of transparency and disclosure in their framework of corporate governance.[46] Initially, the 2005 Guidelines were intended to guide regulatory reforms in developed countries but the documents have since been accepted as an international standard of good corporate governance for all countries where state-owned enterprises (SOEs) are significant market actors.[47] Since 2004, China, which owes its rapid economic development to its numerous SOEs, has been involved with the OECD in a dialogue on corporate governance,[48] and has been participating in the OECD Corporate Governance Committee meetings since 2010. China has also participated in the OECD Working Party on State Ownership and Privatization Practices and has actively discussed the 2015 revision of the Guidelines with other members of that group.[49]

The 2011 UN Guiding Principles on Business and Human Rights,[50] another example of the relevant soft law, addresses transparency by

---

Complements, and Antagonists in International Governance" (2010) 94 Minn. L. Rev. 706 and Andrew Guzman and Timothy L. Meyer, "International Soft Law" (2010) 2 J. Legal Analysis 171.

[45] OECD, *Guidelines on Corporate Governance of State-Owned Enterprises* (Paris: OECD Publishing, 2005). The OECD published *Accountability and Transparency: A Guide for State Ownership* (OECD Publishing, 2010) as a supplementary set of best practices for governments working on implementation of the 2005 Guidelines. In 2015, the Guidelines were revised by OECD countries in cooperation with a number of partners and stakeholders, including non-OECD countries. See the revised 2015 Guidelines at http://www.oecd.org/daf/ca/OECD-Guidelines-Corporate-Governance-SOEs-2015.pdf (accessed 5 January 2017).

[46] Other principles are: ensuring the basis for an effective corporate governance framework, rights of shareholders and key ownership functions, equitable treatment of shareholders, role of stakeholders, and responsibilities of the board.

[47] Daniel Ho and Angus Young argue that China adopted most of the principles of the 2005 Guidelines on SOEs corporate governance. See Daniel Ho and Angus Young, "China's Experience in Reforming its State Owned Enterprises: Something New, Something Old and Something Chinese?" (2013) 2:4 Int'l J. Economy, Management and Social Science 84 at 84.

[48] On the activities of the 2004 China-OECD Corporate Governance Policy Dialogue, see https://www.oecd.org/daf/ca/ChinaOECDCorpGovfinal.pdf (accessed 5 January 2017).

[49] See the revised 2015 Guidelines at http://www.oecd.org/daf/ca/OECD-Guidelines-Corporate-Governance-SOEs-2015.pdf (accessed 5 January 2017).

[50] Report of the Special Representative of the Secretary General on the Issue of Human Rights and Transnational Corporations and Other Business Enterprises, John Ruggie, *Guiding Principles on Business and Human Rights: Implementing the United Nations "Protect, Respect and Remedy" Framework*, OHCRG, 17th Sess,

recognizing states' duties to respect, protect and fulfill human rights and fundamental freedoms.[51] Although not binding on states, the Principles set expectations for states to enforce domestic human rights standards on all businesses operating within their jurisdiction. This includes the possibility of the states enforcing domestic measures with extraterritorial implications.[52] The commentary of the Principles makes it clear that one requirement of states' and businesses' responsibility to respect and protect human rights is that they must have in place transparency policies and measures[53] and that they must share relevant information. The Principles recognize that the obligations of states and businesses to protect individuals against business-related abuse must be matched with appropriate and effective remedies available in case of violations.[54] Next, grievance mechanisms, including a range of remedies, should be available to individuals and groups through efficient state and non-state grievance institutions such as state judicial, administrative and legislative mechanisms.[55] The Principles also propose the establishment of grievance mechanisms administered by business actors, industry, or, collaboratively, by multiple stakeholders on the basis of their codes of conduct and performance standards.[56] They specifically point to the transparency of the grievance mechanisms as a determinant factor in their effectiveness.[57] Generally, China has responded more positively to the UN Guiding Principles than to the OECD initiatives. For example, the China Chamber of Commerce of Metals, Minerals, and Chemicals Importers & Exporters has referred to the Principles in its Guidelines for Social Responsibility in Outbound Mining Investment, calling for its

---

A/HRC/17/31 (2011). The Human Rights Council endorsed the Guiding Principles in its resolution 17/4 of 16 June 2011.

[51] 2011 Guiding Principles, I. The State Duty to Protect Human Rights, A. Foundational Principles, 3–4. Those fundamental rights and freedoms include the protection of the rule of law, accountability, legal certainty and procedural and legal transparency.

[52] 2011 Guiding Principles, I. The State Duty to Protect Human Rights, B. Operational Principles; General State Regulatory and Policy Functions, 4–6.

[53] 2011 Guiding Principles, 3, 24, 35.

[54] 2011 Guiding Principles, III. Access to Remedy, 27.

[55] Ibid. The suggested remedies may include apologies, restitution, rehabilitation, monetary or non-monetary compensation, punitive sanctions (criminal or administrative), injunctions, financial or non-financial compensation and punitive sanctions.

[56] 2011 Guiding Principles, III. Access to Remedy, Non-State-Based Grievance Mechanisms, 31–33.

[57] Ibid. at 33.

member companies to comply with the UN proposed initiative in their mining operations abroad.[58]

The Extractive Industries Transparency Initiative (EITI)[59] is a voluntary initiative launched in 2002 by governments, industry, investors, and civil society in the attempt to create a global transparency standard for the gas, oil and mining sectors around the world.[60] A multi-stakeholder group consisting of representatives of the government, mining companies and civil society performs monitoring and reporting tasks as set out by the EITI Standard of implementation.[61] An EITI country report can provide the basis for transparency reforms. It can ensure in particular that governments work towards the development of all three generations of transparency by fulfilling, first, their own duty to inform all stakeholders of their own rules and policies, then by imposing on mining companies a duty to disclose information about their money matters (targeted transparency), and, finally, by ensuring that civil society is able not only to voice its concerns about government policies and business practices, but also to influence them (collaborative transparency).[62] The EITI Standard also covers all stages of the value chain, contract transparency, government expenditures, revenue transfer to local governments, social expenditure and infrastructure investments. It sets out the requirements that the participating countries must meet in order to become EITI compliant.[63] While China is not one of the participating countries, Peru was the first Latin American country to join the initiative in 2007 and is considered to be a compliant country.[64] At first, the Chinese firms in Peru declined to participate in the initiative, but the two cases below indicate that they have changed their position on the matter.[65]

---

[58] See OECD Insights, *Corporate respect for human rights in the Chinese context*, 18 June 2015, available at http://oecdinsights.org/2015/06/18/corporate-respect-for-human-rights-in-the-chinese-context/ (accessed 5 January 2017).

[59] Ruben Gonzales-Vincente, "Mapping Chinese Mining Investment in Latin America: Politics of Market" (2012) 209 The China Quarterly 35 at 40.

[60] See https://eiti.org/ (accessed 5 January 2017).

[61] The EITI Standard 2016 is the most recent edition and was launched at the EITI Global Conference held in Lima in February 2016, available at https://eiti.org/files/english-eiti-standard_0.pdf (accessed 5 January 2017). For more information on the EITI, see https://beta.eiti.org/about/how-we-work (accessed 5 January 2017).

[62] See https://beta.eiti.org/oversight (accessed 5 January 2017).

[63] Currently, there are 51 countries implementing the EITI but 31 are compliant with the EITI requirements. The EITI Fact Sheet 2016 is available at https://eiti.org/files/document/eiti_factsheet_en.pdf (accessed 5 January 2017).

[64] Ibid.

[65] See also Jill Shankleman, *Going Global: Chinese Oil and Mining Companies*

III. TRANSPARENCY TESTED BY PERU AND CHINA: LAWS, POLITICS AND PRACTICE

The analysis of the evolution of transparency rules and practices with respect to the China-Peru economic cooperation in the extractive industry is organized below as an examination of the impact of the mandatory international transparency rules and voluntary guidelines relevant to the two countries' governance laws and practices. The case study illustrates the impact of China's "win-win", "no strings attached" policy on the development of South-South agreements and the resulting weak transparency provisions in these agreements. It reveals difficulties in managing the implementation of numerous transparency rules imposed by different regulatory bodies through several layers of governance. For several decades both Peru and China have engaged with international and regional organization for which transparency is a condition of membership. This engagement has involved building institutions, processes and means of communication between different layers of governance and developing the three generations of transparency. It is not surprising that transparency has evolved differently in these two vastly different political and social contexts and that the role of state and non-state institutions in monitoring and enforcing the implementation of transparency-related reforms, and in mediating communications and the division of power among the different layers of governance, has been framed differently in these two countries.

Laws regulating foreign investment evolved through interaction among different layers of governance and different sources of law. Therefore, in an analysis of the Chinese investments in Peru consideration must be given to international law as well as to domestic law. That includes rules of international economic law such as that of the WTO and the relevant FTAs, all of which may directly address the rights and duties of states signatories of these agreements, and more specific international law related to the protection of foreign investments (such as the ICSID Convention[66] and BITs), which also provide remedies to foreign investors against states' violation of their treaty rights. Finally, the analysis of the FDI legal regime must include the relevant domestic law, not only commercial, antitrust and tax law but also constitutional, administrative and labour law to name a few related areas, which provide procedures and remedies for both foreign

and the Governance of Resource Wealth (Washington: Woodrow Wilson International Center for Scholars, 2009) 4.

[66] Convention on the Settlement of Investment Disputes Between States and Nationals of Other States (1965), 575 UNTS 159, 4 ILM 532.

investors and domestic private parties seeking protection of their rights against actions of states and foreign investors.

A. China-Peru Economic Cooperation

Since the 1990s, Peru's economic development has rested primarily on resource extraction and trade and investment liberalization.[67] China's investments in developing countries in general, and in Latin American countries in particular, have focused on extractive industry projects.[68] Since 2010, China has replaced the US as Peru's largest trading partner and as the principal investor in the country's mining sector.[69] The important aspect of the China-Peru economic cooperation is China's financial aid to several development projects in Peru. These projects form part of the broader Chinese strategy of investment in Latin American natural resource industries. China's loans to Latin America and the Caribbean exceeded US$22.1 billion in 2014, surpassing the combined financing from traditional sources – the World Bank and the Inter-American Development Bank.[70] Since 2008, China EXIM Bank and the China Development Bank (CDB) have invested more than US$2 billion in Peru.[71] Most of China's lending has been for energy and infrastructure projects, and half of the financing has been in the form of commodity-backed loans.[72]

The two countries' economic cooperation was initially governed by a rather lean 10-year BIT concluded in 1994.[73] When China entered into its

---

[67] Arce (note 16 above).

[68] The gas and oil sector accounts for 69 percent of Chinese M&A investment in Latin America in 2009–13. See Rebecca Ray and Kevin Gallagher, *China-Latin America Economic Bulletin 2015 Edition* (2015) Boston University Global Economic Governance Initiative, Discussion Paper 2015/9, 2, available at https://www.bu.edu/pardeeschool/files/2015/02/Economic-Bulletin-2015.pdf (accessed 5 January 2017). The report finds that China's policy banks have become the largest creditors to Latin American governments: ibid. at 1.

[69] Michael J. McGuinness, "Beijing the Matchmaker" (2013) 32:6 International Financial Law Review 41 at 42.

[70] Ray and Gallagher (note 68 above) at 1.

[71] China-Latin America Finance Database 2013, available at http://www.thedialogue.org/map_list/ (accessed 5 January 2017).

[72] Ibid. See also Jon Brandt, Derek Hottle, Nicole Adams, Nav Aujla, Christina Dinh, Kirsten Kaufman, Devin Kleinfield-Hayes, Wanlin Ren and Andrew Tuck, *Chinese Engagement in Latin America and the Caribbean: Implications for US Foreign Policy*, American University School of International Service (December 2012) 7.

[73] Agreement Between the Government of the Republic of Peru and the Government of the People's Republic of China Concerning the Encouragement

first BIT in the early 1980s in keeping with its economic strategy to attract foreign direct investments (FDIs), it was also trying to enforce regulatory restrictions on foreign investors while supporting domestic SOEs.[74] The 1994 China-Peru BIT was more reflective of China's cautious approach to investing outside of Asia than it was of Peru's interests, which included finding investors for its mining industry projects and securing external financial resources needed for economic development. The 1994 BIT was consistent with the Five Principles of Peaceful Co-Existence of Chinese foreign policy.[75] It included no transparency provisions and made no reference to good governance.

The 2010 China-Peru FTA[76] reflects Peru's experience in negotiating its 2006 FTA with the US, and China's new foreign trade practice of modeling its FTAs on the North American Free Trade Agreement (NAFTA) and on the US FTAs that combine the regulation of trade in goods and services with detailed rules on foreign direct investments.[77] Since 2007, China's regulatory priority has shifted from the regulation of FDIs in China to the protection of Chinese investors abroad. China has become the world's third largest outward investor,[78] and it has focused on concluding IIAs that support its SOE investments in natural resource projects

---

and Reciprocal Protection of Investments (China-Peru BIT) (9 June 1994), available at http://investmentpolicyhub.unctad.org/IIA/country/165/treaty/954 (accessed 5 January 2017).

[74] The first generation of Chinese BITs provided for ad hoc arbitration, with the scope of arbitrability limited to determining the amount of compensation payable for expropriation. It also provided for what was, at best, very limited national treatment for foreign investors. See Alex Berger, *Is China Following the Global Trend Towards Comprehensive Agreements?* (Bonn: DIE Discussion Paper, 2013) 7–8. Berger argues that China uses a restrictive European model of BITs.

[75] The five principles are: mutual respect for each other's sovereignty and territorial integrity, mutual non-aggression, non-interference in each other's internal affairs, equality and mutual benefit, and peaceful co-existence. See Ministry of Foreign Affairs of the People's Republic of China, *China's Initiation of the Five Principles of Peaceful Co-existence*, available at http://www.fmprc.gov.cn/mfa_eng/ziliao_665539/3602_665543/3604_665547/t18053.shtml (accessed 5 January 2017).

[76] Free Trade Agreement Between the Government of the People's Republic of China and the Government of the Republic of Peru (China-Peru FTA), signed and in effect on 1 March 2010, available at http://fta.mofcom.gov.cn/topic/enperu.shtml and http://www.sice.oas.org/TPD/PER_CHN/Texts_28042009_e/index_e.asp (accessed 5 January 2017).

[77] Berger (note 74 above).

[78] Karl P. Sauvant and Victor Zitian Chen, "China's Regulatory Framework for Outward Foreign Direct Investment" (2014) 7:1; China Ec. J. 141 at 141. China is only behind the US and Japan as an outward investor.

overseas.[79] Thus, the 2010 FTA provisions reflect the fact that China's acquisition of minerals from Peru was the primary motivation on its part for the establishment of the FTA between the two countries.[80]

The general transparency provisions of the 2010 China-Peru FTA are included in Chapter 13 and refer only to the obligation of each country to publish the relevant laws and regulations that have already been enacted. There is no requirement for the disclosure of information on new laws.[81] Chapter 13 stipulates that each party shall respond to specific information requests from the other party but not from individual businesses regarding any laws and regulations that it has already enacted.[82] These provisions protect the right to know and impose a limited duty to disclose on the parties and their governments. In contrast, GATT Article X and the subsequent WTO Marrakesh Agreements, such as the WTO Agreement on Technical Barriers to Trade (TBT Agreement)[83] impose, in addition to the obligation for states to publish all laws and regulations already in force, the further obligation for their non-discriminatory, open and predictable administration of trade policies, including the right to appeal all government decisions related to trade policy.[84]

There are no specific transparency provisions in the China-Peru FTA Chapter 10 on investment. Article 139 on investor-state dispute-settlement[85] implies that "any dispute between an investor of one Party and the other Party in connection with an investment in the territory of the other Party", including disputes related to violations of transparency obligations by the other party government, may be submitted to an ad hoc arbitral tribunal for a final and binding resolution. The arbitral tribunal may award to an investor monetary damages as a remedy for a loss caused by the action of a government of the party that violates the FTA provisions.[86] There are no provisions mandating that states or foreign investors must address claims by local communities that their fundamental human rights to health or a safe environment or their labour rights may have had been negatively affected by the Chinese investments or decisions made by the Peruvian government. These last mentioned rights and duties

---

79 Ibid.
80 Shankleman (note 65 above).
81 China-Peru 2010 FTA, Article 167(1).
82 Ibid., Article 167(2).
83 Agreement on Technical Barriers to Trade (TBT Agreement), 1868 UNTS 120, Article 2.
84 GATT, Article X(3).
85 China Peru 2010 FTA, Article 139(1).
86 Ibid., Article 139(7).

are clearly left to be determined by Peruvian and Chinese domestic legislation related to foreign investments, including rules on transparency and good governance.

B. Evolution of Transparency in Peru

Peru's governance reforms were triggered by its binding international obligations undertaken in the 1990s (such as the WTO Agreements) and by political changes on the domestic front over the same period. First, the right of public access to information (the first generation of transparency) was embedded in the 1993 Constitution in order to bring legitimacy to the controversial, autocratic government of Alberto Fujimori.[87] However, this right was not incorporated in legislation until 2003, when the Ministry Council approved the Transparency and Access to Public Information Law ('the Transparency Law')[88] in response to the political instability that peaked upon President Fujimori's resignation in November 2000 amid corruption scandals and allegations of the misuse of public office. The Transparency Law is part of a new targeted transparency policy aimed at democratization. These changes have coincided with the development of the country's new economic policy based on Peru's commitment to the WTO trade rules and the liberalization of rules governing foreign investment.

According to the Transparency Law, all government information is presumed to be public and all people (including non-Peruvian citizens) have the right to request and obtain any information from the state.[89] All public bodies and government agencies are required to establish websites with a transparency section.[90] The statute has imposed an obligation on government agents to respond to information requests from all parties and to provide consultations where necessary.[91] Peru has enacted several subsequent pieces of legislation to complement the Transparency Law,[92] to define the government's obligation to self-report and to determine what

---

87 World Bank, *Implementing Right to Information: A Case Study of Peru* (Washington, 2012) 1, available at http://siteresources.worldbank.org/PUBLICSECTORANDGOVERNANCE/Resources/285741-1343934891414/8787489-1344020463266/RTI-CS-Peru-final.pdf (accessed 5 January 2017).

88 Law No. 27806 *Ley de Transparencia y Acceso a la Información Pública*: 144.

89 Ibid.

90 Ibid.

91 World Bank (note 87 above) at 14.

92 These include Law No. 27444 (the 2007 Law on General Administrative Procedure) and the 2008 Legislative Decree No. 1031 which "aims to improve the efficiency of government business activities. See World Bank (note 87 above) at 10.

information is subject to this obligation. However, the Transparency Law has not been particularly effective because the government has not yet worked out a clear strategy for its implementation.[93] Since the country has lacked both political will and technical expertise in public service matters, it has failed to establish effective implementation and monitoring of compliance at all levels of government.[94]

The Standard Transparency Portal, designed in 2008 by the central government in Lima to facilitate user-friendly public access to information on investment projects undertaken by government bodies, provides what is essentially a one-way flow of information. It is not a forum for the participation of broader society in economic decision-making. The site is technologically difficult to maintain, and it is administratively difficult to coordinate among 13 ministries, 32 decentralized public agencies, nine regional and eight local governments.[95] The time needed to train personnel and secure the technical assistance needed to maintain the portal adds yet another level of difficulty.

Despite the above problems in improving governance and transparency, the 2013 EITI Report for Peru[96] shows that the level of trust between the central government and local authorities and communities has improved. In 2011, Peru became Latin America's first fully EITI-compliant country and the first to enact domestic legislation implementing ILO Convention 169 (Lei 29785), which provides the indigenous population with the right to prior consultation regarding extractive industry projects within their traditional territories.[97] Yet, there is still work to be done. The Report finds that although half of the taxes paid by the extractive industries have been transferred to the regions, tensions remain between the central and local governments with respect to the lack of transparency and the distribution of extractive wealth.[98]

---

93 World Bank (note 87 above) at 43.

94 Ibid.

95 Word Bank (note 87 above) at 16.

96 Available at https://eiti.org/document/2013-peru-eiti-report (accessed 7 January 2017). The Report was published in 2015.

97 Note that Peru ratified ILO Convention 169 in 1994 but until 2011 never introduced domestic legislation to facilitate its implementation (2011 *Ley del Derecho a la Consulta Previa a los Pueblos Indígenas u Originarios, Reconocido en el Convenio 169 de la Organization Internacional del Trabajo*). See further Rebecca Ray, Kevin Gallagher, Andres Lopez and Cynthia Sanborn, *China in Latin America: Lessons for South-South Cooperation and Sustainable Development*, Boston University's Global Economic Initiative (April 2015) 11.

98 See the summary of the 2013 Peru EITI Report at https://eiti.org/news/peru-ten-years-transparency-oil-gas-and-mining (accessed 5 January 2017). Similar

In sum, Peru's transition from first generation of transparency to targeted and collaborative transparency has been slow and its local governments' level of non-compliance with the Transparency Law remains significant. The transition is driven both by external (international and regional laws) and internal pressure. Legitimacy, accountability and efficiency are necessary attributes for the domestic monitoring and enforcement institutions and processes, including remedies to protect the rights of all stakeholders. Without these attributes in place the right to know and access to information has very little impact on the improvement of human rights.

C. Evolution of Transparency in China

Prior to its accession to the WTO, China's regulatory culture of "patrimonial sovereignty" favoured governance under the political authority of the Communist Party and denounced legal accountability and transparency with respect to the actions of state regulators as tools of capitalist states that were inapplicable to Chinese circumstances.[99] In 1997, the WTO Working Party's Draft Protocol of Accession was the first document that raised the question of China's commitment to the regulatory standards of governance, the liberal principles of government accountability, the rule of law and transparency. The Draft Protocol required not only legislative changes but also transformation of China's regulatory culture and practice. The 2001 Protocol of the Accession of the People's Republic of China to the Marrakesh Agreement Establishing the WTO[100] imposed on that country greater obligations related to the transparency principle than have had to be met by any other members.[101] In order to achieve competence and accountability at the central, provincial and municipal

---

comments regarding slow decentralization are provided in *Chinese Investment in the Peru's Mining Sector: Corporate Social and Environmental Responsibility* (American University, 2014) 14, available at https://www.american.edu/sis/gep/upload/Chinese-Mining-in-Peru-Practicum-Final-Report_5_22_14-1.pdf (accessed 5 January 2017).

[99] Pitman B. Potter, *Accessing Treaty Performance in China: Trade and Human Rights* (Vancouver: UBC Press, 2014) 25. The basis of patrimonial sovereignty is that "political leaders and administrative agencies may be responsible *for* society but not to it": ibid.

[100] WT/LI/100 2, 10 November 2001.

[101] See Sylvia Ostry, "China and the WTO: Transparency Issue" (1998) 3 UCLA J. Int'l L. & Foreign Aff. 1; Julia Ya Qin, "'WTO-Plus' Obligations and Their Implications for the World Trade Organization Legal System" (2003) 37 J. World Trade 483; and Karen Halverson Cross, "China's WTO Accession:

government levels and to ensure transparent, simplified and consistent procedures by which individuals and companies can challenge its administrative laws and decisions,[102] a series of administrative law reforms was required. Since 2006, all central, provincial and local government agencies have been required to inform the Ministry of Commerce (MOFCOM) of all changes to trade laws and of the implementation of any trade-related measures. Those new measures are then published in the China Foreign Trade and Economic Co-operation Gazette.

The general duty of public disclosure imposed by the WTO on all levels of government (central and local) does not apply to Party committees. That is unfortunate since it is these committees' decisions that have important legal ramifications.[103] The new regulations have also failed to address adequately the right of a private party to a remedy for a loss caused by unlawful administrative acts. Instead, they focus on determining the precise role that local authorities are to play in making administrative decisions.[104] Thus, in China, although the shift in perception on transparency might not be what is needed in order to achieve transparency as interpreted by the WTO, it is possible to say that the central government has succeeded in combining its stated goal of implementing its WTO transparency obligations with other goals such as ensuring political stability in the country.

In addition to the incorporation of transparency mechanisms into its legislative processes, during the mid-2000s China began developing corporate social responsibility (CSR) rules, including a duty of disclosure regarding the performance of private companies and SOEs.[105] However, legal scholars cannot agree as to the nature and scope of these CSR duties. Some authors indicate that they are not mandatory and that Chinese companies that are involved in FDIs follow them more closely than do companies that are involved in the domestic market. Chinese SOEs have little experience in engaging with local civil society and labour unions and they still see the CSR as an additional business cost that eats into their

---

Economic, Legal, and Political Implications" (2004) 27 Boston College Int'l & Comp. L. Rev. 319.

[102] Ljiljana Biukovic, "Selective Adaptation of WTO Transparency Norms and Local Practices in China and Japan" (2008) 11:4 J. Int'l Econ. L. 803 at 819–21.

[103] On the 2007 Regulations on Government Disclosure of Information see Biukovic, ibid., at 820.

[104] Ibid. at 821.

[105] 2006 Company Law and 2009 Guide Opinion on the Social Responsibility in Implementation for the State-Owned Enterprises Controlled by the Central Government. See also Third Plenary Session of the 18th of the CPC Central Committee (November 2013), available at http://www.xinhuanet.com/english/special/cpcplenum2013/documents.htm (accessed 5 January 2017).

profits.[106] Chinese state banks have modified their codes of conduct to include environmental and sustainable development guidelines but have not developed specific guidelines for transparency.[107] However, neither the Chinese government nor the state banks financing the SOEs that have been investing in Peru's mining sector provide sufficient oversight with respect to the Chinese companies' impact on the social, labour, health and environmental rights of local Peruvian communities.[108] Therefore, Chinese companies operating abroad do comply with local standards and laws if local institutions properly monitor their compliance and enforce those laws and standards.[109]

Despite these changes in China's legislation aimed at providing public access to information and implementing its WTO transparency-related obligations, in a 2009 survey, 55 percent of the participating firms from OECD countries reported "medium to serious" problems in the transparency and predictability of Chinese laws and policies.[110] Furthermore, 59 percent of the firms reported medium to serious problems with the dissemination of information on changes in regulations.[111] The 2013 OECD Report reveals that 96 percent of the central government institutions and most of the local governments have launched official websites but the level of detail varies significantly from site to site.[112] China has also created a special website to provide foreign investors with information related to its laws and regulations on FDIs.[113] A set of updated investment regulations is compiled annually and is posted on this website.[114]

---

106 Embassy of Sweden in Beijing, *A Study on Corporate Social Responsibility Development and Trends in China* (2014) 22, available at http://www.csr-asia.com/report/CSR-development-and-trends-in-China-FINAL-hires.pdf (accessed 5 January 2017).

107 See Kevin Gallagher, Amos Irwin and Katherine Koleski, *The New Banks in Town: Chinese Finance in Latin America* (Report to Inter-American Dialogue, February 2012), available at http://ase.tufts.edu/gdae/Pubs/rp/GallagherChineseFinanceLatinAmericaBrief.pdf (accessed 5 January 2017).

108 Yuan Wang and Simon Zadek, *IISD Report: Sustainability Impact of Chinese Outward Direct Investment: A Review of the Literature* (January 2016) 60.

109 Ibid. at 41.

110 OECD, *Globalization and Emerging Economies: Brazil, Russia, India, Indonesia, China and South Africa* (19 March 2009) 391, available at http://www.oecd-ilibrary.org/trade/globalisation-and-emerging-economies_9789264044814-en (accessed 5 January 2017).

111 Ibid.

112 OECD (note 110 above) at 392.

113 See www.fdi.gov.cn (accessed 5 January 2017).

114 Article 2 of the 1993 Constitution of Peru. See *2007 Peru-China Free Trade Agreement: Joint Feasibility Study* 58, available at http://www.mincetur.gob.pe/

China's WTO accession has strengthened its "right to access" or first generation of transparency policies. This created preconditions for developing targeted transparency and achieving a higher quality of public services in that country. Despite the significant administrative law reforms undertaken, however, problems dealing with remedies available to private parties remain unresolved. The 2014 Communiqué of the Fourth Plenum of the 18th Chinese Communist Party Congress requested public participation in legislative process, but these reforms have yet to be implemented.[115]

The 2015 Regulatory Transparency Scorecard of the US-China Business Council recognizes the areas of improvement of transparency policy but also reveals the need for increased openness in government decision-making. It shows the following two major challenges in measuring the country's progress towards transparency: (i) the lack of clarity about which regulations are subject to the commitment to make information available to the public; and (ii) the government's failure to solicit broad public feedback during the drafting of new laws and regulations.[116] The Scorecard confirms that there is an uneven commitment to government transparency among Chinese regulatory agencies.

On 22 December 2015, Chinese Premier Li Keqiang introduced a new guideline from the State Council mandating increased government transparency and increased public information about government affairs by 2020.[117] China's transparency challenges were discussed at the recent G20 meeting in Shanghai. The culture of secrecy under which the Chinese government operates (under the direct control of the State Council and Chinese Communist Party) was acknowledged.[118] Considerable concern

newweb/portals/0/Peru-China%20JFS%20Final.pdf (accessed 5 January 2017). Article 65 of the Constitution also recognized the right of consumers and users to access information on the goods and services available on the market.

[115] Communiqué of the Fourth Plenary Session of the 18th Central Committee of the Communist Party of China (23 October 2014), available at http://www.china.org.cn/china/fourth_plenary_session/2014-12/02/content_34208801.htm (accessed 5 January 2017).

[116] *USCBC China 2015 Regulatory Transparency Scorecard*, US-China Business Council (March 2015) 2–6, available at https://www.uschina.org/sites/default/files/USCBC%202015%20Regulatory%20Transparency%20Scorecard.pdf (accessed 5 January 2017).

[117] Zhang Yi, "Guideline issued to increase government transparency", *China Daily*, updated on 18 February 2016.

[118] Ben Bernanke and Peter Olson, "China's transparency challenges" (8 March 2016), Brookings Institution (blog), available at https://www.brookings.edu/2016/03/08/chinas-transparency-challenges/ (accessed 5 January 2017).

was expressed over the involvement of the state in economic activity and the possibility of unfair treatment of non-state economic actors and foreign investors. Moreover, despite the fact that China has embraced the internet and computer-based technology, it is still far from committing to collaborative transparency.

As mentioned earlier, China's government is not participating in EITI. China has also been reluctant to accept any voluntary transparency initiatives promoted by the OECD, although it is more open to the UN programs related to the issues of economic development but not human rights in general. China has been promoting South-South cooperation on the basis of the principles of peaceful coexistence, such as the principle of non-interference in the political affairs of developing countries.

Most of China's outward FDIs come from SOEs that are financed by state banks such as China Development Bank (CDB) and China EXIM Bank.[119] The SOEs that make foreign investments are tightly controlled organizations that are subject to centralized state supervision.[120] The Communist Party of China controls the agency that supervises all SOEs, the Party Organization Department appoints the heads and management of all of the big SOEs,[121] and one-third of all SOE employees are party members.[122] The Aluminum Corporation of China (Chinalco), one of the three SOEs that have made the largest investments in other developing countries, started out as an agency that was carved out of the central government structure in 1979. Since 2008, Chinalco's investments have been financed by China EXIM Bank.

D. China's Involvement with Resource Extraction in Peru: Evolution of Transparency in Practice

China's FDIs in extractive projects in developing countries are generally criticized for serious labour standard violations (including low wages, poor safety measures, and a lack of communication with local unions),

---

[119] For the role of China's policy banks in external trade relationships, see Gallagher, Irwin and Koleski (note 106 above); and Deborah Brautigam, *The Dragon's Gift: The Real Story of China in Africa* (Oxford: Oxford University Press, 2009) 142. For more information on China EXIM Bank, see http://english.eximbank.gov.cn/en/ (accessed 5 January 2017).

[120] Li-wen Lin and Curtis J. Milhaupt, "We are the (National) Champions: Understanding the Mechanisms of State Capitalism in China" (2013) 65 Stanford L. Rev. 697 at 699.

[121] Ibid. at 726.

[122] Ibid. at 727.

for withholding information about their investment plans and revenue transfers, and for their failure to address the environmental and development concerns of the affected local communities. The Shougang and Chinalco investment projects in iron ore and copper mines in Peru are no exception.

In Peru, China's first investment in Latin America, the 1992 Shougang acquisition of Hierro Peru, particularly its Marcona mining operations, gained a bad reputation because of irregularities in the privatization process including a lack of transparency, Shougang's poor performance against local labour and environmental standards, and its failure to fulfill its promises to the local community.[123] The company was fined numerous times for violations of labour and environmental standards. In both Peru and China, domestic laws relevant to direct investments were not well developed in the early 1990s. Peru's weak institutions were unequipped to the task of monitoring and enforcing the local laws, and the absence of a consultation process with local communities contributed to the crisis. At the time of the Hierro Peru acquisition, Peru was a party to GATT (from 1951), and a member of one regional trade agreement (the Andean Community, from 1969). It was a party to only two BITs[124] and had not yet entered into any FTAs.

Shougang was China's first state-owned investor in Peru and its first ever major direct investment overseas. At the time of the Hierro Peru acquisition, China was not a participant in the GATT trade system and had had very little experience with outward investments beyond Asia and Africa. In fact, China had not engaged in creation of free trade areas prior to its 2001 accession to the WTO. By 1992 China had signed about 30 investment treaties, primarily with European and Asian countries.[125]

Peru and China did not have a BIT or an FTA in place at the time of Shougang's acquisition of Hierro Peru. Therefore, the transparency rules applicable to this transaction were based on the relevant domestic laws of Peru and China and on general public international law, including customary international law. China did not develop any significant

---

[123] Ibid. See also Amos Irwin and Kevin P. Gallagher, "Chinese Mining in Latin America: A Comparative Perspective" (2013) 22:2 The Journal of Environment and Development 207. The authors argue that other investors in the regions, especially from the US, had similar problems in Peru.

[124] In November 1991 Peru signed BITs with Thailand and Switzerland, see http://investmentpolicyhub.unctad.org/IIA/CountryBits/165#iiaInnerMenu (accessed 5 January 2017).

[125] See http://investmentpolicyhub.unctad.org/IIA/CountryBits/42 (accessed 5 January 2017).

regulations for outward FDIs until the mid-2000s.[126] At the time of Hierro Peru's acquisition the Peruvian government was embroiled in a corruption scandal and had been accused of a lack of transparency. The whole matter of the acquisition of the Marcona mining concession from the government was so problematic that it caused major social conflict in the region. The local government had difficulties containing this unrest. Peruvian President Fujimori had initiated economic reforms by privatizing many state-owned mining companies, including Hierro Peru, for which Shougang paid US$188 million even though the asking price had been only US$22 million. Shougang subsequently failed to live up to its commitments: it invested only US$38 million instead of the promised US$150 million, and it continued to operate the mine without modernizing the facilities, improving workers safety or protecting the environment.[127] Consequently, Hierro Peru had a very high accident rate, caused numerous labour strikes and gained a poor reputation in the local communities. In 2006, the regional government declared a state of "environmental emergency".

Shougang's project in Peru lacked support from the Chinese government because Shougang was a part of an experimental profit-responsibility system devised in the 1980s.[128] As previously mentioned, there was no Chinese regulatory oversight over its overseas investments and CSR programs were absent in China during the 1990s. Shougang's lack of international experience, including, regrettably, its lack of an understanding of and a willingness to engage with the local communities, meant that the company failed to act promptly to remedy consequences of its violation of Peruvian labour and environmental standards. According to some reports, after the acquisition, Shougang invested US$39 million in local utilities. The company also claimed to have paid US$74.75 million in taxes, arguing that half of that should had been given to the community in Marcona.[129] Shoughang was fined an annual average of US$21,000 for environmental standards violations, which was the largest amount ever levied against any

---

[126] Paulina Garzón, *Legal Manual on Chinese Environmental and Social Guidelines for Foreign Loans and Investments: A Guide for Local Communities* (March 2015), Centro De Derechos Económicos y Sociales, CDES, at 11, available at https://www.wcl.american.edu/environment/documents/manualchino15.pdf (accessed 5 January 2017).

[127] For more on the history of Hierro Peru's operations, see Edwin Nieves, "Peru's Environment vs. China's Investment" (2015) 35:19 Washington Report on Hemisphere 4.

[128] Gonzalez-Vincente (note 59 above) at 51–2.

[129] Nieves (note 127 above) at 5.

Chinese firm in Peru.[130] In 2014, Shougang Hierro Peru even agreed to participate in the next EITI report on Peru.[131] In sum, Shougang has paid for its wrongs with respect to labour and the environment and has presented the company as a good corporate citizen on those two fronts, but it still has work to do on transparency. Even after the company's website was launched, information about its operations remains sketchy and it is still having difficulty in gaining the trust of the local communities.

In 2007, 15 years after Shougang acquired Hierro Peru, Chinalco purchased the Toromocho copper mine from Peru Copper. This has been more of a success story. The first investment contract was signed in 2009. It required expansion of the existing excavations, which involved hiring more workers and relocating an old mining city that had already been contaminated by wastewater. The Peruvian government provided support for the project by granting Chinalco a long-term tax holiday.

Chinalco's management made significant efforts to improve relations with the labour unions. It paid its skilled workers wages that were above the market average for the region and has invested in scholarships and training programs for the local population.[132] Despite its investment in workers' safety, Chinalco had several industrial accidents.[133] It benefited from keeping not only Toromocho's advanced mining technology but also the existing management, comprised mainly of North American and Peruvian staff. That strategy helped Chinalco to utilize local management practices and fit in with local business culture more easily.[134] Thus, although Chinalco did not directly adopt international governance standards, it is possible that its more efficient governance would be attributed to their indirect adoption through the hiring of pre-existing management and staff and its style of engagement with the local communities, and by its reliance on pre-existing local practices. In 2013, Chinalco agreed that it would in future participate in Peru's EITI.[135]

Chinalco worked very hard to improve transparency and to consult with the local communities. After acquisition of the mine, it stepped in to build a new town and to ensure voluntary community relocation, the first of its kind in Peruvian history. The process of consultation related to the expansion of the mine and the resettlement took the form of a Dialogue Table,

---

130 Ibid.

131 Ibid. at 4.

132 Sanborn and Chann (note 15 above) at 29 and 31.

133 Sanborn and Chann report one fatal accident in 2011 and two in 2013: ibid. at 30.

134 Gonzales-Vicente (note 59 above) at 52–4.

135 Nieves (note 127 above) at 6.

which is a Peruvian form of governance and negotiations that involves all stakeholders, public and private, and also includes civil society. The resettlement negotiations were in compliance with Peru's domestic laws and its commitment to ILO 169. Despite these consultations, resettlement process of the 5000 Morococha residents did not go smoothly, and even after it was completed in 2013, the local population complained that neither Chinalco nor the local government acted in good faith.[136]

Finally, it must be noted that Chinalco responded in a timely manner to environmental concerns related to a major leak of the contaminated water in the area. It reinforced the waste discharge facilities, built a 400-cubic-meter retention pond in 2013[137] and resumed operations at the mine in 2014.

Chinalco's investment grew out of political and legal circumstances different from those surrounding the Shougang project. Chinalco's operations were subject to multilayered international and domestic standards and laws related to FDIs. Both Peru and China have felt the impact of the "transparency turn" of the twenty-first century. They have participated in the multilateral world trade system as WTO members and have immersed themselves in regional economic integration by concluding many FTAs with other countries.[138] As previously mentioned, almost 95 percent of Peru's exports are covered by FTAs. China has concluded more than 100 BITs, many of them since the Shougang investment in Peru. Peru has also become Latin America's leader in good governance and transparency reforms. It underwent constitutional and administrative reforms in the late 1990s, joined EITI in 2007 and has made a commitment to publish online the extractive companies' revenue flows. It has also reaffirmed its commitment to honour its international human rights obligations (ILO 169) and those to protect the communities living close to extractive projects. The Chinese government has also initiated numerous domestic policy reforms, aimed at improving transparency, increasing the accountability of public and private actors involved in trade and investments, and strengthening the provisions related to government agencies' duties of disclosure to and consultation with private parties in the law-making process.

---

136 McClatchy DC, *High in Peru's Andes, a Chinese firm paid to build a new town*, Editorial, 2 November 2015, available at http://www.mcclatchydc.com/news/nation-world/world/article42274056.html (accessed 5 January 2017).

137 Nieves (note 127 above) at 6.

138 For Peru's FTAs, see http://www.sice.oas.org/ctyindex/PER/PERagreements_e.asp (accessed 5 January 2017). For China's FTA network, see http://fta.mofcom.gov.cn/english/fta_qianshu.shtml (accessed 5 January 2017).

IV. CONCLUSIONS

This chapter has argued that the principle of transparency has been enshrined in international trade and investment treaties primarily to facilitate the implementation of trade policy goals and to ensure the functioning of transparent, accountable and impartial economic governance by states and that its impact on human rights, other than the right of individuals to market access, is difficult to assess. Even the anticipation of international treaty accession can spark domestic law reforms.[139] Moreover, implementation of international laws is a complex process that often takes several years and is affected by domestic legal, political, economic and social circumstances.[140] Therefore, the proliferation of international transparency laws can operate as one factor influencing reforms in domestic governance and can be a catalyst for a worldwide movement to protect all human rights, but it cannot be a substitute for domestic reforms. Similarly, global governance institutions built to monitor and enforce international transparency laws are not substitutes for domestic governance institutions and the remedies available in domestic legal systems. As this chapter reveals, developing countries such as China and Peru have been undergoing significant domestic governance reforms, partially in response to international challenges but also due to their political decisions to strengthen domestic transparency and improve the domestic decision-making process. Despite the fact that both countries have created policies to improve the first two generations of transparency, they are yet to create the processes and institutions needed for the functioning of collaborative transparency.

---

[139] China amended a wide range of its laws, including administrative laws, in anticipation of its accession to the WTO. Canada amended its Investment Canada Act and the related Guidelines for investments by foreign state owned enterprises (SOEs) in 2012 and 2013 (RSC 1985, c. 28), prior to the ratification of Canada-China Foreign Investment and Protection and Promotion Agreement (but after signing it on 8 September 2012). Central and Eastern Europe amended their domestic laws during the process of negotiation of the accession to the European Union and their signing of the Treaty of Accession to European Union. See Frank Emmert and Sinisa Petrovic, "The Past, Present, and Future of EU Enlargement" (2014) 37:5 Fordham Int'l L.J. 1350.

[140] International treaty negotiations often take two to five years, while international trade and investment treaty implementation may take ten to fifteen years. See Leonardo Baccini and Johannes Urpelainen, "International Institutions and Domestic Politics: Can Preferential Trading Agreements Help Leaders Promote Economic Reform?" (2014) 76:1 Journal of Politics 195 at 201.

4. Challenging an investment agreement in Canada: Hupacasath First Nation's application for judicial review against the CCFIPPA*

Naayeli E. Ramírez-Espinosa

I. INTRODUCTION

In December 1960, the United Nations General Assembly adopted the Declaration on the Granting of Independence to Colonial Countries and Peoples,[1] and ever since there has been a continual effort to enact international treaties to protect the land, territories and cultures of Indigenous populations around the world. But these instruments have been difficult to apply and enforce domestically. Moreover, Canada has established laws, policies and programs aimed at the protection of Indigenous peoples' rights and territories, but the justiciability of such rights remains contested. In the words of the United Nations (UN) Special Rapporteur on the rights of Indigenous peoples, James Anaya, "It is difficult to reconcile Canada's well-developed legal framework and general prosperity with the human rights problems faced by [I]ndigenous peoples in Canada, which have reached crisis proportions in many respects".[2] The situation of Indigenous peoples in Canada demonstrates some of the many paradoxes

* This chapter is based on a paper presented to the workshop on 'Mapping the Impact of International Trade and Human Rights on Local Practice', held in July 2014 at the International Institute for the Sociology of Law in Oñati, Spain.

1 The Declaration on the Granting of Independence to Colonial Countries and Peoples, adopted by the United Nations General Assembly on 14 December 1960, is Resolution 1514(XV). See also the Declaration on the Rights of Indigenous Peoples (UNDRIP) adopted by the United Nations General Assembly on 13 September 2007, A/61/295.

2 James Anaya, *The Situation of Indigenous Peoples in Canada*, A/HRC/27/52/ Add.2 (4 July 2014) at para 14.

created by the dominant system of law and the fragmented relationships between constitutionalism, multilevel governance, international economic law, human rights and diversity.

This chapter seeks to illustrate the complexity of the interplay between global and domestic policies in specific local contexts and the impact of the structure of an international investment treaty on local practice framed by a complex constitutional framework through the discussion of one case study: the application for judicial review case brought by the Hupacasath First Nation (Hupacasath) in British Columbia (BC), Canada. In its application, Hupacasath sought a declaration that Canada was required to engage in a process of consultation and accommodation with it and all First Nations, prior to the ratification of the Foreign Investment Promotion and Protection Agreement between Canada and China (CCFIPPA).[3] The application was rejected because, as I argue below, the courts failed to integrate the aim of reconciliation of section 35 of the Constitution Act 1982; the legal context of its existing claim to their ancestral territory; investment law, investment agreements and decisions made by investment tribunals; and Hupacasath laws.

II. THE CONSTITUTIONAL RIGHTS OF INDIGENOUS PEOPLES IN CANADA

All Indigenous peoples, as any other person, enjoy the many rights established by the Constitution. They also benefit from specific rights found in section 35 of the Constitution Act 1982, which recognizes and affirms all Aboriginal and treaty rights. Section 35 acknowledges the "history of legislation and policy designed to terminate Indigenous cultural and social distinctiveness in order to assimilate Indigenous peoples seeking the reconciliation of the pre-existence of Aboriginal societies with the sovereignty of the Crown".[4] This recognition covers the inherent right to self-government, which includes jurisdiction over their ancestral territory and people. However, in order to exercise this jurisdiction, agreements must be negotiated with the federal government, and with the relevant provincial government.

---

[3] Agreement Between the Government of Canada and the Government of the People's Republic of China for the Promotion and Reciprocal Protection of Investments (CCFIPPA), 9 September 2012.

[4] Indigenous Foundations of the University of British Columbia, available at http://indigenousfoundations.arts.ubc.ca/?id=8356 (accessed 5 January 2017), and *R v Van der Peet* [1996] 2 SCR 507, at para 31.

The BC provincial government established the BC Treaty Commission, an agency charged with negotiating treaties with Indigenous peoples, which began its work in 1993. In over 20 years the BC Treaty Commission has only achieved four treaties: Tla'amin, Yale, Tsawwassen and Maa-nulth, of which only the latter two have been implemented.[5] Hupacasath has been in negotiations for an agreement for over 16 years.[6] The significance of achieving an agreement cannot be overstated; all Indigenous peoples' rights are both *band and fact-specific*,[7] making treaties fundamental in the definition, establishment, application and protection of Aboriginal rights in Canada. If Hupacasath had arrived at an agreement in 2012, the decision of the court might have been completely different. The agreements achieved by the Maa-nulth and Tsawwassen First Nations in BC contain a clause that obliges the Government of Canada to consult them prior to making international agreements that may adversely affect their rights. This clause is an example of local adaptation to the conditions set by international law standards in the context of Indigenous peoples' quest to protect their rights in BC, which until now has had no effect since most First Nations in BC remain without a final agreement.

In Canada, achieving an agreement is a complex technical process because provincial governments have jurisdiction over Crown-owned lands and resources, while the federal government has jurisdiction over "Indians and lands reserved for Indians".[8] Moreover, representatives of the federal and the provincial governments come to the negotiation table with a very limited mandate hindering their efforts to directly negotiate their expectations in their own terms within meaningful periods of time.[9]

---

5 BC Treaty Commission website, available at http://www.bctreaty.net/treaties-and-agreements-in-principle (accessed 5 January 2017).

6 According to James Anaya, '[m]any negotiations under these procedures have been ongoing for many years, in some cases decades, with no foreseeable end': (note 2 above) at para 62.

7 *R v Gladstone* [1996] 2 SCR 723, at para 65, and *R v Van der Peet* [1996] 2 SCR 507, at para 69.

8 Constitution Act 1867 (UK), 30 & 31 Vict, c. 3, in VI. 91, 24.

9 Naayeli Esperanza Ramírez-Espinosa, *Indigenous Struggles for Land Rights in Canada, Japan and Mexico: Delgamuukw, Nibutani Dam and Zirahuén* (PhD Dissertation, University of British Columbia, Faculty of Law, 2014), available at https://open.library.ubc.ca/cIRcle/collections/24/items/1.0072155 (accessed 5 January 2017); James Anaya (note 2 above) at para 65 in his report also discusses some of the issues in this respect stating that: 'The Government's stated objective of "full and final certainty" with respect to rights burdens the negotiation process with the almost impossible requirement of being totally comprehensive and anticipating all future circumstances'. See also Judith Sayers, 'Treaties and Tsilhqot'in-Treaties at Risk?' (4 July 2014), *First Nations in BC Knowledge Network* (blog),

In addition, all Indigenous peoples' rights, even those established in the Constitution, can be limited by an undetermined array of standards, such as *compelling and substantive objectives related to development.*[10] This has made it difficult to protect such rights in the past because the interpretation of such standards usually does not include Indigenous peoples' perspectives on development in their territory.

It is true that according to the Constitution of Canada and the *honour of the Crown*, federal and provincial governments are duty-bound to consult Indigenous peoples and accommodate their interests whenever their asserted or established rights may be affected by government conduct.[11] This duty applies to acts of legislation: "The government is required to bear the burden of justifying any legislation that has some negative effect on any [A]boriginal right protected under s.35(1)".[12] However, it is common that federal and provincial legislatures enact and amend legislation that affects Indigenous peoples without properly consulting them,[13] and it is also common for governments to promote the exploration and development of resources on Indigenous peoples' lands without properly complying with their duty to consult.[14] This is why most First

---

available at http://fnbc.info/blogs/judith-sayers/treaties-and-tsilhqot-treaties-risk (accessed 5 January 2017).

[10] *Delgamuukw v British Columbia* [1997] 3 SCR 1010, at para 165.

[11] The duty to consult is a 'constitutional imperative' according to *Nlaka'pamux Nation Tribal Council v British Columbia* (Project Assessment Director, Environmental Assessment Office) [2011] BCCA 78 (CanLII); cited in *Hupacasath First Nation v The Minister of Foreign Affairs Canada and the Attorney General of Canada* 2013 FC 900, at para 46.

[12] *R v Sparrow* [1990] 1 SCR 1075 at 1109–10.

[13] See James Anaya (note 2 above) at paras 47–8: 'In 2012, the federal Government enacted or amended a number of statutes affecting Canada's Indigenous peoples, including the Canadian Environmental Assessment Act, the National Energy Board Act, the Fisheries Act, the Navigable Waters Protection Act and the Indian Act, through two "omnibus" budget implementation acts, the Jobs and Growth Act 2012 (Bill C-45) and the Jobs, Growth and Long-term Prosperity Act (Bill C-38). Despite the vast scope and impact on Indigenous nations of the omnibus acts, there was no specific consultation with [I]ndigenous peoples concerning them.'

[14] *Platinex Inc. v Kitchenuhmaykoosib Inninuwug First Nation et al.*, 272 DLR (4th) 727; [2006] 4 CNLR 152, at paras 95–6: 'Despite repeated judicial messages [compelling the federal and provincial Crowns to address their fiduciary duty in all Crown decisions that affect the rights of Aboriginal peoples] delivered over the course of 16 years, the evidentiary record available in this case sadly reveals that the Provincial Crown has not heard or comprehended this message and has failed in fulfilling this obligation. One of the unfortunate aspects of the Crown's failure to understand and comply with its obligations

Nations, Hupacasath among them, would prefer to have the jurisdiction to enact laws to protect their territory rather than await the government and its agencies to fulfill their duty to consult. This situation has gradually changed, primarily through courts' decisions.[15]

III. INDIGENOUS PEOPLES' RESPONSES TO THE SIGNATURE OF THE CCFIPPA

On 9 September 2012, Prime Minister Stephen Harper signed the CCFIPPA. The CCFIPPA is an agreement that regulates Canada and China's treatment of Chinese and Canadian foreign investors and investments. The agreement deals with rules on non-discriminatory treatment, expropriation, transparency, transfer of funds, and dispute settlement. All investments from both countries in the other country are guaranteed a minimum standard of treatment and the general international law principles of fair and equitable treatment and full protection and security to investors. Also, all investments are to enjoy the same treatment as

---

is that it promotes industrial uncertainty to those companies, like Platinex, interested in exploring and developing the rich resources located on Aboriginal traditional land.'

[15] For example, in *Delgamuukw v British Columbia* [1997] 3 SCR 1010, the Supreme Court of Canada (SCC) established that oral histories were to be given due evidentiary weight, recognizing for the first time in the history of Canada the injustice of disregarding in court cases crucial characteristics of the legal and material realities of Indigenous peoples. In 1973, in *Calder et al. v Attorney General of British Columbia* [1973] SCR 313, the SCC recognized for the first time that the Nisga'a peoples' Aboriginal title had survived until modern times. The *Calder* decision marked a tremendous change in the legal environment of Indigenous claims in BC. The federal government entered a negotiation process with the Nisga'a in the 1970s, and in 1973, it established the first system to deal with comprehensive claims. Such a policy was designed to obtain consensual extinguishments of Aboriginal title and seemed to favor the recognition of inherent Aboriginal rights. This policy has been revised on a number of occasions. In 1990, the provincial government of BC finally joined the negotiation process with the Nisga'a. Land claims are not only about land but also about other Indigenous peoples' rights. There are two kinds of land claims: comprehensive and specific. Most land claims are negotiated through treaty negotiations with state provincial and federal authorities. Comprehensive land claims are claims over land and rights that have never been negotiated. Specific land claims are claims over land and rights that have been addressed through past treaties. The presentation of a specific land claim entails an allegation that the treaty has been violated – not an uncommon situation.

National and Most-Favoured National Companies.[16] There is no mention of Indigenous peoples' rights and interests in the CCFIPPA.

Total Chinese investment in Canada, which is double Canadian investment in China, increased 1075 percent between 2005 and 2011.[17] Most Chinese investments in Canada are in natural resource-based companies. It is reasonable to expect that Chinese investments will continue to focus on this economic sector, and that such investments will have consequences on Indigenous communities.[18] On 25 September 2012, the Assembly of Manitoba Chiefs sent an open letter to the Chinese Ministry of Commerce in Beijing, soliciting a meeting and explaining the Assembly's concerns regarding the CCFIPPA. Such concerns were regarding the diminished scope and implementation of the numbered treaties in the Prairies[19] and the lack of consultation with Indigenous peoples about the exploitation of natural resources in ancestral Indigenous territories.

On 30 October 2012, the Union of BC Indian Chiefs also sent an open letter to then Prime Minister Stephen Harper arguing that there was a lack of information, consultation and public debate regarding the CCFIPPA.[20]

---

[16] For further discussion, see Kathryn Tucker, 'Reconciling Aboriginal Rights with International Trade Agreements: Hupacasath First Nation v. Canada' (2013) 9 *JSDLP – RDPDD* 2 at 109.

[17] Asia Pacific Foundation of Canada, 'Canadian Inward Foreign Direct Investment from Asia', available at http://www.asiapacific.ca/statistics/investment/inward-foreign-direct-investment/canadian-inward-foreign-direct-investment-a-0 (accessed 5 January 2017).

[18] In an Assembly of Manitoba Chiefs, Chief Genaille observed the following: '. . .the foreign investment interests contained within the FIPPA will take precedence over our unresolved Treaty claims and interests in land. . .Given that we still possess unresolved Treaty land claims that contain valuable natural resources. . . [l]et's finish the unresolved Treaty claims that First Nations possess first before Canada enters into and signs investment treaties with foreign governments': Assembly of Manitoba Chiefs' website, http://www.manitobachiefs.com/ and http://amc.manitobachiefs.com/index.php?option=com_content&view=article&id=296:canada-china-foreign-investment-qtreatyq-may-jeopardize-and-threaten-first-nations-treaty-rights-to-land&catid=67:press-release&Itemid=178 (accessed 5 January 2017).

[19] The Numbered Treaties are also known as the Post-confederate Treaties. They comprise 11 treaties signed between Aboriginal peoples in Canada and the British monarchs Victoria, Edward VII and George V between 1871 and 1921. These treaties cover most of the Canadian territory.

[20] 'Open Letter: Canada – China Agreement Abrogates Rights of Indigenous People' (30 October 2012), available at http://www.ubcic.bc.ca/News_Releases/UBCICNews10311201.html# axzz4ZXeMkqRG (accessed 5 January 2017): '[T]he agreement provides far superior protection for Chinese investors' interests than for our First Nations' Aboriginal Title, Rights and Treaty Rights. . .We believe

In this open letter, Grand Chief Stewart Phillip of the Union of BC Indian Chiefs stated that the agreement establishes obligations for Canada that disregard the constitutional position of Aboriginal title, rights and treaty rights in the Canadian Constitution.[21]

On 18 January 2013, Hupacasath applied for a judicial review[22] against the CCFIPPA in a federal court, and in March 2013 also filed an injunction to stop the Cabinet from ratifying[23] the agreement, which was foregone some days later. On 22 April 2013, the New Democratic Party (NDP) entered a motion to block the ratification of the CCFIPPA, a motion that was rejected by a majority in the Parliament of Canada.[24] Hupacasath's

---

the agreement would enable Chinese investors to challenge Canadian regulations, policies and/or legislation designed to protect the environment as well as current reconciliation negotiations, accommodation measures and treaty negotiations.'

[21] Through their website the Chiefs of Ontario have expressed similar views. Lake Huron (Ontario) Regional Grand Chief Isadora Day stated: 'Trade and investment treaties with other countries are very critical and complex endeavors affecting access to lands and resources. Neither China nor any other country should be legally granted delegated access to treaty lands that are still under current arrangements with First Nations in this country': 'First Nations in Ontario continue to oppose the Canada-China Foreign Investment Promotion and Protection Agreement (FIPPA)' (20 February 2013), available at http://www.chiefs-of-ontario.org/node/517 (accessed 5 January 2017).

[22] Many other First Nations have come to the courts asking for the *unlikely*. Previously in Delgamuukw, the Gitksan and the Wet'suwet'en were also denied the opportunity to negotiate their title, and the only open forum to hear their grievances was a court. Most of the progress made in the protection of Indigenous peoples' rights in Canada has been through courts' interpretations and decisions. See also *Calder et al. v Attorney-General of British Columbia* [1973] SCR 313; *Baker Lake (Hamlet) v Minister of Indian Affairs and Northern Development* [1980] 1 FC 518 (TD); *Guerin v The Queen* [1984] 2 SCR 335; 55 NR 161; *R v Sparrow* [1990] 1 SCR 1075; *Delgamuukw v British Columbia* [1997] 3 SCR 1010; *Tsilhqot'in Nation v British Columbia* 2014 SCC 44.

[23] In an interview, a Hupacasath First Nation council member, Brenda Sayers, remarked that the Government of Canada had agreed to hold off on the ratification until due process had taken place in court: Canadian Broadcasting Corporation, 'First Nations Stand Between Canada-China Agreement' (8 November 2013), available at http://www.huffingtonpost.ca/2013/08/11/first-nations-canada-china-fipa_n_3739561.html (accessed 5 January 2017).

[24] The vote in the House of Commons was 170 against and 88 in favor of the motion: Parliament of Canada website, Publications of Debates of the 41st Parliament, 1st Session, Monday, 22 April 2013, available at http://www.parl.gc.ca/HousePublications/Publication.aspx?Language=E&Mode=1&Parl=41&Ses=1&DocId=6094002 (accessed 5 January 2017). Following the session, Green Party leader Elizabeth May declared that the only hope now was for the Hupacasath First Nation to challenge the CCFIPPA. See Chris Lane, 'Parliament rejects NDP motion to stop FIPA' (22 April 2013), available at http://www.

application for judicial review was heard in court on 5–7 June 2013, with a decision dismissing the application rendered on 26 August 2013. The federal cabinet ratified the CCFIPPA on 12 September 2014, and the agreement was brought into force on 1 October 2014.[25]

IV. HUPACASATH FIRST NATION VERSUS THE MINISTER OF FOREIGN AFFAIRS CANADA AND ATTORNEY GENERAL OF CANADA

Hupacasath argued in court that the Government of Canada was required to consult First Nations under section 35 of the Constitution Act 1982. The court applied the test of Rio Tinto, examining three elements: "(1) the Crown's knowledge, actual or constructive, of a potential Aboriginal claim or right; (2) contemplated Crown conduct; and (3) the potential that the contemplated conduct adversely affects an Aboriginal claim or right".[26] The parties in the case conceded the first two elements, thus the court was left to examine if the contemplated conduct might adversely affect Hupacasath rights.

Hupacasath argued that if the investment treaty were ratified, Chinese investors would hypothetically be able to control major assets, such as coal, on its claimed 232,000 hectare territory.[27] It considered that due to current economic and international legal conditions, the rights granted to Chinese companies in the CCFIPPA and their economic power could erode the power of First Nations in their treaty negotiation processes with the governments. Hupacasath also argued that:

> . . .disputes over resource use between them and companies with Chinese investors will be resolved by the application of international trade and investment law, which does not provide the same protections for Aboriginal rights

---

vancouverobserver.com/tags/china-canada-fipa/parliament-votes-against-ndp-motion-stop-fipa (accessed 5 January 2017).

[25] Department of Foreign Affairs, Trade and Development Canada, 'Canada-China Foreign Investment Promotion and Protection Agreement (FIPA) Negotiations', available at http://www.international.gc.ca/trade-agreements-accords-commerciaux/agr-acc/fipa-apie/china-chine.aspx?lang=eng (accessed 5 January 2017). The CCFIPPA will expire in 2045, at least for the investments made in the first 15 years of its duration.

[26] *Rio Tinto Alcan Inc v Carrier Sekani Tribal Council* 2010 SCC 43.

[27] Hupacasath has approximately 300 members, five reserves and claims title to 232,000 hectares of land in central Vancouver Island. Its territory is located in Port Alberni, BC, and is rich in coal.

> and title as Canadian constitutional law and that because measures aimed at protecting the Hupacasath First Nation's rights and title may give rise to significant damage claims, the federal and provincial governments will be less likely to take steps to protect those rights, including engaging in adequate consultation and reasonable accommodation.[28]

The Government of Canada responded that the duty to consult could not be applied so broadly as to apply to the signing of the CCFIPPA. It added that if any declaration was to be granted, it should pertain only to Hupacasath, and should not be a broad declaration concerning the duty to consult owed to other First Nations. The Government of Canada defended the position that the CCFIPPA does not limit the rights of Indigenous peoples in Canada, including those rights that had not been settled through the treaty negotiation process. The Government of Canada also responded that in order to proceed with consultation a causal link must exist between the ratification of CCFIPPA and any adverse effects on Hupacasath's title and rights. Furthermore, it held that no Indigenous group had requested consultation with respect to any of the 24 FIPPA signed by Canada with other countries. Regarding the lack of debate on the CCFIPPA, the Government also argued that some information with respect to the CCFIPPA had been available to the general public via the Department of Foreign Affairs and International Trade website since 2008. An Explanatory Memorandum presented in the court notes that "Consultations on the [CCFIPPA] took place under the ongoing consultation process by the Department of Foreign Affairs and International Trade with stakeholders".[29] Nevertheless, both parties recognized that such consultations did not include Hupacasath or other First Nations,

---

[28] *Hupacasath First Nation v The Minister of Foreign Affairs Canada and the Attorney General of Canada* 2013 FC 900, at para 18(c)(d): 'a. the Hupacasath First Nation may be prevented from exercising its rights to conserve, manage and protect lands, resources and habitats in accordance with traditional Hupacasath laws, customs and practices, and in the best interest of its members; b. the Hupacasath First Nation may be prevented from negotiating a treaty which protects its rights to exercise its authority in the best interest of the Hupacasath people, including to conserve, manage and protect lands, resources and habitats and to engage in other governance activities, in accordance with traditional Hupacasath law, customs and practices, and in the best interest of its members; . . . e. the rights of Chinese investors, and the impact of any potential claim under the CCFIPPA on Canada may be taken into account by the government and courts in determining whether a specific measure the Hupacasath First Nation seeks to protect its rights and title would constitute reasonable accommodation.'

[29] Ibid. at para 11.

including those with treaties with the Government of Canada, which had established such an obligation.

V. THE DECISIONS

Chief Justice Paul Crampton of the Federal Court dismissed the application and awarded costs against Hupacasath. His decision is based on the understanding that the ratification of the CCFIPPA is an exercise of a prerogative power, and that the exercise of this power is subject to review on constitutional grounds.[30] He determined that the standard of review was a standard of correctness. He found *no* "potential adverse impacts" on constitutionally enshrined and judicially recognized Aboriginal rights of Hupacasath by the ratification of CCFIPPA and concluded that the potential adverse impacts asserted by Hupacasath were "non-appreciable" and "speculative" in nature.[31] Chief Justice Crampton agreed with the Government of Canada in that his decision could not address whether a duty to consult is owed to other First Nations, because the application filed by the applicant was not a class action or an action filed by a representative of First Nations in Canada. He also stated that he could not address this issue because "Aboriginal rights in Canada are band and fact specific".[32]

In the decision the court considered the CCFIPPA as highly similar to the North American Free Trade Agreement (NAFTA) between the Governments of Canada, Mexico and the United States.[33] Chief Justice Crampton supported his conclusion that Hupacasath's arguments were speculative on the fact that Canada had violated its international obligations only on very few occasions, that there had been only two judgments or damages rendered in arbitration tribunals against Canada, and that no claims had been filed under any of the current 24 FIPPA signed by Canada, among similar facts. He also supported his conclusions by stating that the CCFIPPA will likely have the same consequences as the other FIPPA, which had no adverse effects on Hupacasath. He also stated there was no evidence that Chinese firms would invest in the Hupacasath claimed terri-

30 Ibid. at para 25.

31 Ibid. at para 59.

32 Ibid. at para 24.

33 Ibid. at para 8. North American Free Trade Agreement between the Government of Canada, the Government of Mexico and the Government of the United States, 17 December 1992, Can TS 1994 No. 2, 32 ILM 289 (entered into force 1 January 1994) (NAFTA).

tory or that measures established by the applicant in its claimed territory could contravene the measures established in the CCFIPPA. Chief Justice Crampton mentioned in several parts of the decision that the Hupacasath will never be a respondent in any action initiated by a Chinese investor under the CCFIPPA.[34]

The judge concluded that the evidence offered by the applicant was not material to its argument. The court ruled that the expert witness offered by the applicant, a law expert in investment treaty arbitration, did not fulfill the expectation of assisting the court impartially and did not materially assist the arguments of the applicant.[35] From his perspective, the addition of international obligations in Canada would not have any adverse consequences for First Nations. He stated that even though the CCFIPPA was a broad, national framework investment treaty, it could not have adverse effects in the asserted Aboriginal rights of the applicant or impact its lands or resources. According to the court, the CCFIPPA allows certain flexibility in the policies applied towards the rights of Indigenous nations. Nonetheless, in my opinion such flexibility cannot be inferred from the text.

Hupacasath appealed, and the Federal Court of Appeal found no evidence that any of Canada's previous FIPPA had caused or were causing Canada to make decisions that did not respect Indigenous peoples' rights, and found that it had no basis to interfere with the Federal Court's factual findings. It held: "the duty to consult is triggered not by imaginings but by tangibilities".[36]

VI. LEGAL UNCERTAINTY AND THE DECISION

The greatest challenge for the applicant was to prove the detriment to its rights: impact and harm. The content of its rights was not settled, the territory it claims is contested, the scope of its self-government remains undecided, the challenged treaty had not been implemented and the political, social and legal discrimination against Indigenous peoples in Canada as the context of the claim was not recognized. Moreover, the

---

[34] Ibid. at para 62.

[35] This was also seen in other cases, such as Delgamuukw, in which the experts offered by the Indigenous communities were considered as biased towards the plaintiffs.

[36] *Hupacasath First Nation v Canada* (Foreign Affairs and International Trade Canada), 2015 FCA 4 (CanLII), at paras 32–70, available at http://canlii.ca/t/gfzcv (accessed 5 January 2017).

decision imposes views of the dominant legal culture on precisely "what is impact" and "what is harm", without taking into consideration the different context and normative perspective of the applicant. Sadly, this is not unusual; most Indigenous communities in BC are in the same fragile legal position.

The decision implies that since the borders of the territory of Hupacasath and the content of its Aboriginal title and rights were unsettled, Hupacasath's claims were speculative.[37] The claims were also characterized as speculative because there is no certainty that Chinese investors would be interested in the ancestral territory of Hupacasath, and that any investment would be approved. Still, the CCFIPPA is a law that directly seeks to change the legal conditions in all land and resources in Canada and China, including the ancestral territory of Hupacasath.[38]

The judge also acknowledged the legal uncertainty of Aboriginal rights, the evolving nature of international trade conditions and international trade decision-making in arguing the speculative nature of the claims. The characteristics of Aboriginal rights as *sui generis* and band and fact specific, which have been fundamental in the rejection and dismissal of a vast number of similar rulings in Canada, were decisive in dismissing and rejecting Hupacasath's claims. The pervading legal uncertainty in this case left Hupacasath without legal opportunities to define what can happen in their claimed territory. The courts also did not examine the context of the difficulty to achieve treaties due to the limited mandate with which the federal and provincial governments continue to negotiate agreements with Indigenous peoples, which makes it difficult to establish the framework necessary for self-government and jurisdiction and create an environment that promotes the protection of the human rights of Indigenous peoples in Canada.

Moreover, the grounds of review available for Hupacasath were insufficient for the correct study of the detrimental situation of the First Nation. The grounds of review available reflect a legal perspective and a policy

---

[37] *Hupacasath First Nation v The Minister of Foreign Affairs Canada and the Attorney General of Canada* 2013 FC 900. I find Chief Justice Crampton's conclusion that the CCFIPPA cannot have an appreciable adverse effect on the Hupacasath First Nations' Aboriginal right unreasonable because while he recognizes that the object of the CCFIPPA is to change the legal conditions to access all land and resources in the territory of Canada, including the claimed territory of Hupacasath, and he admits he does not know the content of the Aboriginal rights of Hupacasath, he dares to decide there cannot be any effect from the CCFIPPA for this First Nation.

[38] Ibid. at para 73, where the court, against mathematical logic (set theory), seems to deny that Hupacasath's territory is included in the territory of Canada.

that allows for the exclusion of Indigenous peoples in the government's decision-making process. Such grounds of review maintain a status quo of legal uncertainty in the matter of Indigenous rights, and thus reinforce the precariousness of the legal position of Indigenous peoples in Canada.[39] If decisions continue to remain decided under these terms (increasing technical difficulty; pervading legal uncertainty about Aboriginal rights; and causes of action and judicial processes defined without taking into consideration the historical, social and political contexts of Indigenous peoples in Canada), courts will continue rejecting and dismissing Indigenous peoples' causes, leaving Aboriginal rights unprotected and unenforced.

VII. INTERNATIONAL LAW AND INDIGENOUS PEOPLES IN CANADA

The judge seems to conclude that the evolving nature of international trade conditions and international trade decision-making will act in favor of Indigenous peoples' rights in the future. Nevertheless there is no evidence or sign to hint that this is the direction that international trade conditions will take in the future. International law has played an important role in the history of the territorial dispossession of Indigenous peoples. From the time of colonization to the contemporary appetite for the natural wealth of their lands, Indigenous peoples have been dispossessed of their lands and their resources through the use of general principles agreed upon by certain nations of the world.[40] Such general principles of law rely on theories such as *terra nullius*, legal concepts such as *sovereignty*, and papal bulls that divided America among European powers. Today the concept of sovereignty and the use of "Westphalian interpretations" of human rights and the limited application and interpretation of international economic law[41] continue to guide and shape many processes of dispossession

---

[39] In *William v British Columbia* 2012 BCCA 285, at para 162, Groberman J of the British Columbia Court of Appeal wrote: 'The technical difficulty of this area of law has exacerbated the problem, and has led to considerable frustration. The efforts of the Nisga'a in Calder, the Gitksan and Wet'suwet'en in Delgamuukw, and the Tsilhqot'in in this case (to this point) all consumed enormous amounts of resources, only to have the cases end inconclusively due to problems with the way they were commenced or pleaded.'

[40] Jérémie Gilbert, *Indigenous Peoples' Land Rights Under International Law: From Victims to Actors* (New York: Transnational Publishers Inc. BRILL, 2006) xiii.

[41] Ernst-Ulrich Petersmann, 'International Economic Law in the 21st Century: Need for Stronger "Democratic Ownership" and Cosmopolitan

that in the short, medium, and long term create human rights problems for minorities and Indigenous peoples. Since international law has been constructed mainly through agreements and treaties among nations and regions, and globalization has provoked the specialization of such agreements and rules, a problem has arisen:

> The problem . . . is that such specialized law-making and institution-building tends to take place with relative ignorance of legislative and institutional activities in the adjoining fields and of the general principles and practices of international law. The result is conflicts between rules or rule-systems, deviating institutional practices and, possibly, the loss of an overall perspective on the law.[42] . . .National laws seem insufficient owing to the transnational nature of the networks while international law only inadequately takes account of their specialized objectives and needs.[43]

By provoking conflicts between rules or rules-systems, deviating institutional practices, and losing an overall perspective on law, fragmentation enables a normative environment that allows the violation of human rights, particularly for communities and persons suffering marginalization from political decision-making processes and social discrimination, such as Indigenous minorities. Moreover, most international courts and arbitral tribunals are specialized, and the adjudication process of arbitration controversies assesses cases with an exclusive oriented perspective, such as that of investment and economic liberalization. Arbitral tribunals are not common, their adjudication processes are not always transparent, and they are not concerned with human or political rights.

VIII. ANOTHER CASE, ANOTHER COMMUNITY

In this respect a recent case is worth mentioning: *Clayton/Bilcon v Government of Canada* (2015)[44] regarding Chapter 11 of NAFTA. The

---

Reforms' (2012) 17 *EUI Working Paper* at 4, available at http://cadmus.eui.eu/bitstream/handle/1814/22797/LAW_2012_17_Petersmann.pdf?sequence=1 (accessed 5 January 2017).

42 Martti Koskenniemi, *Report of the Study Group of the International Law Commission: Fragmentation of International Law: Difficulties Arising from the Diversification and Expansion of International Law* A/CN.4/L.682 (13 April 2006) para 8, available at http://legal.un.org/ilc/documentation/english/a_cn4_l682.pdf (accessed 5 January 2017).

43 Ibid. at para 481.

44 *William Ralph Clayton, William Richard Clayton, Douglas Clayton, Daniel Clayton and Bilcon of Delaware Inc. vs Government of Canada*, Chapter 11 of

arbitral tribunal in this case found Canada liable for denying national treatment to the investment because:

> the 'community core values' approach adopted by the JRP [Joint Review Panel] was not a 'rational government policy'; it was at odds with the law and policy of the CEAA [Canadian Environmental Assessment Act, SC 1992, c. 37 (in force until 6 July 2012)]. The approach of the JRP was not consistent with the investment liberalizing objectives of NAFTA; indeed the Tribunal has found it to be incompatible with Article 1105.[45]

The "community core values" to which the citation refers included matters such as "Aboriginal peoples resource use, community history and heritage resources, community character and attitudes, and community health and wellness".[46] The arbitral tribunal in *Clayton/Bilcon* implied that the JRP assessment must have been consistent with the liberalizing objectives of NAFTA, thus overriding local regulations and normative views. The arbitral tribunal was unable to recognize and integrate the local normative environment and the relevance of *community core values* in environmental assessments, indicating one of the many ways in which international economic laws may deviate from national institutional practices, thus illustrating fragmentation.

It is true that in the *Clayton/Bilcon* case, neither the municipal government nor the community had to pay the award or act as respondents in the

---

NAFTA and UNCITRAL Rules, PCA 2009–04. In this case, the investors (Clayton/Bilcon) contended that the treatment they received at every stage of the Environmental Assessment (EA) was unfair, politically biased and discriminatory. The arbitral tribunal decided that indeed they were treated unfairly and awarded damages of US$101 million. See Global Affairs Canada, Cases Filed Against the Government of Canada, Clayton/Bilcon v. Government of Canada, available at http://www.international.gc.ca/trade-agreements-accords-commerciaux/topics-domaines/disp-diff/clayton.aspx?lang=eng (accessed 5 January 2017).

[45] Ibid. at paras 724–5. The JRP was the agency in charge of assessing the application of EA that the investors (Clayton/Bilcon) applied for regarding the Whites Point Quarry and Marine Terminal Project (their investment). The JRP applied laws of Canada and the province of Nova Scotia and concluded that the project was likely to cause significant adverse environmental effects that could not be justified. At the end of 2007, the governments of Nova Scotia and Canada rejected the project on environmental grounds in line with the recommendations of the JRP.

[46] Donald McRae, *Dissenting Opinion In the Matter of an Arbitration under Chapter Eleven of NAFTA and the UNCITRAL Rules of 1976 between William Ralph Clayton, William Richard Clayton, Douglas Clayton, Daniel Clayton and Bilcon of Delaware Inc. vs Government of Canada*, PCA 2009–04, at para 16, available at http://www.pcacases.com/web/sendAttach/1288 (accessed 5 January 2017).

case. Nevertheless, as Donald McRae expressed in his dissenting opinion, the decision will impose "a chill on environmental review panels which will be concerned not to give too much weight to socio-economic considerations or other considerations of the human environment in case the result is a claim for damages under NAFTA Chapter 11".[47] Since most processes of consultation of Indigenous peoples in Canada for investment projects in their territories is done through Environmental Assessments (EA) and regulated by environmental law, the decision rendered in *Clayton/Bilcon* can also be seen as a step backwards in the protection of Indigenous peoples' rights.[48]

IX. CONCLUSIONS AND POLICY RECOMMENDATIONS

Indigenous peoples in BC are at a considerable disadvantage, not only in socio-economic terms due to poverty, social discrimination and their situation as a political minority, but also in legal terms due to the lack of agreements with both levels of governments that define their band and fact-specific rights as well as the lack of causes of action and grounds of review that take into consideration the legal conditions of First Nations in Canada. This is why Hupacasath was and continues to be in a precarious position to defend its interests against Canada and BC governments' economic and investment decisions over its territory.

No court can deny that the CCFIPPA covers and affects the entire jurisdictions of Canada and China, including Hupacasath's ancestral territory, and that the treaty, as all laws, subordinates Hupacasath's claimed rights to a set of externally imposed legal rights and principles, and the predominant legal culture in which such treaty was designed. The imposition of the CCFIPPA in its territory places a burden upon its claimed jurisdiction. Still, the courts that heard Hupacasath's application were unable to see how all these seemingly separated normative orders in the

---

[47] McRae (note 46 above) at para 51.

[48] Many communities and the governments of Canada, Mexico and the United States have expressed their disappointment with the decision due to the failure of the tribunal to 'adequately address nationality-based discrimination when determining whether the Claimants were in like circumstances with alleged comparators'. Second Submission of the United States of America in the case of *Mesa Power Group, LLC, Claimants/Investors vs Government of Canada* (PCA Case No. 2012–17), 13 June 2015, at para 4, available at http://www.pcacases.com/web/sendAttach/1455 (accessed 5 January 2017).

context of Hupacasath affect it, thus promoting fragmentation that will in the short, medium and long term have an undesirable effect on the people and territory of this First Nation. In this case, a fragmented interpretation of the law led to the dismissal of its communal political and legal will to exempt its territory from coverage by the CCFIPPA.

One of the expressions of fragmentation occurs in the courts when legal reasoning is made without building sufficient systemic relationships among different areas of law taking into consideration the context and justification of such different laws, envisaging them as parts of a society's normative aim and purpose. The constitutional aim to reconcile with Indigenous minorities, as well as the many sources on the legal and political context of Indigenous peoples in Canada, appears as a structure that provides judges, policy-makers, governments and citizens with ample tools to apply and protect the rights of Indigenous peoples. However, as Professor Anaya's above-cited report tells us, this is not enough. It is crucial that systemic relationships be built with Aboriginal law in Canada at all levels. This process requires a fundamental turnaround of the Canadian legal system and the re-education of judges, academics, arbitrators and policy-makers about Indigenous laws and normative systems, their constitutional relevance and how these principles ought to make space within international investment law, among other areas of law.

In order to promote an environment that nurtures the protection of human rights, achieves legal certainty and promotes justice through international trade and investment in Canada, courts and arbitral tribunals must adjudicate disputes with the aim of building relationships with local Indigenous legal and normative concepts, thus creating a better understanding of the social, political and legal contexts of Indigenous peoples. This integration ought to be conscious and it is the only way in which fragmentation can be counterbalanced.

At the same time, Canada and BC must improve the current policy to achieve agreements and broaden the mandates of negotiators in order to settle the meaning of Indigenous peoples' rights and provide more legal certainty in this area of law. Jurisdiction of Indigenous peoples needs to be recognized in the courts while the final agreements are being settled in order to achieve self-government and Indigenous jurisdiction. Academics, policy-makers and experts agree that "self-government is essential to improving their social and economic situation and sustaining healthy communities".[49]

---

[49] Anaya (note 2 above) at para 38. See also James Anaya, *Report of the Special Rapporteur on the Rights of Indigenous Peoples*, A/HRC/21/47 (July 2012) at paras 29, 78, 86.

Granting jurisdiction to Indigenous peoples to regulate themselves and their territories will provide effective structures to empower them to participate in the decisions that they consider necessary to improve their situation. The bridge to reconciling the tensions between international standards and local contexts and interests should be constructed from below, through local initiatives such as the construction of self-government that allows the reinterpretation of a community's rights according to its own needs and context. The danger of not advancing in this direction might be irreversible: four Indigenous nations in BC that have been in treaty land entitlement negotiations "for so long that there are almost no available lands left for the First Nations to select".[50]

[50] Ibid. at para 65.

5. The impact of Mexico's 2011 human rights constitutional amendment on arbitral practice: a view from local actors*

Erika Cedillo

I. INTRODUCTION

The 2011 'Human Rights Amendment' (hereinafter, 'Amendment') to the 1917 Constitution of Mexico (hereinafter, 'Constitution') has significantly changed the constitutional approach to the guarantees and rights of persons in Mexico. Prior to that Amendment, the Constitution established 'guarantees' for all persons within the territory. Today, the Government of Mexico must guarantee the protection of those 'human rights' recognized in the Constitution *and* in the international treaties it ratifies, guided by the principles of universality, interdependency, indivisibility and progression. These principles are now established in the Constitution and have also been interpreted by the Mexican Supreme Court of Justice. Although this Amendment was a major reform with a paramount impact on the administration of justice in Mexico, few have considered the effects that it could have in trade-related topics, such as arbitration practice.

Using Mexico as a case study, this chapter illustrates the dilemmas of local performance of international standards on trade and human rights that local 'interpretive communities'[1] encounter. The perspectives from local actors shed light on the mutual interactions between international legal rules and the local context where interpretive communities face

* This chapter is based on a paper presented to the workshop on 'Mapping the Impact of International Trade and Human Rights on Local Practice', held in July 2014 at the International Institute for the Sociology of Law in Oñati, Spain.

[1] Stanley Fish, *Is There a Text in This Class? The Authority of Interpretive Communities* (Cambridge: Harvard University Press, 1982).

challenges of interpretation, implementation and coordination of norms from these two areas of law.

After offering some background on normative trade and human rights conditions in Mexico, this chapter presents the key elements of the Amendment and discusses a controversial decision from the Mexican Supreme Court of Justice. In that decision, the court recognized the Constitution and international treaties to be at the same level in the hierarchy of sources of law, but, in case of conflict, mandated that constitutional restrictions prevail over international treaties. The final section presents some perspectives from local actors – arbitrators, party counsellors and federal judges – regarding the Amendment and the potential effects it could have in the practice of arbitration in Mexico. Their views expose how the engagement with local knowledge, culture and perspectives affects the possibilities for coordinating local compliance with international trade and human rights standards.

II. MEXICO: ON TRADE AND HUMAN RIGHTS

For 25 years starting from the 1950s, Mexico had an industrialization model based on imports substitution and state intervention to promote national growth and development. Mexico sustained this closed economic model until the 1980s, when it started a series of legal reforms focused on the promotion of trade, financial liberalization, privatization of state-owned enterprises, deregulation and the promotion of foreign direct investment. Mexico eliminated the anticipated import permit for most of its products and opened its internal markets, mainly to capital and intermediate goods.[2] In 1986, Mexico joined the General Agreement on Tariffs and Trade (GATT) and enhanced its position in the international arena, becoming an important actor, particularly on trade matters. Between 1988 and 1994, Mexico consolidated its transformation to an open market economy. Numerous privatizations were advanced; there was a strong focus on national economic growth based on exports, and

---

[2] Subsecretaría de Industria y Comercio, 'Evolución del Comercio Exterior de México' [Evolution of Mexican foreign trade] (2009), available at http://www.siicex.gob.mx/portalSiicex/Pagina%20principal/EVOLUCION%20DEL%20COMERCIO%20EXTERIOR.pdf (accessed 5 January 2017); Misión de México ante la Unión Europea, '200 Años de Comercio Exterior de México' [200 years of foreign trade in Mexico] (2010) 8:9 Trade Links Lazos Comerciales, available at http://www.economia-snci.gob.mx/sic_php/pages/bruselas/trade_links/esp/sepesp2010.pdf (accessed 5 January 2017).

trade liberalization became a fundamental objective to support economic development.[3] One of the iconic developments in this market liberalization process was the signature of the North American Free Trade Agreement (NAFTA) with Canada and the United States, which entered into force in 1994.[4]

As part of its new economic model and focus on trade liberalization, Mexico looked for opportunities to diversify its trade relations. In 1994, Mexico became the first Latin American country to enter the Asia-Pacific Economic Cooperation (APEC) and the first developing country to be admitted into the Organization for Economic Cooperation and Development (OECD). In the following years, Mexico extended its trade partnerships through numerous trade agreements, making itself more attractive as a trading partner and destination of foreign direct investment.[5] By 2014, Mexico had signed 10 free trade agreements, 30 bilateral agreements for the promotion and protection of investments and nine agreements of limited scope (within the framework of the Latin American Integration Association, or ALADI) with 49 different trade partners. In 2013, Mexico also joined the negotiations for the Trans-Pacific Partnership (TPP).

Throughout this process of economic transformation, Mexico has constantly been adapting its legal system to offer a legal framework that supports these policy changes. In 1971, Mexico ratified the New York Convention for the Recognition and Enforcement of Foreign Arbitral Awards.[6] It fully embraced arbitration in 1993 by incorporating the United Nations Commission on International Trade Law (UNCITRAL) Model Law for Commercial Arbitration in its Commercial Code.[7] Mexico was one of the first countries to use the same set of laws for national and international arbitration, which reflects its commitment to incorporate international standards in its legal framework and

---

[3] Roberto Ortiz de Zárate, ed., *Carlos Salinas de Gortari*, available at http://www.cidob.org/es/documentacio/biografias_lideres_politicos/america_del_norte/mexico/carlos_salinas_de_gortari (accessed 5 January 2017).

[4] North American Free Trade Agreement Between the Government of Canada, the Government of Mexico and the Government of the United States, 17 December 1992, Can TS 1994 No 2, 32 ILM 289 (entered into force 1 January 1994).

[5] Ibid.

[6] Convention on the Recognition and Enforcement of Foreign Arbitral Awards, 10 June 1958, 330 UNTS at 3; 7 ILM 1046 (1968) (entered into force 7 June 1959).

[7] Commercial Code, published in the Federal Official Gazette 7 October 1889 (entered into force 1 January 1890).

to offer clarity and certainty to its trade partners. In 2008, there was an amendment made to Article 17 of the Constitution,[8] according to which national laws should provide for alternative dispute-settlement mechanisms. Some scholars considered this the establishment of the human right to arbitration,[9] as this article falls within the section of the Constitution that provides for individual guarantees. Within Mexico's legal system this provision granted a higher status (constitutional rank) to alternative dispute-resolution mechanisms, including arbitration. In 2011, an amendment to the Commercial Code called the Arbitration Amendment[10] clarified issues on the execution of arbitral awards, the cooperation of the courts with arbitral procedures and the granting of interim measures, and created special summary procedures for certain topics, like nullity and recognition and enforcement of arbitral awards.[11] Overall, Mexico has been recognized as a pro-arbitration jurisdiction because of its progressive legal framework and the usually positive attitude from its courts towards arbitration.

Mexico is also an active participant in the international human rights framework. It has ratified over 171 international agreements on human rights and is a member of a number of international organizations on the issue.[12] Among these is its membership of the Inter-American Commission and the Inter-American Court on Human Rights (IACHR), both autonomous organs of the Organization of American States. Mexico has explicitly recognized the jurisdiction of the IACHR, and its decisions are binding on the Mexican State and its authorities at all levels. There is an increased awareness of this jurisdiction, and between 2008 and 2010 there were six cases against Mexico before the IACHR. The Mexican State

---

[8] Decree reforming and adding to various provisions of the Political Constitution of the United Mexican States (Mexico) published in the Federal Official Gazette, 18 June 2008.

[9] Francisco González de Cossío, 'El Derecho Humano Arbitral' [The human right to arbitration] (2008), available at http://www.gdca.com.mx/ (accessed 5 January 2017).

[10] Decree reforming, adding to and repealing various provisions of the Commercial Code published in the *Federal Official Gazette*, 27 January 2011.

[11] For a brief on the Arbitration Amendment, see Santamarina and Steta, 'Reforma Legal en Apoyo al Arbitraje Comercial' [Legal amendment in support or commercial arbitration] (2011), available at http://www.s-s.mx/site/?p=2336 (accessed 5 January 2017).

[12] For a full list, see Suprema Corte de la Justicia de la Nación (Supreme Court of Justice of the Nation), 'Tratados internacionales de los que el Estado Mexicano es parte en los que se reconocen derechos humanos' [International treaties in which Mexico is a party and that recognize human rights], available at http://www2.scjn.gob.mx/red/constitucion/inicio.html (accessed 5 January 2017).

has been found responsible on several issues and has been obliged to take specific actions, including amending its laws.[13]

III. THE HUMAN RIGHTS AMENDMENT

Mexico's Constitution has been constantly reformed over the last 30 years. One of the most relevant reforms in recent years is the 'Human Rights Amendment' of June 2011. Article 1 of the Mexican Constitution was the central focus of the amendment and today it reads as follows (emphasis added):

> Article 1. In the United Mexican States all individuals are granted the *human rights* recognized in this Constitution and *in the international treaties* that the Mexican State has ratified; as well as the guarantees for their protection, their exercise cannot be restricted or suspended, except in those cases and under the conditions that this Constitution establishes.
>
> The norms related to human rights will be interpreted according to this Constitution and the international treaties in this matter, *granting the individual the most ample protection at all times*.
>
> All the authorities, within their jurisdiction, have the obligation to promote, respect, protect and guarantee human rights according to the principles of *universality, interdependency, indivisibility and progression*. As a consequence, the State shall prevent, investigate, sanction and repair violations to human rights, according to the terms specified in the law.

The wording change from 'individual guarantees' to 'human rights and its guarantees' conveys a new paradigm of how individuals are granted protection of their rights. The main elements of the new paradigm, which are emphasized in the quote above, include: the diffused control of conventionality through the application of conforming interpretation; the supremacy of the *pro personae* principle; and the four principles that should guide the protection of human rights (universality, interdependency, indivisibility and progression). It expands human rights protection beyond those rights granted in the Constitution to those established in the international treaties that Mexico has ratified. These rights were already part of the Mexican legal framework since the treaties were ratified by the Mexican Senate. However, with this Amendment all judges now need to

[13] For cases against Mexico, see Miguel Carbonell, 'Mexico ante la Corte Interamericana de Derechos Humanos' [Mexico before the Inter-American Court of Human Rights], available at http://www.miguelcarbonell.com/docencia/nter americana_de_Derechos_Humanos.shtml (accessed 5 January 2017).

apply the new paradigm and analyze *ex officio* whether a person's human rights are at risk, in consideration of the expansion of the set of rights now covered by this provision.

The concept of 'diffuse control of conventionality' was introduced by the IACHR. It refers to the assessment of compatibility of the national law of a country with the Inter-American Convention on Human Rights, its additional protocols and the jurisprudence of the IACHR. This is a minimum standard created by the IACHR for member states to offer a broader protection of human rights through national legislation.[14] The implementation of this paradigm comes with the application of 'conforming interpretation', which requires judges to harmonize the national law with the Convention, its protocol and jurisprudence. National judges, within their own jurisdiction, have a constitutional mandate to interpret national laws in conformity with these international treaties whenever human rights are involved. The Amendment brought this paradigm to the forefront, and the Supreme Court ratified it when it reframed the interpretation of Article 133 of the Constitution[15] regarding the hierarchy of sources of law.

In the second paragraph of Article 1, the Constitution reflects the adoption of the principle *pro personae*, according to which individuals ought to be protected by the norm which grants the most ample protection, either by the most extensive interpretation of rights, or by the most restrictive interpretation of its limitations.[16] According to Ximena Medellín Urquiaga, this paradigm 'implies, among other things, the rethinking of structures and categories of thought traditionally used by jurists, in addition to the profound reflection on the role of the administration of justice in a democratic, constitutional and rule-of-law State'.[17] The Supreme Court of Justice, in its discussion of the Radilla Pacheco Case,[18] argued

---

14 Eduardo Ferrer Mac-Gregor, 'Interpretación conforme y Control Difuso de Convencionalidad. El nuevo paradigma para el juez mexicano' [Conforming interpretation and diffuse control of conventionality: the new paradigm for the Mexican judge] (2011) 9:2 Estudios Constitucionales 531 at 532.

15 See section A below.

16 Ximena Medellín Urquiaga, 'Principio pro persona' [*Pro personae* principle] (Mexico, D.F.: Comisión de Derechos Humanos del Distrito Federal, Suprema Corte de Justicia de la Nación, Oficina en México del Alto Comisionado de las Naciones Unidas para los Derechos Humanos, 2013) 18–19.

17 Ibid. at 4 (translation by the author).

18 In this case, the IACHR found the Mexican State responsible and it gave origin to the landmark decision from the Supreme Court explaining the application of the new paradigm and the principles that should guide judges and providing the interpretation and implications of the Amendment. See 'Caso Radilla

that the *pro homine* principle of interpretation brings the individual to the center of the analysis, and declared that all the organs of the Mexican State shall find the most favourable interpretation of a norm, pursuant to Article 1 of the Constitution.

The third element relates to the incorporation of the four principles that should inform the criteria of courts in deciding on issues involving the protection of human rights: universality, interdependency, indivisibility and progression. These principles have become the basis of the human rights system in Mexico. This chapter looks mainly at the mandate of the judges, but when the Constitution refers to 'all the authorities' it includes all those within any of the three branches of government and on any of the three levels of government, that is, federal, provincial and municipal. Universality, interdependency and indivisibility, in addition to informing the actions of national authorities, should guide projects and public policy design to ensure the guarantee and protection of the human rights of persons in Mexico.[19] As for progression, this is a call to authorities to take the necessary actions to ensure that the guarantee and protection of human rights gradually increase overtime.[20]

The Amendment had an overarching impact on how human rights are conceived and protected in Mexico. It has been declared, in the words of the Federal Congress, as a step forward for the full harmonization of national legislation with international human rights laws.[21] Along with the amendment to the Amparo Law,[22] it aspires to procure a more effective and efficient administration of justice in accordance with the international

---

Pacheco, Crónicas del Pleno y de las Salas' [Radilla Pacheco Case, Chronicles of the Plenary and Chambers], Sinopsis de Asuntos Destacados del Tribunal y del Pleno, Sesiones del 4, 5, 7, 11, 12 y 14 de julio del 2011, Suprema Corte de Justicia de la Nación, available at http://www.sitios.scjn.gob.mx/codhap/sites/default/files/cronicas_pdf_sr/TP-140711-MBLR-912.pdf (accessed 5 January 2017).

[19] These principles have been established in diverse international treaties, one of the more recent being the Vienna Declaration and Programme of Action of the World Conference on Human Rights of 1993.

[20] For a detailed analysis, see Luis Daniel Vázquez and Sandra Serrano, 'Los principios de universalidad, interdependencia, indivisibilidad y progresividad. Apuntes para su aplicación práctica' [Principles of universality, interdependence, indivisibility and progression. Notes for their practical application] (2012) Biblioteca Jurídica Virtual del Instituto de Investigaciones Jurídicas de la UNAM, available at http://biblio.juridicas.unam.mx/libros/7/3033/7.pdf (accessed 5 January 2017).

[21] 'Declaratoria' [Declaration], transcript from the Federal Congress Session held on 1 June 2011, which approved the Amendment.

[22] An amparo is a constitutional remedy that protects individuals against human rights violations by any act of authority. The protection of an amparo is

standards that Mexico has accepted in the many treaties it has ratified on this matter.

A. The Controversial Criteria from the Mexican Supreme Court of Justice

In 2013, the Plenary of the Supreme Court of Justice (SCJ) issued two new jurisprudences[23] in resolving Contradiction 293/2011.[24] This contradiction emerged from the conflicting rulings of two circuit courts on two topics: the normative hierarchy between international treaties and the Constitution as sources of law in regards to human rights issues; and the guiding or mandatory character that national judges should give to the jurisprudence from the IACHR.

Regarding the normative hierarchy, in a ruling from 2007, the SCJ established that international treaties were hierarchically above general and federal laws but below the Constitution.[25] Even though at that time the issue was revisited with an increased awareness of the number of international treaties that Mexico had incorporated, the SCJ concluded that from the interpretation of Article 133 of the Constitution, and in harmony

---

provided pursuant to Articles 103 and 107 of the Constitution and is regulated in detail by the Amparo Law that entered into force on 3 April 2013.

[23] Jurisprudence in Mexico is binding interpretive criteria issued by specific courts authorized to do so, that is, the Supreme Court of Justice, the Plenary of Circuit Courts and Collegiate Circuit Courts. It can be created by one of three methods: reiteration, contradiction or substitution. For details on the three types of jurisprudence, see Miguel de Jesús Alvarado Esquivel, 'La jurisprudencia en la nueva ley de amparo' [Jurisprudence in the new Amparo Law] (2013) 35 Revista del Instituto de la Judicatura Federal 189.

[24] Contradiction no. 293/2011 between rulings from the First Collegiate Circuit Court on Administrative and Labour Matters from the 11th Circuit and the Seventh Collegiate Court on Civil Matters from the First Circuit, solved by the Plenary of the Supreme Court, 2 September 2013. A jurisprudence by contradiction, according to Article 225 of the Amparo Law, is issued to clarify conflicting criteria held between the Chambers of the Supreme Court of Justice, between Plenary of Circuit Courts or between Collegiate Circuit Courts in matters within their competence. The court decides on the contradiction and issues a jurisprudence that becomes the new mandatory interpretive criteria. In its decision on Contradiction 293/2011, the SCJ issued two jurisprudences.

[25] Tesis P. IX/2007, 'Tratados Internacionales. Son parte integrante de la ley suprema de la Unión y se ubican jerárquicamente por encima de las leyes generales, federales y locales. Interpretación del artículo 133 Constitucional' [International treaties. They are an integral part of the supreme law of the Union and are located hierarchically above general, federal, and local laws. Interpretation of Article 133 of the Constitution], 9th Epoch, SJF XXV, 2007, 6.

with the principles of international law that are included in diverse articles in the Constitution, the 'Supreme Law of the Union' are the Constitution, international treaties and general laws, with international treaties hierarchically above the general and federal laws.[26]

In Contradiction 293/2011, the Supreme Court declared that, from the interpretation of the law after the Human Rights Amendment of 2011 and in accordance with its spirit:

> . . .the human rights laws, regardless of their source, do not relate in hierarchical terms, and only when the Constitution establishes an express restriction on the exercise of certain human rights, the authority must act in accordance with the Constitution. In this sense, human rights, regardless of their source, are the *parameter of control of the constitutional regularity*, according to which the validity of all the norms and acts of authority that are part of Mexican law must be analyzed.[27]

This decision supported the shift from a hierarchical approach to a constitutional set of norms that must guide judges in deciding on the validity of a specific law or authoritative act. It was an important step to changing the way Mexican law is understood and interpreted. The judges would be able to choose the norm that offered the most ample protection in deciding on a case, using the constitutional set of laws as the parameter for the control of constitutional regularity.[28] However, the SCJ also decided that if there were a conflict on any restriction of a human right, the constitutional restriction should prevail.

Regarding the jurisprudence from the IACHR in Contradiction 293/2011, the SCJ decided that it was mandatory for Mexican judges to apply it if doing so would provide more ample protection to the individual. With this decision, Mexico is fully incorporating the whole body of jurisprudence from the IACHR, giving judges an extended framework to decide on cases in which human rights are involved. One of the consequences of this expanded framework is the need for more specific training for judges, which includes an extended awareness of the sources of law available to them. This represents an important change for the Mexican

---

26 Justice of the Supreme Court Olga Sánchez Cordero de García Villegas, 'La jerarquía de los tratados internacionales en el orden jurídico mexicano' [Hierarchy of international treaties in the Mexican juridical system], presentation at the Tecnológico de Monterrey, 27 November 2008, Toluca, State of Mexico.

27 Contradiction no. 293/2011 (note 24 above) (translation and emphasis by the author).

28 Miguel Carbonell, '¿Constitución o Tratados Internacionales?' [Constitution or international treaties?], El Universal, 20 February 2014, available at http://www.miguelcarbonell.com/articulos_periodicos/Constituci_n_o_tratados_internacionales.shtml (accessed 5 January 2017).

judiciary given that, generally, judges did not consider looking outside of Mexican law and case law in deciding their cases.

While the SCJ ratified the superiority of the *pro personae* principle in its decision on Contradiction 193/2011, it also limited it to a great extent. The SCJ ratified its superiority by granting a mandatory character to the IACHR jurisprudence and by providing more tools for judges to grant the most ample protection. It is expected that granting this protection grounded on international standards will promote better dialogue between national courts and the IACHR, and modernize the practice of law in Mexico.[29] However, the SCJ also limited the *pro personae* principle when it established that any constitutional restriction on human rights should prevail. The whole spirit of the Amendment was to offer the individual the most ample protection available from the Constitution and the international treaties that Mexico had ratified, but with this decision the Supreme Court is moving away from that.

This jurisprudence generated negative reactions in the Mexican legal community because judges were left with a limited range of action when it came to human rights restrictions established by the Constitution. Even if an international treaty provides better protection, the restrictions established in the Constitution must be enforced.[30] While the Amendment showed a shift towards an internationally based conception of human rights, the SCJ issued a restrictive interpretation that limited the actual reach of the Amendment and the *pro personae* principle it embraces.

The dissenting perspective regarding this jurisprudence by contradiction is explained in great detail by Justice José Ramón Cossío Díaz in his individual vote[31] on Contradiction 293/2011.[32] Justice Cossío Díaz

---

29 Ibid.

30 For media reactions, including references to the reactions of international institutions like Amnesty International, see CNN Mexico, 'La SCJN aprueba límites a derechos humanos en tratados internacionales' [The Supreme Court approves limits to human rights in international treaties], 3 September 2013, available at http://expansion.mx/nacional/2013/09/03/la-scjn-aprueba-limites-a-derechos-humanos-en-tratados-internacionales (accessed 5 January 2017); also, Jesús Aranda, 'La Constitución prevalecerá sobre tratados internacionales en derechos humanos: SCJN' [Supreme Court: the Constitution will prevail over international treaties on human rights], *La Jornada*, 4 September 2013.

31 The Plenary of the Supreme Court, composed of 11 justices, makes its decisions by majority. Justices have the prerogative of issuing extended reasoning for their votes, which are incorporated into the official file of the court's decision. For Contradiction 293/2011, the SCJ issued one jurisprudence for each topic. Justice Cossío Díaz voted against the first jurisprudence regarding normative hierarchy.

32 José Ramón Cossío Díaz, 'Voto particular que formula el Ministro José Ramón Cossío Díaz en la Contradicción de Tesis 293/2011' [Individual

explained that the new Article 1 of the Constitution gives way to a completely different normative operation in which hierarchy is not a factor. According to this new normative operation, judges need to apply the *pro personae* principle when deciding on an issue by using the human rights contained in the Constitution and in international treaties, without establishing a hierarchy between them. Justice Cossío Díaz affirmed that the Supreme Court, by adding an exception for those restrictions contained in the Constitution, was creating a rule of interpretation in which the international treaties were placed beneath the Constitution, thus abandoning the possibility of deciding on a case-by-case basis by effectively applying the *pro personae* principle because both sources of rights were not being treated as equals: one was given precedence over the other. Even though the standing criteria is that the Constitution is above international treaties, by exposing these arguments Justice Cossío Díaz left on the official record the approach by which the Constitution and international treaties are considered a 'constitutional set,' with the aspiration that further discussion will be raised in the Supreme Court.

IV. LOCAL ACTORS: ON THE AMENDMENT AND ARBITRATION

This section presents the views of Mexican local actors regarding the Amendment and its possible effect on arbitration practice. The interviewees are lawyers based in Mexico City (the nation's capital) and were invited to participate based on their experience in one of three roles: counsellor of a party, arbitrator or federal judge. There were a total of twelve participants in this study, four in each category. Eight of twelve of these interviewees obtained their law degrees from public universities and four from private universities. In addition to their many years of experience, ten completed post-graduate studies – from specialties to masters – and five interviewees had doctorate degrees. Seven of those with post-graduate studies obtained their degrees from universities in the United States, Europe and one in Nicaragua.

The counsellors are lawyers that have been representing private parties – Mexican and foreign – in international arbitration cases. They averaged over 20 years of experience in the field. The arbitrators have participated in cases involving Mexican and foreign parties, averaging over 22 years of

vote issued by Justice José Ramón Cossío Díaz in Contradiction 293/2011], 3 September 2013.

experience, and have participated as both sole arbitrators and on arbitral tribunals. In both categories, they were highly experienced individuals with international credentials; some of them represented Mexico or were part of groups that participated in UNCITRAL conferences on arbitration and negotiations over NAFTA, among other similar international fora.

The federal judges were invited to participate based on their experience with arbitration cases – specifically, with the public policy exception. All were members of a Collegiate Circuit Court in the First Circuit (Mexico City) and averaged 34 years of experience in the judiciary. Circuit Courts decide on appeals to decisions from District Courts and reviews to indirect and direct amparos.[33] They are the second highest level of the judiciary, just below the Supreme Court, and can create jurisprudence. Because of their geographic location, Circuit Courts of the First Circuit receive the majority of the arbitration-related cases that reach the judiciary.

The main objective of the interviews was to obtain the points of view of experienced local actors regarding the application of the public policy exception in Mexico within the context of arbitration. The general purpose was to understand how local actors construct the meaning of public policy for deciding on the recognition and enforcement of foreign arbitral awards. The interview questions touched upon the actors' experiences with the application of the exception, their opinions on how Mexican courts have applied it, whether they considered it necessary to have a clearer interpretive criterion on the concept of public policy from the Supreme Court, and, in that case, what elements ought to be taken into consideration for constructing such a concept. Their opinions were also queried regarding whether international standards on the public policy exception had influenced the local application of the exception, and if such standards were being used by the courts. They were asked their thoughts on the role of local legal culture in defining public policy and the key elements of the Mexican legal culture that should be taken into consideration.

The topic of the Human Rights Amendment was not a pre-designed question for the interviews but it was brought up early on by one of the arbitrators who used it to highlight the changes that the Mexican legal system was undergoing at the moment. Arbitrator 2 affirmed that 'the distinctive feature of the Mexican legal system at [that] point in time [was] its openness to international conventionality and change'.[34] As a result

---

[33] An indirect amparo challenges a law, acts or omissions of authorities that are not part of a trial, and acts or omissions derived from a trial that are not the final decision on a case. A direct amparo challenges the final decision on a case.

[34] Author interview, Arbitrator 2, 21 May 2012, Mexico City, Mexico.

of the Amendment, he explained, the judges now have to apply a 'diffuse control of conventionality', leaving behind the 'legality control model'. This was a significant observation and, when interviewing the judges, the relevance of the Amendment for the Mexican legal system at that time was made more evident. Therefore, in subsequent interviews, the participants were asked to offer their perspectives on the Amendment and the potential effect that it might have on arbitration practice given that it was changing the local approach to international treaties in the context of human rights significantly.

Counsellors and arbitrators who commented on the Amendment generally shared the idea that it would not have a direct effect on arbitration, mainly because the Amendment concerned human rights, and arbitration was a commercial matter. For the most part, they continued to see these two bodies of law as unrelated. The perception from one of the counsellors, who has also acted as arbitrator in several cases, is that 'regarding international commercial traffic, the legal framework available suffices [him] to decide if a party acted according to the law and the contracts signed between them'.[35] Therefore, he considered it difficult to think of a case in which he would need to refer to the San Jose Pact (Inter-American Convention on Human Rights) to decide, as an arbitrator, on an international commercial case.

Nevertheless, some practitioners remained open to the development of this topic. Arbitrator 2 could foresee it having an impact but was uncertain where it would lead because the Amendment was significantly changing the way judges decide all types of cases, even those related to arbitration. He brought attention to, and showed concern about, the fact that now even lower court judges could decide not to apply a law if they considered it in violation of international treaties that Mexico had ratified. One counsellor was of the opinion that judges were not well informed on the international conventions or treaties available and limited themselves to national law, to the extent that oftentimes counsellors had had to brief a judge on how a certain issue was regulated in an international treaty that Mexico has ratified and its applicability to a particular case. This counsellor was hopeful that the Amendment was now binding them to take into consideration the international treaties Mexico has ratified on human rights topics.

The judges elaborated more on the effects that the Amendment could have on arbitration practice as it is having a larger effect on their primary

[35] Author interview, Counsellor of a Party 3, 6 June 2012, Mexico City, Mexico.

duties. Circuit courts felt it more directly because they decide on direct and indirect amparos,[36] which directly involve the protection of individual guarantees and human rights. The following paragraphs present the perspectives and concerns of these experienced individuals who provided local views of the challenging task of applying the Amendment in their everyday practice. It is important to note the implications that they consider the Amendment has on their legal system; the connections they make between how their legal system works and the risks and challenges it has brought; and how international treaties, with their accompanying standards, are positioned differently in their mindset.

Federal Judge 1 considered the Amendment to have completely transformed the law in Mexico – a change for which federal courts felt unprepared at the time. His main concern was the uncertainty, and thus the need for clarification, about what body of law they should apply, the Constitution or international treaties. He perceived pressure from those on the side of international treaties to make them prevail when there was a conflict between them and the Constitution, and that the Amendment was making an exception to Article 133 of the Constitution. For him, the Constitution and international treaties were at the same level only for human rights purposes; in any other matter, the Constitution still held precedence over international treaties.

Federal Judge 1 drew attention to cases where an extreme interpretation of the Amendment could have a negative effect on arbitration. He made reference to the 2011 Arbitral Amendment by which the legislature clarified the constantly debated issue regarding the remedies available against judicial decisions on two topics – nullity and the recognition and enforcement of arbitral awards.[37] Instead of filing these cases as connected

[36] Amparos are filed against courts decisions, not against an arbitral award, such as a judicial decision on the recognition and enforcement of a foreign arbitral award, or on its nullity. The SCJ has ruled that arbitrators cannot be considered authorities for the purpose of amparo, thus, the remedy is filed against a judicial decision pertaining to an arbitral award. See Justice Guillermo Ortiz Mayagoitia, 'Arbitraje privado, ¿Procede el amparo en contra del laudo que le pone fin?' [Private arbitration, Can the amparo remedy proceed against the award that decides it?], message delivered before the Arbitration Commission of the Mexican Chapter of the International Chamber of Commerce (ICC Mexico), 23 April 2013, available at http://www.iccmex.mx/uploads/arbitraje/arbitro/Discurso%20Ministro%20Ortiz%20Mayagoitia%20La%20Ley%20de%20Amparo.pdf (accessed 6 January 2017).

[37] The question was which amparo, direct or indirect, was the correct way to challenge a court's decision on these two topics because, depending on the type of amparo, it would affect, most of all, the length of the procedure and the number of steps needed to finally have an award enforced or nullified.

procedures,[38] they are now filed as the principal action in the newly created 'arbitral special trial'. Conforming to the amended Commercial Code (Article 1476), no ordinary remedy can be filed against the decisions of such trials, only a direct amparo before a circuit court. Federal Judge 1 explained that there could be a conflict of interpretation because, pursuant to Article 25 of the San Jose Pact, all individuals have the right to an effective and fast remedy; thus, a judge could argue that this constitutes a violation of that Pact. However, if within an international context, the amparo is considered a remedy, then there is no such violation. The problem, he explained, is that in Mexico the amparo is not considered a remedy but a '*sui generis* trial' in which the judge decides on the act of the authority (court decision), not on the particular act. If the mandate is to harmonize national and international laws, there should be no considerations for violation of the Pact. However, this would depend on the interpretation of the court. This is leaving too much leeway for the subjective interpretation of the judge, which, combined with strong, nationalist views about amparo, could pose a challenge.

In general, for Federal Judge 1, the whole idea of the diffuse control of constitutionality and conventionality could pose a risk not only to arbitration but to the entire system. The Amendment is also causing unrest because any judge or authority can now decide not to apply a law in favour of a convention, the Constitution or an individual. This was an exclusive faculty of the federal judiciary, and the judge feared that this could lead to cases of 'corruptive interpretation' that could affect the legal system. Concerned about judges taking a protagonist role, he suggested that each judge or authority should continue to act within their own jurisdiction and that this new approach should not be used as a justification to go beyond it. International law does not want each judge and authority to break the jurisdiction order, but to do what is mandated to them by law and follow the new principles.

Federal Judge 2 considered international law as having received a naturalization letter by this Amendment, becoming equivalent to national law. Nonetheless, he invited judges not to abuse the principle of conventionality and to avoid the 'new tool effect', which could induce judges to justify everything on these grounds. He emphasized that the tools for interpretation and application of the law must be borne in the minds of

38 See Francisco González de Cossío, 'La Modificación a Derecho Arbitral Mexicano – Un comentario' [The amendment to the Mexican Arbitration Law – a comment] (2012) 1(1) Revista de Derecho Privado 289, available at https://revistas.juridicas.unam.mx/index.php/derecho-privado/article/view/8972/11022 (accessed 11 January 2017).

judges; they must look at an issue to the entire extent that the Constitution allows, and if, and only if, the constitutional interpretation is insufficient, then they should resort to the principle of conventionality; judges should not proceed directly to this principle.

Federal Judge 2 saw the need for training of federal judges on human rights, international treaties, and their application to human rights issues. He recognized a trend towards applying international law in an unrestricted way and suggested that national rights should evolve as a more universal conception. The judge considered himself an advocate for international treaties, and, to fulfill his duty, he referred first to national law, using international law only when national law did not provide an adequate answer; if national law provided an answer, the issue was solved:

> I believe that in our country we are living through a paradigm shift. For me this is very important; it is not only a word, but a different concept of the law. We have to develop a different legal culture that must begin from the universities. The schools and the faculties of law have not taken charge of this fundamental change that has to permeate to judges, magistrates, justices, notaries and lawyers. This also influences arbitration, because arbitrators now have more liberty for interpretation of the norms to solve the cases presented before them.[39]

The judges, he added, now have more freedom – to a certain extent – to interpret the law; thus, the methods of interpretation have to change, for example, with the incorporation of the *pro personae* principle. Other principles, such as the judge taking a leading role in a process, will now take priority, demanding that judges be more proactive rather than mere observers of the process; this is something Federal Judge 2 does not see being taught in the universities. For him, arbitration is opening new horizons and possibilities for the Mexican legal system, thus arbitrators need to take the Amendment into account and how any award might affect the human rights of the parties involved. Arbitrators are immersed in the same legal framework, and they have to apply international conventions and treaties, just like judges. Interestingly for him, arbitration is usually seen as a very costly option, but those who do so lose sight of the amount of resources needed to move the judicial system. This Amendment and its principles, he added, require the best qualities from parties, judges and arbitrators: 'they should take seriously the responsibility given to them by exercising the great virtues of prudence, justice, and the prudent and just interpretation of the law'.[40]

---

39 Author interview, Federal Judge 2, 29 May 2012, Mexico City, Mexico.
40 Ibid.

For Federal Judge 2, national and international actors will trust arbitration and Mexico if Mexico shows respect for international arbitrations regardless of the arbitral forum or nationality of the arbitrators. Individuals will feel confident that whatever the judgment, it will be respected in Mexico:

> Mexico has to be aware that it is an element within an international concert and if it wants to be taken seriously by other countries, if it wants to be a protagonist along with other countries, it has to give answer to that responsibility with criteria that accords with the general principle.[41]

Federal Judge 3 considered that there was no real change because such rights existed in the legal framework even before the Amendment. He did not feel that this was something new; the courts already had this perspective of enforcing rights. He only saw that for those who did not have this point of view, they ought now to follow it. For this judge, what needed to be taken into consideration was that Mexico has had a tradition of incorporating international treaties in its national law; therefore, if the answer is in the national law, judges need not refer to treaties because the national law suffices.

Federal Judge 4 observed that there was not a large legal culture on the use of international treaties in Mexico as a direct source of law; the view prevailed among Mexican judges that the Mexican legal system and Constitution provided all the normative elements contained in the ratified international treaties. It was not a common practice to consider treaties directly to decide on a case. However, with the Amendment, judges now recognized their obligation to consider international treaties as part of Mexican positive law.

For him, the Amendment would have an impact on arbitration and on the recognition and enforcement of arbitral awards because it would necessarily broaden the concept of public policy. Judges now have to be careful not to take extreme positions, and the concept of public policy has to comply with the international standards contained in the Constitution and international treaties. Federal Judge 4 was convinced that Mexico would acquire that culture (of using international treaties as a direct source) once judges understood that public policy was related to the respect for fundamental rights. However, both public policy and fundamental rights have to fit like a perfect gear into a juridical-political system, to aim, in every case, for effective justice, not simply to resolve cases according to

---

41 Ibid.

the law. He warned that judges must attend to the law and to Mexican reality, and be cautious of not being too localist, while at the same time not losing sight of what is happening beyond Mexico. In his opinion, due to the Amendment there is now a view of justice occupied with the protection of human rights in other parts of the world. However, he warned, such an outlook should not import ideas that do not adjust to Mexican reality. He had seen Mexico adopting juridical systems (institutions or models) that were successful in other countries, but generated great problems in Mexico due to the lack of proper consideration of the Mexican context.

Regarding the normative hierarchy and the debate between a 'constitutional set' and a 'legality set',[42] Federal Judge 4 considered that the 'constitutional set' approach better aligns with the international trend. Mexico's acceptance of the jurisdiction of the IACHR and the fact that this Court can order the Mexican State to reform its Constitution, was a clear indication that the international treaties on human rights would necessarily need to take precedence over the Mexican Constitution.

V. CONCLUSIONS

Arbitration, the mechanism par excellence for resolving commercial disputes, can be considered a fundamental expression of the autonomy of commercial law. Business parties are generally of the opinion that it does not have an effect on the field of human rights, and vice versa; however, the findings presented here support the idea that these two fields – arbitration and human rights – cannot be considered unrelated. The mere conceptualization of arbitration as a human right – as suggested by Gonzalez de Cossío – creates a bridge between the two. With the Human Rights Amendment, Mexico showed again its openness and desire to engage with international trends on the protection of human rights. Mexico is working towards the convergence of international law with Mexican laws through the constitutionalization of international law. Nevertheless, operational challenges surface in the implementation stage at the court level, which exemplifies the impact that the underlying tension between international law and standards of local performance has on local interpretive communities.

---

42 In the 'legality set', as it was also explained by Justice Cossío Díaz in section III.A above, the Constitution is still at the top of the pyramid of sources of law, with international treaties beneath it. In a 'constitutional set' the Constitution and international treaties are considered all together, without any hierarchy, and are applied depending on which of these might grant better protection to the individual.

The interviews detailed in this chapter illustrate the ideas and perspectives on the implementation of the Human Rights Amendment of the people on the 'frontline'. Here have been presented the main concerns of law practitioners regarding the possible effects that the Mexican Human Rights Amendment might have on local arbitration practice. Even though counsellors and arbitrators see very little possibility (and are to some extent reluctant) that the Amendment will have an impact on arbitration, they are also aware and are hopeful that it will position international treaties differently in the minds of Mexican judges. This would be a positive development underpinning Mexico's efforts to maintain its position as a pro arbitration jurisdiction.

The judges' points of view presented in this chapter were significant for their insightful and in-depth reflections. Through them, we can see that the hierarchical approach to the interpretation and application of the law is at the center of their concerns. They still think of the legal framework in terms of a hierarchical order, in which they need an interpretation from the Supreme Court to determine which instrument is at which level. In Contradiction 293/2011, the Supreme Court stayed with the hierarchical approach, rather than moving on to a constitutional set that would better support the application of the *pro personae* principle now embraced by the Constitution in its Article 1. Justice Cossío, in his dissenting vote, made a call to the Supreme Court to consider its previous rulings, which aimed at creating a constitutional set; yet the court still maintained the hierarchical model. Progressive views, like those of Justice Cossío, are still more of an exception than a general perspective. As can be appraised from the interviews, it is difficult for the judges to embrace a model in which the Constitution and international treaties are considered as one constitutional set. It will take a considerable amount of training to get them to adopt this perspective and is something that needs to be addressed in the training and education of judges and legal professionals.

Cases of 'extreme interpretation' by the courts are one of the main challenges noted by the judges. Such cases can have a negative effect on arbitration practice; nonetheless, it is necessary to observe how actual practice evolves before calling them a real risk and not just a potential area of concern. And caution should be taken before considering one case of extreme interpretation to be a general trend within the courts.

In the fields of human rights and arbitration, there is vast international scholarship and legislation that demand an openness of mind of local actors; it demands from them the willingness to abandon purely localist views. Studies on how local actors are dealing with the tensions between global standards and local practices are limited, though emerging. In this case, we can see how the traditional conception of the amparo as a trial and not a remedy might be an ignition point for an extreme interpretation. If Mexican judges hold too tightly to the traditional conception of the amparo, this could clash with the trend Mexico is demonstrating of embracing international standards, both on human rights and arbitration, but the same would apply to any other subject matter. It was significant, and a positive sign, that Federal Judge 4 called for the adoption of international institutions and practices, as long as they are suited to local practices and realities. Judges are holding tight to their national law and, for the most part, this is part of their role. However, in order for more progressive ideas to permeate the system, it is desirable that local actors continue to embrace approaches that aim at finding ways to engage, coordinate and integrate national and international laws and standards.

PART III

The impact of communities and local culture

6. Demarcating the international community: where do international practices come from?*

Mor Mitrani

I. INTRODUCTION

The end of the Cold War, coupled with processes of globalization, has envisaged eminent political challenges for the international arena. Subsequently, political actors, especially state agents, have had to respond to these challenges and adjust and adapt their international practices, including in the legal context. The reconstruction of international law and its future trajectories have been the subject of extensive debates in recent decades. Most of these debates revolve around the extent to which the basic constituents of international law – mainly the notion of sovereignty – have shifted and, as a result, propelled changes not only in the notional and normative frameworks of contemporary international law but also in their practical manifestations at the local level.

The interplay between the local and international arenas sits at the core of this book. Focused on the tensions between international law and standards for local performance, it assesses the tension between the international and domestic levels. Nonetheless, any attempt to scrutinize the meeting point between local and international practices requires first a depiction of the realm of international practices, namely to ask from where international practices derive. It is necessary to understand not only how the characteristics of local communities determine the adaptation of international practices, but also how the notion of a grander international community shapes them to begin with. This outlook is essential in order to suggest a full picture of the various vectors that describe the interplay between the international and the local.

* This chapter is based on a paper presented to the workshop on "Mapping the Impact of International Trade and Human Rights on Local Practice", held in July 2014 at the International Institute for the Sociology of Law in Oñati, Spain.

Along with the growing literature over the last decades aiming to theorize international (legal) practices, this chapter attempts to focus on the communal framing of international practices, specifically on the common notion of the international community. The concept of the international community epitomizes the idea that states can hold common values and standards of conduct as well as having some capacity to act in the international arena in a collective manner for collective goals. Although the term "international community" is widely and frequently used by scholars, practitioners and international political leaders and is an integral part of the political vocabulary, most usages of the term either take its existence for granted or use it in order to understand other phenomena, like international law or international legitimacy. Only a few have sought to explore the international community as a subject in its own right, let alone define it, identify its members and characterize the ways it acts and the sources of its legitimacy.[1]

The significance of exploring and theorizing the international community in general, and in the attempt to understand the meeting point between international law and local standards in particular, lies in the notion that the latter cannot emerge in a complete vacuum and therefore requires a wider community context with which to correspond. The extensive usages of the term suggest that community, or at least conceptions of community, play an important role in the social relationship between international actors and in shaping their particular practices in the greater social setting of the international arena. In this way, this chapter provides an illuminating example of this book's core theme: the local performance of international standards, here understood not as a legal standard, but as a social construct. This social construct shapes and is shaped by international actors' particular practices, which together comprise their collective self-perception as a community.

The questions for us as international scholars are first, how to typify the social relationship in the international arena, and more importantly,

---

[1] See for example Georges Abi-saab, "Whither the International Community?" (1998) 9:2 Eur J Int'l L 248; Adene Addis, "Imagining the International Community: The Constitutive Dimension of Universal Jurisdiction" (2008) 31:1 Hum Rts Q 129; Gennadi M. Danilenko, "The Changing Structure of the International Community: Constitutional Implication" (1991) 32:2 Harv Int'l LJ 353; David C. Ellis, "On the Possibility of 'International Community'" (2009) 11:1 Int'l Stud Rev 1; Gleider I. Hernandez, "A Reluctant Guardian: The International Court of Justice and the Concept of 'International Community'" (2013) 83:1 Brit YB Int'l L 13; Colin Warbrick and Stephen Tierney, *Towards an International Legal Community?: The Sovereignty of States and the Sovereignty of International Law* (London: British Institute of International and Comparative Law, 2006).

how to identify how collective perceptions of these social relationships, as the term international community embodies, construct the practices and behavior at the local level. To this end, this chapter will first discuss the application of the concept of community at the international level, which essentially lacks formal authority or rule of law. It will then focus on normative and descriptive socio-legal perspectives on the international community, as they are entwined with historical and political aspects as supplementary perspectives. This examination will survey whether and to what extent these are viable lenses for comprehensively gauging the implications on state behavior in the framework of international practices, namely on the ability to use international practices as guidelines and demarcations for the array of legitimate conduct.

II. THE CONCEPT OF COMMUNITY AT THE INTERNATIONAL LEVEL

Essentially, the concept of the international community denotes the ability of international actors to form social relationships and to associate in a meaningful and deep degree that yields a community. Therefore, the first step in understanding international community requires a preliminary discussion of the prerequisites of applying the sociological concept of community to the international level. The sociological concept of community is widely perceived as a human association in which individuals interact based upon shared common features of identity. It was mainly developed in the nineteenth century by German sociologists and is most identified with the work of Ferdinand Tonnies, namely his seminal book *Gemeinschaft und Gesellschaft.*[2] Tonnies renders social relationships as forming collective association, a social entity that both internally and externally manifests itself and acts as a unit. The book presents two ideal types of social associations, *Gemeinschaft* ("community") and *Gesellschaft* ("society"). While both types of association are constructed through social relations that are based on "rational and human will", they are differentiated by their origins: real and organic (kinship-based) relationships indicate a community, while artificial, imaginary and mechanical connections stand for a society.[3]

---

[2] Ferdinand Tonnies, *Community and Society: Gemeinschaft Und Gesellschaft* (New York: Harper and Row, 1963).

[3] See also Dino Kritsiotis, "Imagining the International Community" (2002) 13:4 Eur J Int'l L 961 at 962.

Entrenched in the notions of nature and rationality as establishing social norms and values, Tonnies maintains that a community is united by will. Human will not only generates and constructs shared understandings, identity and interests, but also the possibility of a collective action based on an authentic sense of unity and shared moral imperatives. One of the main assumptions is that this sense of unity can be maintained even when the members of the community are separated. However, whereas Tonnies referred to rather small-scale type of communities, hence to organic communities that are founded upon kinship,[4] an application to the international level envisages a community on a greater scale. An international community, or even political communities in general, which are by definition an imagined and artificial construction, require tailored theorization of the nexus between politics and community. Political theorists portrayed diverse, sometime contradicting, frameworks of the political community, focusing mostly on the relations and tensions between individuals, greater authority and social order as constituting specific socio-political spaces of association.[5] Echoing Rousseau, like-mindedness is conceived as the main feature of a political community. Like-mindedness among people instigates solidarity and identification,[6] and thus maintains and supplements political order through a known and acknowledged array of the rules of the game.[7] At the domestic-local level, it is possible (sometimes) to point to social or cultural similarities (mainly based on national or ethnic elements) that can tie individuals and form a political community, which may form an authentic (even if not organic) sense of unity.[8] It is much more challenging to envision such a construct at the international level.

A conception of the international community as a community of communities in general and of states in particular[9] asserts that groups of states (or other international actors) are capable of both sharing a certain level of communal feeling and acting on behalf of these shared feelings. It thus bestows upon the international community some agential capacities

---

4 Tonnies (note 2 above) at 37.

5 Russell Buchan, "International Community and the Occupation of Iraq" (2007) 12:1 J Conf & Sec L 37 at 43.

6 Karl W. Deutsch, *Political Community and the North Atlantic Area: International Organization in the Light of Historical Experience* (Princeton: Princeton University Press, 1957) 26.

7 Nicholas Greenwood Onuf, "International Legal Order as an Idea" (1979) 73:2 Am J Int'l L 244.

8 Anthony P. Cohen, *The Symbolic Construction of Community* (London: Ellis Horwood and Tavistock Publications, 1985).

9 Addis (note 1 above); David R. Mapel and Terry Nardin, *International Society: Diverse Ethical Perspectives* (Princeton: Princeton University Press, 1999).

to either act or to legitimate members' actions.[10] Can states, in what we have learnt to portray as an anarchical society, genuinely form such an association and hold a sense of identity that constructs a collective "We" of states, or is the international community as we have come to know it no more than a fiction or a political myth? The answer to these questions is of course contingent upon the paradigmatic and theoretical positions one adopts. The most dominant framing of the international community is a socio-legal depiction that portrays the international community as the normative, even constitutional, source of international practices in general and of international law in particular. The following section will elaborate on the theoretical linkage between the international community and international (legal) order. Further, it discusses how the notion of international community as a moral agent of progress and liberalism might reflect changes in world politics and the challenges they bear to states' practices in the international arena.

III. THE INTERNATIONAL COMMUNITY AS THE SOCIAL FOUNDATION OF INTERNATIONAL LAW

The socio-legal perspective is the most dominant way of depicting the international community. It envisages it as the fundamental prism for understanding and framing international law, by conceiving the international community as the sociological – some would say constitutional – context in which international law emerges. The linkage between international law and international community goes back decades. It resonates with the socio-legal framework of Hugo Grotius (1583–1645), who portrayed international society as a community of those who take part in an international legal order that is governed (also) by the institution of international law.[11]

The articulation of the international community as a notional foundation of international law flourished during the inter-war period of the 1930s. Coinciding with the establishment (and then failure) of the League of Nations, the international community was conceived as a normative and structural means to foster greater compliance through a persuasive

---

[10] Barry Buzan and Ana Gonzalez-Pelaez, "'International Community' after Iraq" (2005) 81:1 Int'l Aff 31 at 32–3.

[11] Hedley Bull, *The Anarchical Society: A Study of Order in World Politics* (New York: Columbia University Press, 1977) 2; Warbrick and Tierney (note 1 above).

narrative of a community.[12] In this context, Hersch Lauterpacht's work, *The Function of Law in the International Community*,[13] offers a legal perspective on the tripartite interplay between law, politics and sovereignty by rejecting the tendency to refer to law and politics as being in juxtaposition. Lauterpacht's account can be seen as a first – and early – endeavor to reconcile the notion that while territorial sovereignty is one of the main constituents of international law, the more embedded international law is, the less it is contingent merely on the consent of sovereign states. Following World War I, such an account was clearly an answer to a specific political situation that required formulating avenues to explore international law not as the representation of separate and independent sovereign states but rather as an emerging normative order of its own, of an international community.[14]

The rationale is straightforward. Since law as a legal system essentially requires some sort of legal community that would be committed to both formulate and comply with law, an international community is a prerequisite to the operation of international law.[15] Based on this logic, the mere existence of international law insinuates the existence of an international (legal) community exclusive to states, at least while states are both the principal law-making authority of international law and the principal legal subjects of international law.[16] The community in this respect is more than the sum of its units. It holds "a distinct personality from its members"[17] as it operates as a separated hub that manifests a higher unity

[12] Martti Koskenniemi, "The Fate of Public International Law: Between Technique and Politics" (2007) 70:1 Mod L Rev 1 at 2.

[13] Hersch Lauterpacht, *The Function of Law in the International Community* (Oxford: Clarendon Press, 1933).

[14] Harold Hongju Koh, "Why Do Nations Obey International Law?" (1997) 106:8 Yale LJ 2599; Warbrick and Tierney (note 1 above).

[15] Andreas Paulus, "The Influence of the United States on the Concept of the 'International Community'" in Michael Byers and Georg Nolte, eds, *United States Hegemony and the Foundations of International Law* (Cambridge: Cambridge University Press, 2003) 266.

[16] John Charvet, "International Society from a Contractarian Perspective" in David R. Mapel and Terry Nardin, eds, *International Society: Diverse Ethical Perspectives* (Princeton: Princeton University Press, 1999) 114.

[17] N. Tsagourias, "International Community, Recognition of States, and Political Cloning" in Colin Warbrick and Stephen Tierney, eds, *Towards an "International Legal Community"? The Sovereignty of States and the Sovereignty of International Law* (London: British Institute of International and Comparative Law, 2006) 211 at 212.

and capacities of its own,[18] that facilitate it as some sort of a normative (imagined) entity.

The international community therefore exhibits common bonds and a consensus on shared values among its members. As such, it operates as a normative and structural source that can mitigate and frame particular (domestic) features within collective (international) ones. This effect of the greater societal setting on the practices and behavior of the individual members echoes the longstanding debates regarding the social role of international law in international relations and world politics. One of the main debates concerns why and under what conditions states obey or comply with international law,[19] given the lack of formal international authority. This debate ranges from the assertion, at one extreme, that international compliance is a unique and binding characteristic of the rule-governed social relationships among states, and, at the other extreme, that it should be reckoned merely as another policy preference contingent upon one's political needs.[20]

Thomas Franck[21] argues that states' tendency voluntarily *not* to violate international law manifests a shared belief that public obligations should be respected and adhered to. Franck offers a sociological framework emphasizing the role of common understandings and a state's ability to predict that "state conduct will definitely be constrained by the commitments states have accepted".[22] Such a condition is contingent upon the existence of an international community as a notional framework that generates common understanding and perceptions. In this respect, the (international) community is more than a catchy phrase. It is an institutionalized hub of rule-governed interactions. According to Franck, these rules embody the operation of normativity in inter-state

---

18 Bruno Simma and A.L. Paulus, "The 'International Community': Facing the Challenge of Globalization" (1998) 9:2 Eur J Int'l L 266.

19 See for example Thomas M. Franck, *Fairness in International Law and Institutions* (Oxford: Oxford University Press, 1995); Andrew T. Guzman, "A Compliance-Based Theory of International Law" (2002) 90:6 Cal L Rev 1823; Benedict Kingsbury, "The Concept of Compliance as a Function of Competing Conceptions of International Law" (1997) 19 Mich J Int'l L 345; Koh (note 14 above); Beth A. Simmons and Allison Danner, "Credible Commitments and the International Criminal Court" (2010) 64:2 Int'l Org 225.

20 Thomas M. Franck, "The Power of Legitimacy and the Legitimacy of Power: International Law in an Age of Power Disequilibrium" (2006) 100:1 Am J Int'l L 88.

21 Thomas M. Franck, *The Power of Legitimacy among Nations* (Oxford: Oxford University Press, 1990); Franck (note 19 above); Franck (note 20 above).

22 Franck (note 20 above) at 92.

interactions[23] and thus render the existence of an international community as a grander collective whose members not only share these understandings but also act in awareness of them. Importantly, a state's awareness of the common rules does not necessarily mean that it constantly complies with these rules, but rather that it is mindful of what is considered a lawful and unlawful act.

States' collective awareness of an international community is showcased in the ever-growing references to such a community in legal and political texts. Since the 1960s, and coinciding with the consolidation of the United Nations system, the notion that international law is a manifestation of the international community has migrated to the practical arena.[24] This is evident in various legal texts that aim to define and set the scope of international law and entwine the essence of international law with the idea of the international community. Notable examples are the Draft Declaration on the Rights and Duties of States (1949), which contends that "the States of the world form a community governed by international law", and the Declaration on Principles of International Law (1970), asserting that all states "are equal members of the international community". The clearest example in this regard is probably the Vienna Convention on the Law of Treaties (1969), which presents the notion of *jus cogens* as those norms that are "accepted and recognized by the international community of states as a whole",[25] hence acknowledging not only the hierarchy among rules in international law, but also – and more importantly – of the social existence of the international community of states as a whole. A similar indication is presented in the International Criminal Court's Rome Statute (1998), which limits the Court's jurisdiction to "the most serious crimes of concern to the international community as a whole".[26]

The frequent adoption of the international community vocabulary by legal and political texts may seem a negligent and fictitious habit that lacks any explanation as to who or what it references.[27] However, the

---

23 Franck (note 19 above) at 42; see also Kritsiotis (note 3 above) at 962; Iain Scobbie, "Tom Franck's Fairness" (2002) 13:4 Eur J Int'l L 909.

24 Koskenniemi (note 12 above).

25 Ulrich Fastenrath, "Relative Normativity in International Law" (1993) 4 Eur J Int'l L 305.

26 See also Edward Kwakwa, "The International Community, International Law, and the United States: Three in One, Two against One, or One and the Same?" in Michael Byers and Georg Nolte, eds, *United States Hegemony and the Foundations of International Law* (Cambridge: Cambridge University Press, 2003).

27 See for example Philip Allott, "The True Function of Law in the International Community" (1998) 5:2 Ind J Glob Legal Stud 391; Katarzyna Kaczmarska, "The Powerful Myth of International Community and the Imperative

penetration of the term, and mainly its dominance, actually reinforce the assertion that states are minded to a communal setting and thus act, or at least claim to act, in its context, and therefore use it as means to legitimize and de-legitimize action in the international arena. In this respect, the idea of an international community, more than inducing international law per se, induces and constitutes the legitimacy of international law and of the virtues it entails.[28] As such, the idea of an international community rests on the role of legitimacy as the ability "to command acceptance and support from the community so as to render force unnecessary".[29] As a common reference point, the international community reflects states' common *will* to act in a legitimized way, on the one hand, and to condemn illegitimate conduct of fellow states, on the other.

IV. INTERNATIONAL COMMUNITY AND THE CONSTITUTION OF INTERNATIONAL LAW

According to Franck, the sense of an international community exists in a substantive manner as a social contract that states constantly aim to maintain and preserve. The sense of the community as shared by actors in the international arena[30] serves as the prerequisite of a structured, reciprocal and rule-governed relationship that is based on shared moral imperatives and values and also includes mechanisms to resolve disagreements over rules.[31] Franck specifically argues that one of the motives for states' compliance is their interest in empowering the rule of law and perpetuating the state of rule-governed and rule-ordered inter-state relations through habitual compliance.[32] In this respect, the heralding of the international community in both academic and legal texts not only stresses elements of solidarity and unity, but also reinforces a rule-based constitutive perspective of world politics.

The international community is portrayed not only as regulated by

---

to Build States" in Berit Bliesemann de Guevara, ed., *Myth and Narrative in International Politics: Interpretive Approaches to the Study of IR* (London: Palgrave Macmillan, 2016) 209.

[28] Franck (note 19 above); Scobbie (note 23 above).

[29] Daniel Bodansky, "The Legitimacy of International Governance: A Coming Challenge for International Environmental Law?" (1999) 93:3 Am J Int'l L 596 at 600, n 24.

[30] Scobbie (note 23 above) at 909.

[31] Franck (note 19 above); see also Koh (note 14 above); Kritsiotis (note 3 above) at 962; Scobbie (note 23 above).

[32] Franck (note 20 above).

international law but also as constituted by it, and especially by customary international law.[33] The existence and scope of operation of the legal community depends on the extent to which states conceive themselves as part of a realm that is governed by common law that constrains practices, and thus as members in a voluntary association of those who accept the rules.[34] A state that sees itself as a member of the community therefore accepts the array of legitimate rules of conduct in its context. These rules perpetuate the patterns of lawful (and mainly unlawful) behavior and maintain social order and therefore exercise the legitimate authority of the community on its member states, even when there is lack of specific consent.[35] Diehl, Ku and Zamora argue that the international community, through international institutions, sets the normative framework of the acceptable and expectable standards of behavior and operations in various issue areas of the international system.[36] The international community can be reckoned a reference point of the two main functions – normative and structural – of international law.[37]

This is however a somehow circular conceptualization as international law is both the indicator and the originator of the international community.[38] Moreover, if legitimacy creates compliance, and compliance creates legitimacy, and bundled together they deepen the sense of the international community, how can we tell what precedes what, and how can we know what was the normative and communal source from which international law emerged to begin with? Therefore, even if we accept the argument that any attempt to explain authority and order is entrenched in societal and communal explanations as an international legal order presupposes certain rules of the game,[39] it is not enough just to acknowledge the international community as an indicator for a legal order, and there is

---

[33] Terry Nardin, "Legal Positivism as a Theory of International Society" in David R. Mapel and Terry Nardin, eds, *International Society: Diverse Ethical Perspectives* (Princeton: Princeton University Press, 1999) 17.

[34] Mapeland Nardin (note 9 above); Fredrick G. Whelan, "Legal Positivism and International Society" in David R. Mapel and Terry Nardin, *International Society: Diverse Ethical Perspectives* (Princeton: Princeton University Press, 1999) 36.

[35] Kritsiotis (note 3 above); Scobbie (note 23 above).

[36] Paul F. Diehl, Charlotte Ku and Daniel Zamora, "The Dynamics of International Law: The Interaction of Normative and Operating Systems" (2003) 57:1 Int'l Org 43.

[37] Prosper Weil, "Towards Relative Normativity in International Law" (1983) 77:3 Am J Int'l L 413.

[38] Simma and Paula (note 18 above).

[39] Onuf (note 7 above) at 247.

a great need to account for its contents and for the meanings of the rules that it constitutes and is being constituted by.

The United Nations (UN) is naturally understood as the source of substance of the international community, and its various organs repeatedly refer to the concept, often as a synonym for the UN itself.[40] It is thus not surprising that the UN Charter is often considered, mainly by proponents of the constitutional strand of international law scholarship, as the constitutional text of the international community. According to this, the international community was constituted by the establishment of the UN in 1945, and the articulation of the UN Charter is the binding covenant of the existing and normatively desired international community and constitutes (at least some parts of) the normative system that states supposedly follow.[41] From this perspective, the Charter can be seen as a manual for the operations of the international community. It names and specifies concrete areas of cooperation and the values it is supposed to advance and thus manifests, practically and discursively, a degree of unity that has deepened "areas of cooperation", and radically shifted the structure and substance of international law.[42]

According to Abi-saab, the degree of community shared by members of a certain international society implies the legal position to which a certain international society will ascribe, ranging from a core of "law of coexistence" to a core of "law of cooperation". In this regard the "degree of community" is treated as a dynamic variable that, once it changes, "in relation to a given subject, at a given moment", affects the socio-legal position of states regarding world politics.[43] As such, and corresponding with Tonnies, the international community can be reckoned as an association of specific types of states in which the degree of unity depends on political currents and circumstances, and which may affect in turn the infrastructure of international law. In this regard, the end of the Cold War and the dissolution of the Eastern Bloc in the early 1990s are seen as drivers of

---

[40] Simma and Paula (note 18 above).

[41] For example, Abi-saab (note 1 above); Antonio Cassese, "The International Community's 'Legal' Response to Terrorism" (1989) 38:3 Int'l & Comp LQ 589; M.P. Dupuy, "The Constitutional Dimension of the Charter of the United Nations Revisited" (1997) 1 Max Planck YB UNL 1; Bardo Fassbender, "The United Nations Charter as Constitution of the International Community" (1998) 36 Colum J Transnat'l L 529; Simma and Paula (note 18 above); Attila Tanzi, "Remarks on Sovereignty in the Evolving Constitutional Features of the International Community" (2010) 12:2 Int'l Com L Rev 145.

[42] See Dupuy (note 41 above).

[43] Abi-saab (note 1 above).

change in the structure of the international community, manifested in the ever-growing scope of international law.

V. RE-DEMARCATING THE INTERNATIONAL COMMUNITY AS AN HISTORICAL OUTCOME

It would be hard to argue against the assertion that since the end of the Cold War the scope, magnitude and independence of international law has expanded, deepened and strengthened (although it is, of course, still far in terms of formality and authority from domestic legal arenas).[44] These processes of change, however, could not emerge in a vacuum, but rather as a response to either a specific need or to a fundamental change in the international community and its constitutive elements. The main debate in this respect revolves around the implications for national sovereignty; and the extent to which this has been diminished or marginalized as an international community has arguably constitutionalized.[45] Political changes created a gap between the normative frameworks of the international community and the existing international legal order and necessitated the adaption of central international law measures to conform the legal order to the changes in the international community.[46] The end of the Cold War is thus portrayed as progressing the international community by transforming it from a framework based on states' sovereignty and thus of consent to a framework designated by forces of community.[47]

This depiction combines to a great extent both historicist and legal ontologies, as the international community is seen on the one hand

---

44 See note 36 above.

45 See for example J.L. Dunoff and J.P. Trachtman, *Ruling the World? Constitutionalism, International Law, and Global Governance* (Cambridge: Cambridge University Press, 2009); Martti Koskenniemi, "Constitutionalism as Mindset: Reflections on Kantian Themes about International Law and Globalization" (2007) 8:1 Theor Inq L 9; Jeremy A. Rabkin, *Law without Nations? Why Constitutional Government Requires Sovereign States* (Princeton: Princeton University Press, 2005); Christoph Schreuer, "The Waning of the Sovereign State: Towards a New Paradigm for International Law" (1993) 4 Eur J Int'l L 447; Tanzi (note 41 above).

46 Abi-saab (note 1 above); Gennady M. Danilenko, "The Changing Structure of the International Community: Constitutional Implications" (1991) 32:2 Harv Int'l L J 353.

47 David Armstrong, "Law, Justice and the Idea of a World Society" (1999) 75:3 Int'l Aff 547; Scobbie (note 23 above); Warbrick and Tierney (note 1 above).

as a historical construct shaped in light of historical political changes, and on the other hand as a normative framework that subscribes the contexts in which practices of international law shall be reconstructed in light of historical processes. The socio-historical ontology of the international community discerns it as evolving through history as a result of the inter-state system formation and consolidation process that began with the Peace of Westphalia (1648). From a historicist perspective, the international community is not a new concept, and one can find multiple references dating back to the early twentieth century that allude to the formulation or potential formulation of an international community, albeit not necessarily a cohesive one. These accounts are usually linked to the field of integration studies, striving to place the development of a community at the international level as part of the wider process of political community formation. By applying a transaction-based concept, the main argument is that, over time, states establish nets of communication and social transaction that integrate them around common norms of *peaceful* state conduct that indicate states' ripeness for an international community.[48] The most notable work in this respect is Karl Deutsch's seminal work, *Political Community and the North Atlantic Area*,[49] which tracks the evolution of the polity and sets the criteria that allowed it – in different historical periods – to form a community, focusing on the prospects of establishing a supranational (security) community. All the works cited above discern the idea of community at the international level as a historical construct, and the "sense of community" as both the generator of (peaceful) historical change and the result of historical changes.

When Deutsch's vision was revived in Adler and Barnett's seminal study, *Security Communities*,[50] the emphasis on the "sense of community" deepened. In one of the book's chapters, Russett links the concept of security communities and the concept of the international community, and points to the peaceful end of the Cold War as an historical moment that realized the three components of the Kantian triangle at once: consolidation of democracy, economic interdependence and transnational institutions, leading to a shift of the core of international politics from the

---

[48] Roger W. Cobb and Charles D. Elder, *International Community: A Regional and Global Study* (New York: Holt, Rinehart and Winston, 1970); J. Leo and S.J. Martin, "Forces for an International Community Integrating" (1943) 4:4 Am Cath Sociological Rev 194.

[49] Deutsch (note 6 above).

[50] Emanuel Adler and Michael Barnett, *Security Communities* (New York: Cambridge University Press, 1998).

idea of sovereignty to the Kantian triad[51] – a shift that both describes and prescribes (from a neo-Kantian perspective) a partial, uneven and nascent global security community sustained by democratic peace, which in turn affects the embedment of reconstructed notions of international law.

According to Grewe, the development of an international community that transcends the traditional nation-state means that the community's interests, rather than pure national ones, could now play a role in the evolution of international law and in reshaping its foundations.[52] The question in this regard is who the post-Cold War community is, and whether it goes globally beyond the state-centric depiction of the international community or whether the change is within the social fabric of states themselves.

For example, the idea of universal jurisdiction asks that the subject of international law be recast based on a cosmopolitan idea. Universal jurisdiction is "a process through which the international community imagines its identity", since it both constitutes the international community and regulates the legal behavior of its members,[53] and is seen as the constitutive function through which the contemporary international community as a collective (legal) identity is being enacted. This international community is genuinely different from that associated with the international community of states. It is a community of humankind as a whole, constituted from the bottom up, through the formation of a cosmopolitan network of relations between a variety of actors, including individuals, non-governmental associations and sub-national communities.[54] Nonetheless, ideas like universal jurisdiction are still challenging as they do not fully meet the assertion that external jurisdiction over states is contingent upon a state's consent, and therefore that law beyond the state still resides completely in the realm of sovereignty.[55]

---

51 Bruce Russett, "A Neo-Kantian Perspective: Democracy, Interdependence and International Organizations in Building Security Communities" in Adler and Barnett (note 50 above).

52 W.G. Grewe, *The Epochs of International Law* (Berlin: Walter de Gruyter, 2000). See also Michael Byers, "Introduction: The Complexities of Foundational Change" in Michael Byers and Georg Nolte, eds, *United States Hegemony and the Foundations of International Law* (Cambridge: Cambridge University Press, 2003).

53 Addis (note 1 above) at 133; see also Anne-Marie Slaughter, "Disaggregated Sovereignty: Towards the Public Accountability of Global Government Networks" (2004) 39:2 Gov Opp 159.

54 See Berit Bliesemann de Guevara and Florian P. Kühn, "'The International Community Needs to Act': Loose Use and Empty Signalling of a Hackneyed Concept" (2011) 18:2 Int'l Peacekeeping 135; Tanzi (note 41 above); Tsagourias (note 17 avove).

55 Armstrong (note 47 above).

A state-centric perspective to the contemporary international community is presented, for example, by Buchan,[56] who claims that since the end of the Cold War liberal states have instituted an international community exclusive to liberal-democratic states and dedicated to the advancement of a specific doctrine and identity. The most significant impact of the emergence of an international community of liberal democracies is that it breaks the principle of equality among sovereign states and creates hierarchy between liberal and non-liberal states. The international law of such an international community is oriented towards specific liberal values, such as human dignity, arguably at the expense of the principle of sovereignty, thus expounding progressive unity within a greater fragmentation that reinforces a new sense of normative superiority and dichotomy between liberal and non-liberal states.

The tension between the interest of the community and the interests of its members is to a great extent the tension between greater and growing solidarity and the need to address new and unfamiliar lines of conflict and contention among the members that were generated with the end of the Cold War. This is exactly the context in which the discourse of international community became more and more prevalent and reiterated the 1930s' ideas of international law as a solution to growing political problems, especially in light of voices that criticized processes of expanding notions of legalization and of the over-formalization and technicality of international law.[57] This is probably the main peril in the ontologies that portray the international community as either a normative-legal construct or as an historical outcome. Both lack a concrete political perspective as they pay less attention to the political settings that establish the international community and to the implications the concept has for political behavior. In this regard, neither the more legal nor the historical perspective provides the theoretical tools to envisage not only who the international community is, but also how it may inform state practices. This is the case mainly since while acknowledging its role in the international political arena, they fail to underscore it as a political phenomenon in its own right. They employ the concept of "international community" as a theoretical conduit to explain certain political outcomes, like international law or peace and stability, but evade the need to explain the international community itself as a political outcome that operates in a

---

56 Buchan (note 5 above); Russell Buchan, "A Clash of Normativities: International Society and International Community" (2008) 10:1 Int'l Com L Rev 3.

57 See, for example, Fastenrath (note 25 above); Koskenniemi (note 12 above); Weil (note 37 above).

political environment. Given the fact that there is no single representative or ruler of "the international community as a whole", particular political elements intrinsically stand behind any notion of it.[58] The international community cannot be reduced solely to a legal-normative entity that serves as the social foundation of international law, but should also be perceived as a political project of its own that "is nonetheless a form of politics that has some particular virtues".[59] Since we cannot and should not ignore the political aspects of legal issues and debates, we should ask what the political component of the international community is and how it operates. We thus need to acknowledge the unique political elements of the international and the power-infused relations among units.

VI. THE INTERNATIONAL COMMUNITY AS A POLITICAL CONSTRUCT

From a political perspective, it seems natural to focus on the English school of international relations as a framework for the international community. To a great extent the English school allows for the bridging of the legal and historical depictions, as it is both infused by Grotian thought regarding international law while recognizing the role of historical context in the evolution of patterns of state conduct.[60] This agglomeration is the basis for one of the main theoretical notions of the English school – that states are capable of sharing common interests, rules and values in the framework of "international society".[61]

The affinity between the theoretical concept of international society and the concept of the international community clearly invites an attempt to use the former as an effective leverage to portray the latter. Interestingly, however, the concept of the international community is not very common among English School scholars, and only a few accounts have attempted to theorize the commonalities and linkages between the theoretical framework of international society and the concept of the international

---

[58] Martti Koskenniemi, "International Law and Hegemony: A Reconfiguration" (2004) 17:2 Cam Rev Int'l Aff 197.

[59] Robert Wai, "Countering, Branding, Dealing: Using Economic and Social Rights in and around the International Trade Regime" (2003) 14:1 Eur J Int'l L 35, cited by Koskenniemi (note 58 above) at 214.

[60] Hermann Mosler, *The International Society as a Legal Community* (Alphen aan den Rijn: Sijthoff and Noordhoff, 1980).

[61] Hedley Bull, *The Anarchical Society: A Study of Order in World Politics* (New York: Columbia University Press, 1977).

community as it is being used in the political arena.[62] The conventional conceptualization of international society supposedly refers to an association of states that lacks (or at least does not necessarily hold) a degree of unity, and therefore cannot be automatically equated with the concept of the international community. Brown, for example, argues that the international community is not a feasible political construct because it stands in contradiction to the main ordering principle of the international society – sovereignty.[63] Nonetheless, the English school's conceptualization of international society does not necessarily render international society and the international community as mutually exclusive. The common premise that international society is not confined to particular substantial features does not preclude an identity or a "we-ness" feature, and thus does not stand in contradiction to the possibility that members of international society might collectively unite around a certain issue area or norm in processes that formulate at least nascent (international) community.

The concept of international society can therefore be seen, at least theoretically, as the political framework that enables a certain international community, as a specific – a thicker and denser, perhaps even solidarist – type of international society.[64] Buzan and Gonzalez-Pelaez recognize the possibility of multiple international communities at the sub-global level, and depict international communities as smaller hubs within international society in which one can find a "tighter net of states within international society that share a higher degree of integration defined by a strong common identity".[65] This net ties single actors via a greater (though not necessarily global) external environment in which they seek to act, serving thus as "a political function for those who act in its name".[66] The international community thereby is a political construct that states are aware of and minded to, whether or not they operate in its context. Ontologically, this political perspective provides a structural framework for understanding the international community as a political construct as it gives extra leverage to answer how the international community can be recognized, but again the question "what is the international community?" remains open.

To summarize, the three ontologies provide lenses for viewing how the international community can be recognized and how it can be seen as a

---

62 Buzan and Gonzalez-Pelaez (note 10 above).

63 Chris Brown, "International Theory and International Society: The Viability of the Middle Way?" (1995) 21:2 Rev Int'l Stud 183.

64 Buzan and Gonzalez-Pelaez (note 10 above) at 35.

65 Ibid. at 38.

66 Ibid. at 31.

normative structure that explains peace, international law and political legitimation. All three fail, however, to shed light on the substances that constitute it (let alone on the dynamics in these substances) and on its agential features. I suggest therefore to go one step further from the basic sociological notion that states are capable of constructing an international community – a political construct whose mere existence can account for historical changes and of socio-legal developments – and face the challenge of developing tools to understand the interactions, content and patterns of the political behavior of the states that constitute the international community. This challenge requires one to push the ontological questions aside and focus on the notion that the international community emerges through rhetoric, namely that it exists only once a political agent refers to its existence and attributes to it certain values, rules and virtues, or depicts it as an agent that is called into action or assigned responsibility.[67]

Processes of change, especially since the end of the Cold War, require states to constantly adjust and adapt their practices as well as the main referential frameworks being used to legitimize these changes. The underlying premise is that perceptional shifts are translated into doctrines and policies and thus further yield functional and practical shifts. Consequently, changes in international law can be assessed not only through measures of compliance and violation, but also through "the extent that the change is generally approved and applied by the international community"[68] via the common perceptions regarding rightful and lawful conduct. Therefore, perhaps the attempts to reveal the nature of the international community and the conditions of its existence[69] are essentially redundant. It might be more conducive to focus on its epistemological features and the discursive roles it plays. In this respect, the concept and term "international community" can be understood as a speech act[70] – as holding the capacity to perform action in rhetorical processes of communication. The normative values and practical measures that are accepted and recognized by the international community of states as a whole, and are affiliated with it,

---

[67] Bliesemann and Kühn (note 54 above); Toni Erskine, "'Blood on the UN's Hands'? Assigning Duties and Apportioning Blame to an Intergovernmental Organization" (2004) 18:1 Global Society 21; Toni Erskine, "Locating Responsibility: The Problem of Moral Agency in International Relations" in Christian Reus-Smit and Duncan Snidal, eds, *The Oxford Handbooks of International Relations* (Oxford: Oxford University Press, 2008).

[68] Franck (note 20 above) at 105.

[69] Ellis (note 1 above).

[70] Nicholas Greenwood Onuf, *World of Our Making: Rules and Rule in Social Theory and International Relations* (Columbia: University of South Carolina Press, 1989).

can illuminate the contents that infuse the international community. They can also shed light on processes of change and continuity through the discursive choices state agents make while reconstructing and re-demarcating the international community and its "referential boundaries" through linguistic conventions and public discursive choices.[71]

VII. THE INTERNATIONAL COMMUNITY AS RHETORICAL CONSTRUCT

Often, the international community is seen as an empty concept that is used ubiquitously and is therefore rendered as nothing more than a political myth, as an instant and fictitious model of cooperation and problem-solving in contemporary world politics.[72] It is tempting to be skeptical towards the concept of the international community and discount it due to its abstract and reductionist features that preclude the identification of its true essence – who or what the international community is. However, precisely because there is no organic community at the international level, and that, to a great extent, community "exists in the eye of the beholder"[73] makes the notion of community the perfect vessel for making legal and political claims in the dynamic and changing environment of world politics,[74] and therefore to be used as a reference point for the standardization of local practices.

At the rhetorical level, the international community offers a specific reading of the international sphere as ordered through communal relations.[75] The content and meanings of international community can help us further scrutinize the role that the international community plays in the construction of identity and behavior of individual states as actors in a greater setting by casting substance to state practices in various contexts and situations.[76] Moreover, changes in the ways the international community is being recognized and understood may reflect changes in how states position themselves in this communal setting. They can further

---

71 Fastenrath (note 25 above).

72 Kaczmarska (note 27 above); Kritsiotis (note 3 above).

73 Martti Koskenniemi, Steven Ratner and Volker Rittberger, "Comments to Chapter 1 and 2" in Michael Byers and Georg Nolte, eds, *United States Hegemony and the Foundations of International Law* (Cambridge: Cambridge University Press, 2003) 91.

74 Koskenniemi (note 58 above).

75 Tsagourias (note 17 above).

76 Franck (note 20 above).

point to conceptual reconstructions of state practices in general, and of international law in particular,[77] and shed light on practical changes and on the power calculations that infuse them.

Compliance in itself is not sufficient to determine degrees of legitimacy, deliberation and argumentations that are purposed to create or sustain legitimacy. However, it can illuminate important "backstage" performative patterns and sources of legitimacy.[78] The framing of these changes (also) occurs through changes in how the international community is narrated both as they reflect various (but collective) experiences of unity and fragmentation and as being used to make specific legal claims. The operation of legal claims and legal discourse is essential for publicizing the common understandings of the division of rights and duties in a certain social setting. This is a strong social mechanism that allows establishing and enacting who is in and who is out and what rules membership entails. The engagement with specific legal claims allows the identification of the legal entities, which rights and duties they carry, and to which community structure they are accountable. From such a perspective, both the international community and international law embody a translation and articulation of specific political preferences and contentions into legal and ethical claims.[79]

VIII. CONCLUSIONS

The international community is an open concept. Different disciplines offer different, though not necessarily separate, ways of understanding and defining it and characterizing its members. This chapter has surveyed the main depiction of the international community as a socio-legal construct, and has pointed to socio-historical and socio-political supplementary depictions of it. The various characterizations of the international community can be broadly distinguished from normative perspectives that are focused on the role of shared values in engendering solidarity and descriptive perspectives that portray it as some sort of historical outcome. Both normatively and descriptively the international community is often equated with the West or with the sub-group of liberal democracies.[80] This myriad of ontologies accentuates the role of the international com-

[77] Hernandez (note 1 above).
[78] Jens Steffek, "The Legitimation of International Governance: A Discourse Approach" (2003) 9:2 Eur J Int'l Relat 249.
[79] Koskenniemi (note 58 above).
[80] Bliesemann and Kühn (note 54 above).

munity as an ethical framework and a moral agent that serves institutional and political functions for legitimizing the practices of those who act in its context and on its behalf.[81] Since the international community is dynamic in essence, changes in state practices can therefore be explained through changes in the fabric of the international community. However, I have argued throughout this chapter that while many of these accounts track back to questions regarding the dynamic nature of the international community, at the end of the day these are futile attempts since the international community is an imagined construct that first and foremost exists at the discursive level. Therefore, there is more merit in asking what the international community serves and in what contexts, than in the ontological attempt to discern who or what it is.

Optimists describe the international community as normative wishful thinking that helps to paint political reality in positive and bright colors; skeptics as a political myth and even as no more than a deceptive rhetorical device. Neither of these readings inquires normatively why and under which conditions it became such a dominant element in the communication between states and in the ways scholars account and explain international relations. The international community serves as a discursive device for political leaders that frames and legitimizes their actions on its behalf. It provides one broad reference point for binding, socializing and recruiting actors for collective action.[82] It is also a rhetorical device for scholars who aim to theorize it as a communal source for international law and can easily frame it to different arguments and assertions.

As a mediating term it is used in both academic and political discourses to bridge, or at least mask, paradigmatic and ideological gaps and to consolidate and link internal and external audiences. However, both political leaders and academic scholars should be aware and mindful of the discursive choices they make when referring to the international community. Accordingly, we cannot and should not dismiss the international community as a cheap rhetorical device, since in spite of (and probably because of) not having any fixed or pre-determined content, its constant presence in day-to-day international discourse is a vital part of institutionalization and of the practices with which it is affiliated. The dominance of the concept insinuates the great social role it plays and the pragmatic needs of states to use it as a narrative of organized and rule-governed international relations that involves collective commitments. At least while political leaders and academic scholars are mindful of and accountable to this

81 Buzan and Gonzalez-Pelaez (note 10 above).
82 Bliesemann and Kühn (note 54 above).

discursive choice, there is no real harm in using it. This, however, requires assuming responsibility, not for the international community but for the discursive choice of using it as a referential anchor.

The discursive choice of the international community, and the fact that states – individually and collectively – portray themselves and judge their fellow states based on their conduct in the framework of the international community are therefore key components for understanding the international community. Echoing Tonnies, the discursive affiliation with the international community can be understood as representing the sense of unity that binds members in a specific communal setting. It thus insinuates that alongside complex legal and political processes of interplay between domestic and international practices, there is an impact to belonging in a wider collective *we* of states.

Taking a socio-discursive approach, I have argued that the international community is essentially a discursive construct that materializes only once political agents refer to it and attribute to it certain values, rules and virtues. However, the international community is not only ideational; it is both a discursive choice and a discursive practice. On the one hand, it is created and sustained by the acknowledgment of various agents, and on the other hand, it is entrusted with agential capacities to act in the international arena. Therefore, by exploring the ways political agents refer and narrate – namely, talk about – the international community, we can learn what it is, and how the agents that arguably act in its context are perceiving it. The main premise in this regard is that words shape concepts and concepts construct shared knowledge and reality, and therefore construct concrete practices and institutions. The discursive epistemology of the "international community" as a construct that is constituted through agents' dialogue is not necessarily unique, and we can specifically identify similar notions with regards to international law.[83] However, the great interest lies, in my opinion, not merely in understating the discursive construct, but in the exploration of these dialogues and how they portray the interplay between such discursive constructs – for example, international community and international law. In doing so, we can gain a unique point of view on the patterns of state transactions and relations and further understand how states themselves conceive, experience and narrate interstate relations and practices of inter-state relations. Further, exploring the various conceptions, interpretations and discursive choices of individual

---

[83] For example, Ryan Goodman and Derek Jinks, "How to Influence States: Socialization and International Human Rights Law" (2004) 54:3 Duke LJ 621; Koh (note 14 above).

states and the way they negotiate them with other states allows us to evaluate the creative tension and feedback between local and international perceptions. This creative tension is yet another example of the complex relationship between local and global culture.

7. Local communities, cultural heritage and international economic law*

Valentina Vadi

I. INTRODUCTION

What role do local communities play in the making of international economic law? Do local cultural heritage and values matter in the adjudication of international economic disputes? Where there is a conflict between the objective of global economic liberalization and the pursuit of local cultural policies, should the local give way to the global? Like other branches of international law, international economic law treats each state as one unit and does not typically focus on the different subparts within states. As a result, local communities do not appear in the text of international economic law treaties. Only recently have local communities gradually emerged in the adjudication of international economic disputes. Despite their gradual appearance, they still remain significantly absent or marginalised in mainstream international economic law discourse. This chapter aims to fill this gap in legal literature investigating the impact of economic globalization on local communities and the role that local communities play in international economic law and adjudication. The clash

* This chapter is based on a paper presented to the workshop on "Mapping the Impact of International Trade and Human Rights on Local Practice", held in July 2014 at the International Institute for the Sociology of Law in Oñati, Spain. The author wishes to thank Ljiljana Biukovic, Moshe Hirsch and Pitman Potter for their comments on an earlier draft. The usual disclaimer applies. Earlier versions of this chapter were presented at the International Law Association British Branch Spring Conference, and at the Socio-Legal Studies Association Annual Conference, both held at the Law School, Lancaster University, United Kingdom, on 5 April and 8 April 2016 respectively. The research leading to these results has received funding from the European Research Council under the European Union's ERC Starting Grant Agreement n. 639564. The chapter reflects the author's views only and not necessarily those of the Union.

between local cultural values and international economic governance is one example of the tension between international law and state autonomy and of the subsequent local adaptation of, and/or local resistance to, international law standards. It illustrates the challenge of implementing international law at the local level.

Socio-legal approaches to international economic governance reveal that, substantively, a clash of culture can emerge between an international economic culture aimed at productivity and development and local cultural practices. Procedurally, international economic courts may not be the most appropriate tribunals for disputes adjudicating cultural heritage-related issues. After briefly discussing these findings, this chapter highlights two different yet complementary avenues for integrating local communities' concerns into the fabric of international economic law. On the one hand, *de lege ferenda*, since international investment treaties are renegotiated periodically, there is scope for inserting ad hoc clauses within these treaties to protect local communities. Analogously, World Trade Organization (WTO) law is not written in stone; rather, amendments and waivers are legal instruments to reconcile conflicting norms and interests. On the other hand, *de lege lata*, international economic courts can take into account local entitlements within the current framework of international economic law.

This chapter proceeds as follows. First, it explores the promises and pitfalls of socio-legal analysis in international economic law. In fact, socio-legal approaches can illuminate the relevance of social factors in the creation and implementation of international economic law. Second, the concepts of local communities and cultural heritage as well as their interplay will be sketched out. Third, the international economic governance will be briefly described. Reference to the WTO[1] and investment law regimes and their effective and sophisticated dispute-settlement mechanisms will be made. Fourth, the clash between local cultural values and international economic governance will be analysed and critically assessed. Finally, some conclusions shall be drawn.

II. SOCIO-LEGAL APPROACHES TO INTERNATIONAL ECONOMIC LAW

In the past decades, international economic law has come to the fore, becoming a sophisticated field of academic study and legal practice.

---

[1] Marrakesh Agreement Establishing the World Trade Organization, 15 April 1994, 33 ILM 1144 (1994).

The move from the periphery to the core of public international law has required the use of various methods of inquiry to map the field. Among these various methods, ranging from law and economics[2] to legal realism,[3] from critical theory[4] to global administrative law,[5] only recently have socio-legal approaches made their way into international economic law.[6]

While socio-legal approaches are not the sole – let alone the ultimate – method for investigating international economic law (IEL), they contribute to illuminate this field of study. Socio-legal approaches can "offer valuable insights into IEL and broade[n] our understanding of social factors involved in the creation and implementation of IEL rules".[7] They can also have "implications for policy-making", and "suggest some better mechanisms for coping with the modern challenges faced by IEL".[8]

Socio-legal approaches to international economic law acknowledge that international economic activities and their regulation are social phenomena and have pervasive effects on everyday life.[9] As traders and investors "cross boundaries", "settle in new communities" and commercialize their products and services, international trade and foreign direct investments spread "knowledge, norms, and values".[10] Not only do socio-legal

---

[2] Guido Calabresi, *The Future of Law & Economics – Essays in Reform and Recollection* (New Haven and London: Yale University Press, 2016).

[3] Gregory Shaffer, "A New Legal Realism: Method in International Economic Law Scholarship" in Colin B Picker, Isabella Bunn and Douglas Arner, eds, *International Economic Law – The State and the Future of the Discipline* (Oxford: Hart Publishing, 2008).

[4] BS Chimni, "Critical Theory and International Economic Law" in John Linarelli, ed., *Research Handbook on Global Justice and International Economic Law* (Cheltenham and Northampton: Edward Elgar, 2013).

[5] Benedict Kingsbury, Nico Krisch and Richard B Stewart, "The Emergence of Global Administrative Law" (2005) 68 Law & Contemp Probs 15.

[6] Moshe Hirsch, "The Sociology of International Economic Law: Sociological Analysis of the Regulation of Regional Agreements in the World Trading System" (2008) 19 EJIL 277; Stephan W Schill, "W(h)ither Fragmentation? On the Literature and Sociology of International Investment Law" (2011) 22 EJIL 875; Sergio Puig, "Social Capital in the Arbitration Market" (2014) 25 EJIL 387.

[7] Hirsch (note 6 above) at 278.

[8] Ibid.

[9] Amanda Perry-Kessaris, "What Does It Mean to Take a Socio-legal Approach to International Economic Law?" in Amanda Perry-Kessaris, ed., *Socio-Legal Approaches to International Economic Law* (Abingdon: Routledge, 2013) 3.

[10] Hirsch (note 6 above) at 280–1 (highlighting that "International economic relations are not only affected by socio-cultural factors, they often influence the socio-cultural features of the communities involved").

approaches investigate legal provisions, but they also examine the contexts in which legal texts operate.[11] In fact, international economic law is much more than the mere sum of its provisions.[12] Socio-legal approaches to IEL explore the role that both public and private actors play in international economic relations considering economic interactions as "part and parcel of social life".[13] Like other "law and . . ." linkages, the link between law and society can be a fertile one, allowing some cross-fertilization across international law and sociology – meant as the study of society.[14]

While seminal studies have investigated the role of multinational corporations,[15] international tribunals[16] and non-governmental organizations (NGOs)[17] in the making of global economic governance, very little attention has been paid to local communities. For centuries, law has consisted of the state law, and public international law has consisted of the law governing states.[18] International economic law was no exception to this state-centric approach. While states remain an important focus of international economic law, state sub-units have increasingly participated in international economic law regimes. In parallel, international economic law has a pervasive character, having an impact on the life of local communities. Moreover, current global economic trends can be fostered or resisted by local cultural aspirations. This chapter contributes to the emerging literature shedding light on the interplay between local communities and global economic governance. Due to space limits, it has an exploratory character.

---

11 Perry-Kessaris (note 9 above) at 6.

12 Ibid. at 7.

13 Ibid. at 9.

14 See Moshe Hirsch, *Invitation to the Sociology of International Law* (Oxford: Oxford University Press, 2016).

15 See Peter Muchlinski, *Multinational Enterprises and the Law* (New York: Oxford University Press, 2007) 82–9; Francesco Francioni, *Imprese Multinazionali, Protezione Diplomatica e Responsabilità Internazionale* (Milan: Giuffrè, 1979).

16 Miguel Poiares Maduro, *We the Court: The European Court of Justice and the European Economic Constitution* (Oxford: Hart Publishing, 1998).

17 Sergey Ripinsky and Peter Van den Bossche, eds, *NGO Involvement in International Organizations* (London: British Institute of International and Comparative Law, 2007).

18 See William Twining, *General Jurisprudence: Understanding Law from a Global Perspective* (Cambridge: Cambridge University Press, 2008) 362 (calling this double assumption the "Westphalian duo").

III. WHY DO LOCAL COMMUNITIES MATTER?

Local communities can be defined as groups of individuals, living in a common location and organized around common values. "Local" indicates the fact that these communities are rooted in "particular contexts of experience".[19] The word "community" derives from the Latin *communitas* (comprising *cum*, meaning "with/together", and *munus*, meaning "duty")[20] and refers to a social group and its "syste[m] of interests, values or beliefs".[21] Local communities are characterized by different types of links. Local communities are the first ambit in which human beings connect; they count for most in the daily lives of people and create a sense of identity.

Local communities are not legal subjects of international law, as states formally remain the only subjects of international law.[22] If local communities by definition are not subjects of international law, why should they matter to international economic law discourse? If one accepts the conception of international economic law as a branch of international law aimed at fostering peaceful and prosperous relations among nations for the commonweal of the international community, then local communities matter because they are the social units or building stones of the international community itself. According to this view, international economic law would be rooted in, and express the aspirations of, the international community as a whole.

Exploring the human dimension of international economic law requires scholars not only to focus on macroeconomic notions of growth but also to consider the impact that international economic activities and their regulation have on the commonweal. In other words, "balancing economic and wider social – non-economic – values and interests requires that we no longer naturally exclude the latter from our conceptions of international economic law, and that we re-evaluate the values inherent to international economic law".[23] The very text of international economic law instruments

---

19 Roger Cotterell, "A Legal Concept of Community" (1997)12 CJLS 75 at 79.

20 See Roberto Esposito, *Communitas. Origine e destino delle comunità* (Torino: Einaudi, 1998).

21 Cotterell (note 19 above) at 78.

22 Roger Cotterell, "Transnational Networks of Community and International Economic Law" in A. Perry-Kessaris, ed., *Socio-Legal Approaches to International Economic Law* (Abingdon: Routledge, 2013) 133 (noting that international law "builds from a heritage of thought that focuses on nation states as legal actors").

23 Cecilia J Flores Elizondo, "Reflexive International Economic Law – Balancing Economic and Social Goals in the Construction of Law" in A Perry-

refers to non-economic values.[24] For instance, the preamble to the WTO stresses the importance of "raising standards of living" and "sustainable development".[25] Therefore, the WTO should not be exclusively identified with trade liberation in goods and services; rather "liberalization is a means to an end, and not an end in itself".[26]

Even accepting the idea that local communities matter, and that international economic law should have a human face, states remain the interlocutors, makers and subjects of international economic law. States sign international treaties and have to comply with international law commitments. States represent their population, and *a fortiori*, also local communities. Why then should analysis focus on local communities as sub-units of states? What is the added value of focusing on local communities?

In most cases, states have filed claims before international economic law tribunals to defend key interests of their local communities. For instance, in the recent seal products dispute before the WTO panel and Appellate Body, Canada vigorously defended the economic and cultural interests of its coastal communities, in practising seal hunting and commercializing seal products, that had been affected by the EU ban on seal products.[27] In the *Glamis Gold* arbitration, concerning the development of a gold mine in California, the United States vigorously and successfully defended the cultural interests of the indigenous tribes in protecting sacred sites.[28]

However, "States rarely comprise one homogenous legal culture",

---

Kessaris, ed., *Socio-Legal Approaches to International Economic Law* (Abingdon: Routledge, 2013) 127–8.

[24] Brigitte Stern, "The Future of International Investment Law: A Balance between the Protection of Investors and the States' Capacity to Regulate" in José E Alvarez and Karl P Sauvant, eds, *The Evolving International Investment Regime* (New York: Oxford University Press, 2011) 192 (noting that international investment agreements have multiple goals usually expressed in their preambles).

[25] Marrakesh Agreement Establishing the World Trade Organization, Preamble.

[26] Thomas Cottier, "Poverty, Redistribution, and International Trade Regulation" in Krista Nadakavukaren Schefer, ed., *Poverty and the International Legal System* (Cambridge: Cambridge University Press, 2013) 48 (suggesting that "the principal goals of the WTO are directed towards social justice in the new deal tradition").

[27] *European Communities – Measures Prohibiting the Importation and Marketing of Seal Products*, Reports of the Panel, WT/DS400/R and WT/DS401/R (25 November 2013); *European Communities – Measures Prohibiting the Importation and Marketing of Seal Products*, Appellate Body Report, WT/DS400/AB/R and WT/DS401/AB/R (22 May 2014).

[28] *Glamis Gold, Ltd v United States of America*, Award of 8 June 2009, [2009] 48 ILM 1039 (International Centre for Settlement of Investment Disputes).

and people living in a state can be divided into different groups because of economic, social and cultural reasons.[29] In certain cases, states and given local communities may have diverging interests. While states may pursue aggressive developmental policies, local communities affected by such plans might prefer a more sustainable approach to developmental objectives.[30]

IV. INTERNATIONAL ECONOMIC GOVERNANCE

International economic law is a well-developed field of study and is characterized by sophisticated dispute-settlement mechanisms. While the dispute-settlement mechanism of the WTO has been defined as the "jewel in the crown" of this organization,[31] investment treaty arbitration has become the most successful mechanism for settling investment-related disputes.[32]

The creation of the WTO Dispute Settlement Body (DSB) determined a major shift from the political consensus-based dispute-settlement system of the GATT 1947 to a rule-based architecture designed to strengthen the multilateral trade system.[33] The WTO Dispute Settlement Mechanism (DSM) is compulsory, exclusive and highly effective.[34] Panels and the Appellate Body interpret and apply the WTO treaties, preserving the rights and obligations of the WTO members.[35] Their decisions are binding

---

[29] See Colin B Picker, "Islands of Prosperity and Poverty: A Rational Trade Development Policy for Economically Heterogeneous States" in Yong Shik Lee, Gary Horlick, Won-Mog Choi and Tomer Broude, eds, *Law and Development Perspective on International Trade Law* (New York: Cambridge University Press, 2011).

[30] Yu Kanosue, "When Land is Taken Away: States Obligations under International Human Rights Law Concerning Large-Scale Projects Impacting Local Communities" (2015) 15 Hum Rts L Rev 643 at 657 (noting that land acquisitions by foreign investors can affect peasants and people living in rural areas).

[31] Amrita Narlikar, *The WTO: A Very Short Introduction* (Oxford: Oxford University Press, 2005).

[32] Susan Franck, "Development and Outcomes of Investor–State Arbitration" (2009) 9 Harv Int'l LJ 435.

[33] Steven P Crowley and John H Jackson, "WTO Dispute Procedures, Standard of Review, and Deference to National Governments" (1996) 90 AJIL193.

[34] Peter Van Den Bossche and Werner Zdouc, *The Law and Policy of the World Trade Organization* (Cambridge: Cambridge University Press, 2013).

[35] Understanding on Rules and Procedures Governing the Settlement of Disputes, Marrakesh Agreement Establishing the World Trade Organization, Annex 2, 1869 UNTS 401, 33 ILM 1226, art 3.2 (1994) [hereinafter "DSU"].

on the parties, and the Dispute Settlement Understanding (DSU)[36] provides remedies for breach of WTO law. Only WTO member states have *locus standi* in the DSM, i.e. individuals cannot file claims before panels and the Appellate Body.[37] When trade disputes emerge, Article 23.1 of the DSU obliges Members to subject the dispute exclusively to WTO bodies.[38]

In parallel, as there is no single comprehensive multilateral investment agreement, investors' rights are defined by a plethora of international investment agreements, customary law and general principles of law. International investment law provides extensive protection to investors' rights in order to encourage foreign direct investment (FDI) and to foster economic development. At the substantive level, investment treaties provide for, inter alia: adequate compensation for expropriated property; protection against discrimination; fair and equitable treatment; full protection and security; and assurances that the host country will honor its commitments regarding the investment. At the procedural level, investment treaties provide investors direct access to an international arbitral tribunal. The use of the arbitration model is aimed at depoliticizing disputes, avoiding potential national court bias and ensuring the advantages of confidentiality and effectiveness.[39] Arbitral tribunals review state acts in the light of their investment treaties.

Given the structural imbalance between the vague and non-binding dispute-settlement mechanisms provided by international treaties protecting various types of cultural heritage,[40] on the one hand, and the highly effective and sophisticated dispute-settlement mechanisms available under international economic law, on the other, cultural disputes involving investors' or traders' rights have often been brought before international economic law *fora*.[41]

One may wonder whether the fact that cultural disputes tend to be

---

[36] Ibid.

[37] Henrik Andersen, "Protection of Non-Trade Values in WTO Appellate Body Jurisprudence: Exceptions, Economic Arguments, and Eluding Questions" (2015) 18 J Int'l Econ L 385 at 391.

[38] DSU, art 23.1.

[39] Ibrahim FI Shihata, "Towards a Greater Depoliticization of Investment Disputes: The Role of ICSID and MIGA" (1986) 1 ICSID Rev 1.

[40] On international cultural law and its dispute-settlement mechanisms, see Valentina Vadi, "The Cultural Wealth of Nations in International Law" (2012) 21 Tulane J Int'l & Comp L 87.

[41] Clearly, this does not mean that these are the only available *fora*, let alone the superior *fora* for this kind of dispute. Other *fora* are available such as national courts, human rights courts, regional economic courts and the traditional state-to-state *fora* such as the International Court of Justice or even inter-state arbitration.

adjudicated before international economic law *fora* determines a sort of institutional bias. Treaty provisions can be vague and their language encompasses a potentially wide variety of state regulation that may interfere with economic interests. Therefore, a potential tension exists when a state adopts regulatory measures interfering with foreign investments or free trade, as regulation may be considered as violating substantive standards of treatment under investment treaties or the WTO covered agreements and the foreign investor may require compensation before arbitral tribunals or spur the home state to file a claim before the WTO organs.

More specifically, with regard to the WTO DSB, "it is quite uncontroversial that an adjudicatory system engaged in interpreting trade-liberalizing standards would tend to favor free trade".[42] According to some empirical studies, there is a consistently high rate of complainant success in WTO dispute resolution[43] and authors have theorized that "the WTO panels and the WTO Appellate Body have interpreted the WTO agreements in a manner that consistently promotes the goal of expanding trade, often to the detriment of respondents' negotiated and reserved regulatory competencies".[44] In particular, given the fact that about 80 percent of the cases have been settled in favor of the claimant, Colares highlighted that "the DSB has evolved WTO norms in a manner that consistently favors litigants whose interests are generally aligned with the unfettered expansion of trade".[45]

In the parallel domain of investor–state arbitration, some scholars contend that such mechanism is biased in favor of corporate and economic interests, and "excludes consideration of vital non-commercial interests".[46] Certainly, given the architecture of the arbitral process, significant concerns arise in the context of disputes involving local communities and their cultural concerns. While arbitration structurally constitutes a private model of adjudication, investment disputes present public law

---

Some of these dispute-settlement mechanisms may be more suitable than investor–state arbitration or the WTO DSM to address cultural concerns.

[42] Joel P Trachtman, "The Domain of WTO Dispute Resolution" (1999) 40 Harv Int'l LJ 333.

[43] John Maton and Carolyn Maton, "Independence under Fire: Extra Legal Pressures and Coalition Building in WTO Dispute Settlement" (2007) 10 J Int'l Econ L 317.

[44] Juscelino F Colares, "A Theory of WTO Adjudication: From Empirical Analysis to Biased Rule Development" (2009) 42 V and J Transnat'l L 383 at 388.

[45] Ibid. at 387.

[46] Robin Broad, "Corporate Bias in the World Bank Group's International Centre for Settlement of Investment Disputes – A Case Study of a Global Mining Corporation Suing El Salvador" (2015) 36 U Pa J Int'l L 851 at 854.

aspects.[47] Arbitral awards ultimately shape the relationship between the state, on the one hand, and private individuals, on the other.[48] Arbitrators determine matters such as the legality of governmental activity, the degree to which individuals should be protected from regulation, and the appropriate role of the state.[49]

Investor–state arbitration, however, distinguishes between two types of non-state actors: (1) foreign investors; and (2) the FDI impacted-local communities.[50] International investment treaties generally delegate the resolution of disputes arising from the investment within the territory of the host state to an international dispute-settlement mechanism, thus bypassing national courts.[51] Furthermore, court decisions in the host state upholding complaints brought by private parties against a foreign investor may be challenged by the investor before an arbitral tribunal on the grounds that they constitute wrongful interference with the investment.[52]

The increasing impact of FDI on the social sphere of the host state has raised the question of whether the principle of access to justice, as successfully developed to the benefit of investors through the provision of binding arbitration, ought to be matched by a corresponding right to a remedial process for local communities adversely affected by the investment in the host state.[53] While the recognition of multinational corporations (MNCs) as "international corporate citizens" has progressed,[54] by comparison, the procedural rights of local communities have remained unchanged. The following section addresses the question as to whether cultural entitlements play any role in the context of international disputes before international economic fora.

---

47 Gus Van Harten, "The Public-Private Distinction in the International Arbitration of Individual Claims against the State" (2007) 56 ICLQ 371 at 372.

48 Gus Van Harten, *Investment Treaty Arbitration and Public Law* (Oxford: Oxford University Press, 2007) 70.

49 M Sornarajah, "The Clash of Globalizations and the International Law on Foreign Investment" (2003) 10 Can Foreign Pol'y 1.

50 Noemi Gal-Or, "The Investor and Civil Society as Twin Global Citizens: Proposing a New Interpretation in the Legitimacy Debate" (2008–2009) 32 Suffolk Transnat'l L Rev 271.

51 Francesco Francioni, "Access to Justice, Denial of Justice, and International Investment Law" in Pierre-Marie Dupuy, Francesco Francioni and Ernst-Ulrich Petersmann, eds, *Human Rights in International Investment Law and Arbitration* (Oxford: Oxford University Press, 2009) 72.

52 Ibid. at 72.

53 Ibid. at 71.

54 Peter Muchlinski, "Global Bukovina Examined: Viewing the Multinational Enterprise as a Transnational Law Making Community" in Gunther Teubner, ed., *Global Law Without a State* (London: Dartmouth, 1997) 79.

V. A CLASH OF CULTURES?

Culture represents inherited values, ideas, beliefs and traditions which characterize social groups and their behaviour. Culture is not a static concept but rather a dynamic force, which evolves through time and shapes countries and civilizations. As such, culture has always benefited from economic exchange. International trade in recent times has spurred a more intense dialogue and interaction among nations: thus, it offers unprecedented opportunities for cultural exchange. In parallel, FDI can promote cultural diversity and provide the funds needed to locate, recover and preserve cultural heritage.

Nonetheless, economic globalization can also jeopardize cultural diversity and determine the erosion of cultural heritage. While states actively compete for FDI and liberalize trade to promote growth, foster competition and attract transfers of technology, FDI and trade can affect the cultural heritage and deeply held cultural practices of local communities. While trade in cultural products can lead to cultural homogenization, certain investments, such as those in the extractive sector, have the ultimate capacity to change landscapes and erase memory.

Despite its significant relationship to international economic law, culture receives very limited attention in the text of trade and investment treaties. In the General Agreement on Tariffs and Trade 1947 (GATT),[55] two provisions address cultural matters. Article IV GATT allows WTO member states to establish screen quotas – i.e. policies requiring a minimum number of screening days of domestic movies each year to protect the national film industry – by exempting cinematographic films from the national treatment principle. Article XX(f) GATT allows member states to adopt or enforce measures to protect "national treasures of artistic, historic or archaeological value". Nonetheless, the restrictive requirements of the introductory part (*chapeau*) of Article XX have de facto limited the successful application of Article XX of GATT 1994. Notoriously, the *chapeau* of Article XX requires that the measures restricting trade must not be applied in a manner which would constitute a means of arbitrary or unjustifiable discrimination between countries where the same conditions prevail, and they must not constitute a disguised restriction on international trade.

In international investment law, discussions about a cultural exception were pivotal to the Multilateral Agreement on Investment (MAI) negoti-

---

55 General Agreement on Tariffs and Trade (GATT 1947), 30 October 1947, 55 UNTS 194.

ations. At the time, France and Canada had pursued the insertion of an exception to enable all parties to protect cultural diversity and enterprises engaged in cultural activities. The United States' opposition to such a clause, however, could not be overcome and the whole project ultimately failed.

This was not the end of "cultural exceptions" – the idea to treat cultural goods and services differently from commercial products and consider them as exceptions – in international investment law. Some international investment agreements present ad hoc provisions protecting relevant communities and/or their cultural interests. For instance, in the Annex of the US–Lithuania bilateral investment treaty (BIT), Lithuania reserved "the right to make or maintain limited exceptions to national treatment" with regard to, inter alia, "monuments of nature, history, archaeology and culture as well as the surrounding protective areas", and the land of the Curonian Spit – a landscape of sand dunes that is a World Heritage site.[56] More recently, the Trans-Pacific Partnership stipulates that:

> [p]rovided that such measures are not used as a means of arbitrary or unjustified discrimination against persons of the other Parties or a disguised restriction on trade in goods, trade in services and investment, nothing in this agreement shall preclude the adoption by New Zealand of measures it deems necessary to accord more favourable treatment to Maori in respect of matters covered by this agreement, including in fulfilment of its obligations under the Treaty of Waitangi.[57]

Until recently, international economic law had developed only limited tools for the protection of cultural heritage through dispute settlement. Cases like *UPS v Canada*[58] show that the existence of a cultural exception can facilitate the consideration of cultural concerns in international economic disputes. However, in the absence of a cultural exception, it seems more difficult to integrate cultural concerns into the fabric of international economic law.[59] Finding the proper balance between the need of investors and traders "for the rule of law" and due process, on the one hand, and

---

[56] Treaty between the Government of the United States of America and the Government of the Republic of Lithuania for the Encouragement and Reciprocal Protection of Investment, 14 January 1998, Annex at para 3 (entered into force 22 November 2001).

[57] Transpacific Partnership Agreement, 4 February 2016, art 29.6.1.

[58] *United Parcel Service of America Inc v Government of Canada*, 24 May 2007, 46 ILM 922 (2007).

[59] WTO Panel Report, *Canada – Certain Measures Concerning Periodicals*, WT/DS31/R (15 March 1997); WTO Appellate Body Report, *Canada – Certain Measures Concerning Periodicals*, WT/DS31/AB/R (30 June 1997).

states' desire to preserve their policy space to pursue their legitimate interests, on the other, is the key challenge that international economic law faces "in the interest of its own legitimacy".[60]

VI. CRITICAL ASSESSMENT

Socio-legal approaches to international economic law reveal the interplay between local communities and global economic governance. Not only are local communities "important sources and carriers of identities",[61] they also constitute "powerful units of analysis" because they "bring human beings to the centre of the analytical frame".[62] "Community lenses" applied to international economic law can contribute to the theoretical study of the field and suggest paths for improvement.[63] Socio-legal approaches reveal that, substantively, a clash of culture can emerge between an international economic culture aimed at productivity and development and local cultural practices. Procedurally, international economic fora may not be the most appropriate tribunals for disputes adjudicating cultural heritage-related issues. After briefly discussing these findings, this section proposes two avenues for facilitating the consideration of local communities' entitlements in international economic disputes: (1) a text-driven approach and (2) a judicially driven approach.

At the substantive level, FDI and trade can have both positive and negative effects on the lives of local communities. Among the positive spillovers there is economic growth, competition, knowledge transfers and well-being. Development analysts point to trade and extractive projects as anti-poverty measures, and advocate trade and FDI as major catalysts for development.[64] However, "for the most part, the peoples in the areas where the resources are located tend to bear a disproportionate share of the negative impacts of development through reduced access to resources and direct exposure to pollution and environmental degradation".[65]

---

60 Karl P Sauvant and José E Alvarez, "Introduction – International Investment Law in Transition" in José E Alvarez and Karl P Sauvant, eds, *The Evolving International Law Regime* (Oxford: Oxford University Press, 2011) xlii.

61 Ting Xu, "Global Legal Transplants through the Lens of Community" in Amanda Perry-Kessaris, ed., *Socio-Legal Approaches to International Economic Law* (Abingdon: Routledge, 2013) 170.

62 Ibid. at 169–70.

63 Cotterell (note 22 above) at 145.

64 OECD, *Foreign Direct Investment for Development* (Paris: OECD, 2002) 3.

65 Lila Barrera-Hernández, "Indigenous Peoples, Human Rights and Natural

At the procedural level, arbitral tribunals constitute an uneven playing field: while foreign investors have locus standi – i.e. the right to act or be heard – before these tribunals, local communities do not have direct access to these dispute-settlement mechanisms. Rather, their arguments need to be espoused by their home government. Nonetheless, for a variety of reasons, states do not always adequately represent local communities.[66] In fact, the cultural entitlements of local communities often compete with the economic development plans of both investors and states. Therefore, despite the formal premise of equality between the parties, there are structural power asymmetries between MNCs and local communities that governments may not mitigate. Not only does investor–state arbitration fail to take into account the eventual conflict of interest between the cultural entitlements of local communities and the economic needs of the state, but it also confers distinct procedural advantages to foreign investors vis-à-vis other private actors.

While local communities can (and have) present(ed) friends of the court (*amicus curiae*) briefs reflecting their interests, investment tribunals and the WTO panels and Appellate Body are not legally obligated to consider such briefs – rather, they have the faculty to do so should they deem it appropriate.[67] The requests are granted if the friends of the court can demonstrate that they could assist tribunals without unduly delaying arbitrations.[68] As *amici curiae*, local communities cannot ask for final or interlocutory remedies to preserve their cultural entitlements before arbitral tribunals and the WTO DSM.

Moreover, investors' and traders' claims "are adjudicated faster, sooner, and with greater potential for immediate state liability" than the claims of local communities before domestic courts.[69] Furthermore, "any strictly pecuniary quantification of damages is likely to favour foreign investors" and traders at the expense of the competing interests

---

Resource Development: Chile's Mapuche Peoples and the Right to Water" (2005) 11 Ann Surv Int'l & Comp L 1 at 6.

[66] William Shipley, "What's Yours is Mine: Conflict of Law and Conflict of Interest Regarding Indigenous Property Rights in Latin American Investment Dispute Arbitration" (2014) 11 Transnat'l Disp Management 1.

[67] In some cases, arbitral tribunals have denied the participation of non-disputing parties. See *Bernhard von Pezold and Others v Zimbabwe*, 26 June 2012, ICSID Case No. ARB/10/15 (2012) para 49 (stating that *amici curiae* should be independent of the parties and "bring a perspective, particular knowledge or insight that is different from that of the parties").

[68] Lucas Bastin, "*Amici Curiae* in Investor–State Arbitrations: Two Recent Decisions" (2013) 20 Austl Int'l LJ 101.

[69] Shipley (note 66 above) at 53.

of local communities.[70] In fact, mere pecuniary valuation may not accord significant weight to "permanent alterations to landscape" or change of lifestyle.[71] Finally, the fear of costly litigation can prevent states from protecting the entitlements of local communities determining a regulatory chill.[72]

Two avenues can facilitate the consideration of local communities' entitlements in international economic disputes: (1) a "treaty-driven approach"; and (2) a "judicially driven approach".[73] First, the text-driven approach relies on the periodical renegotiation of the international economic law *acquis*. As international investment treaties are renegotiated from time to time, treaty drafters can expressly accommodate local communities' entitlements in the text of these treaties.[74] Analogously, WTO agreements are not written in stone; rather, rounds of negotiations regularly take place, and WTO members have adopted amendments and/or interpretative statements to better accommodate non-trade concerns into the fabric of the WTO.[75] For instance, renegotiation of international investment agreements might take account of the requirements of free prior informed consent and benefit sharing. Such requirements, which have been developed in the context of indigenous peoples' rights, could be extended to other social groups, enabling local communities to participate in the decision-making that can affect them and share the benefits that derive from given economic activities. In parallel, investors should take into account the existence of protected groups when assessing the economic risks of the given investment[76] and consider incorporating local communities as part of multi-actor contracts.[77]

Second, the judicially driven approach relies on the interpretation and

---

[70] Ibid.

[71] Ibid.

[72] Mihail Krepchev, "The Problem of Accommodating Indigenous Land Rights in International Investment Law" (2015) 6 J Int'l Disp Settlement 42 at 43–4.

[73] Ibid. at 45.

[74] Ibid.

[75] Joost Pauwelyn, "WTO Compassion or Superiority Complex?: What to Make of the WTO Waiver for 'Conflict Diamonds'" (2003) 24 Mich J Int'l L 1177 (critically assessing the WTO waiver for conflict diamonds); Isabel Feichtner, "The Waiver Power of the WTO: Opening the WTO for Political Debate on the Reconciliation of Competing Interests" (2009) 20 EJIL 615 (discussing the WTO waivers as tools for reconciling conflicting norms and interests).

[76] Krepchev (note 72 above) at 71.

[77] Ibironke T Odumosu-Ayanu, "Governments, Investors and Local Communities: Analysis of a Multi-Actor Investment Contract Framework" (2014) 15 Melbourne J Int'l L 473.

application of international economic law by arbitral tribunals, WTO panels and the Appellate Body (AB). International economic courts can take into account local entitlements within the current framework of international economic law.[78] Arbitral tribunals, WTO panels and the AB are tribunals of limited jurisdiction and lack the jurisdiction to hold states liable for breach of their human rights obligations. Rather, they can only determine whether the protections in the relevant investment treaty or WTO covered agreements, respectively, have been breached.

However, this does not mean that human rights should be irrelevant in the context of investment disputes. Arbitral tribunals, WTO panels and the AB can and should interpret international economic law in conformity with *jus cogens*[79] and a state's obligations under the United Nations Charter.[80] Some norms protecting human rights have acquired *jus cogens* status, such as the prohibitions of racial discrimination and of genocide. Moreover, international economic law is not a self-contained regime, but constitutes an important field of international law. As such, it should not frustrate the aim and objectives of the latter, which include the protection of human rights and fundamental freedoms as expressed, inter alia, in the Universal Declaration of Human Rights (UDHR),[81] the International Covenant on Civil and Political Rights (ICCPR)[82] and the Covenant on Economic, Social and Cultural Rights (ICESCR).[83] Rather, international economic courts should interpret international economic law taking into

---

[78] Krepchev (note 72 above) at 45.

[79] Vienna Convention on the Law of Treaties (VCLT), 23 May 1969, United Nations Treaty Series, vol. 1155 at 331, art 53 (entered into force 27 January 1980) (recognizing a *jus cogens* norm as one "accepted and recognized by the international community of states as a whole as a norm from which no derogation is possible").

[80] On *jus cogens* and international investment law, see Andrea K Bjorklund, "Mandatory Rules of Law and Investment Arbitration" (2007) 18 Am Rev Int'l Arb 175; Valentina Vadi, "*Jus Cogens* in International Investment Law and Arbitration" (2015) 46 Nethl YB Int'l L 357. On *jus cogens* in WTO adjudication, see Gabrielle Marceau, "WTO Dispute Settlement and Human Rights" (2002) 13 EJIL 753.

[81] Universal Declaration of Human Rights (UDHR) (entered into force 10 December 1948).

[82] International Covenant on Civil and Political Rights (ICCPR), adopted and opened for signature by General Assembly Resolution 2200A (XXI) of 16 December 1966; 999 UNTS 171; 6 ILM 368 (entered into force 23 March 1976).

[83] International Covenant on Economic, Social and Cultural Rights (ICESCR), adopted and opened for signature by General Assembly Resolution 2200A (XXI) of 16 December 1966; 993 UNTS 3; 6 ILM 368 (3 January 1976).

account "any relevant rules of international law applicable in the relations between the parties".[84]

Several international human rights rules refer to collective values and cultural entitlements. These provisions include both hard law and soft law.[85] Examples of binding cultural entitlements abound. For instance, Article 1 of both the ICCPR and the ICESCR recognizes the right of self-determination, i.e. the peoples' right to "freely determine their political status and freely pursue their economic, social and *cultural* development".[86] The same provision also clarifies that international economic cooperation is "based upon the principle of mutual benefit, and international law" and that "in no case may a people be deprived of its own means of subsistence".[87] Significantly, the principle of self-determination is commonly regarded as a *jus cogens* rule. For example, Article 27 of the ICCPR recognizes the individual right of persons belonging to ethnic, religious or linguistic minorities "to enjoy their own culture, to profess and practise their own religion, or to use their own language", "in community with the other members of their group". This provision is binding on the parties to the ICCPR.

There are even more instances of non-binding cultural entitlements. For instance, Article 27(1) of the UDHR states that "Everyone has the right freely to participate in the cultural life of the community, to enjoy the arts and to share in scientific advancement and its benefits".[88] Indigenous culture plays a central role in the United Nations Declaration on the Rights of Indigenous Peoples (UNDRIP).[89] Although neither the UDHR nor the UNDRIP are binding, and therefore include soft law norms, they can coalesce in customary international law and therefore become binding.

In conclusion, while international economic law does not give too much attention to culture – at least when it comes to texts of the WTO covered agreements and international investment agreements – and therefore international economic courts have limited or no specific mandate to protect cultural entitlements, such entitlements are a significant component of

---

84 VCLT, art 31.3.c.

85 Due to space limits, this section can provide only a limited number of examples of human rights law provisions recognizing cultural entitlements.

86 ICCPR, art 1.1 and ICESCR, art 1.1 (emphasis added).

87 ICCPR, art 1.2 and ICESCR, art 1.2.

88 UDHR, art 27.1.

89 United Nations Declaration on the Rights of Indigenous Peoples (UNDRIP) GA Res. 61/295, UN Doc. A/RES/61/295 (entered into force 13 September 2007).

human rights law. Arguably, provisions such as Article 27 of the UDHR, which provides the right of individuals to freely participate in the cultural life of the community and to enjoy and share cultural life, can influence the interpretation and application of international economic law. This is even more the case with regard to cultural entitlements that are binding or have a peremptory character.

VII. CONCLUSIONS

The clash between local cultural values and international economic governance is one example of the tension between international law and state autonomy and of the subsequent local adaptation of, and/or local resistance to, international law standards. FDI and free trade can represent a potentially positive force for development. Still, state policy and practice concerning economic activities must be mindful of the implications for the culture of local communities. The interplay between the promotion of free trade and FDI, on the one hand, and the protection of local cultural heritage, on the other, highlights a fundamental clash between local and global dimensions of governance. Heritage is local and belongs to specific places and local communities: economic governance has an international character. At the same time, both foreign investments and international trade can affect the traditional lifestyle and cultural values of local communities.

Disputes involving the conflict between the protection of cultural heritage and the promotion of economic interests have been brought before international economic fora. International economic fora may not be the most suitable fora to settle this kind of dispute. They are courts of limited jurisdiction, and cannot adjudicate on state violations of local communities' entitlements. This does not mean, however, that they should (or do) not take cultural considerations into account. Rather, international economic courts ought to hear the voices of these communities.[90]

This chapter highlights two different yet complementary avenues for integrating local communities' concerns into the fabric of international economic law. On the one hand, *de lege ferenda*, since international investment treaties are renegotiated periodically, there is scope for inserting ad hoc clauses within these treaties to protect local communities.

---

[90] For an analogous argument in the context of European integration, see Fernanda Nicola, "Invisible Cities in Europe" (2011–12) 35 Fordham Int'l LJ 1285.

Analogously, WTO law is not written in stone; rather, amendments and waivers are legal instruments to reconcile conflicting norms and interests. On the other hand, *de lege lata*, international economic courts can take into account local entitlements within the current framework of international economic law.

8. Identity matters: the enforcement of global human rights treaties by European Union trade instruments*

Moshe Hirsch

I. INTRODUCTION

One of the major factors feeding the process of fragmentation of international human rights law is the parallel operation of global and regional legal frameworks, both in terms of substantive treaties and institutional arrangements. Ample literature discusses various aspects of fragmentation of international human right *instruments*, certain differences between the jurisprudence of different *courts* (such as the European Court of Human Rights and the Inter-American Court of Human Rights) and some coordination problems between different human rights *treaty bodies* (for example, the UN Human Rights Committee and the Committee on the Rights of Persons with Disabilities).[1]

* This chapter is based on a paper presented to the workshop on "Mapping the Impact of International Trade and Human Rights on Local Practice", held in July 2014 at the International Institute for the Sociology of Law in Oñati, Spain. I am indebted to Yuval Shany and Guy Harpaz (Hebrew University) for helpful comments on earlier drafts. I am grateful to Anna Lechermann (Hebrew University and Ruprecht Karl University Heidelberg) and Ohad Abrahami for their excellent research assistance. This chapter expands on Moshe Hirsch, *Invitation to the Sociology of International Law* (Oxford: Oxford University Press, 2015) Section IV(B), Ch 4, 106–116.

[1] See, for example, Martti Koskenniemi, "Conclusions of the work of the Study Group on the Fragmentation of International Law: Difficulties arising from the Diversification and Expansion of International Law" ILC, 58th Sess, UN Doc A/CN.4/L.682 (2006) paras 161 et seq., available at http://legal.un.org/ilc/texts/1_9.shtml (accessed 9 January 2017); Malgosia Fitzmaurice, "Interpretation of Human Rights Treaties" in Dinah Shelton, ed., *The Oxford Handbook of International Human Rights Law* (Oxford: Oxford University Press, 2013) 739 at 741–2, 752 et seq.; Yuval Shany, "International Human Rights Bodies and the Little-Realized Threat of Fragmentation" (2016) Hebrew University of Jerusalem Legal Research

Unlike these cases of international legal fragmentation, this chapter addresses a significant development which operates in the reverse direction: attempts undertaken by a major *regional* organization to promote compliance with *global* human rights treaties in areas outside the region, and the ensuing tensions between international human rights law and *local* standards of performance. The European Union (EU) employs certain trade instruments (mainly regional trade agreements and trade preferences granted to developing countries) to promote compliance with global human rights law. The use of these trade mechanisms to enforce global human rights law is significantly motivated by the collective identity and perceived social role of the EU in the international community as a promoter of human rights worldwide. As elaborated below, these EU identity-driven measures illustrate the adaptation of global human rights standards to the local (European) level and may also affect the identity of other international actors targeted by such measures. Thus, the interactions between the EU and non-members in this sphere exemplify also the potential impact and constraints of the European Community's trade-human rights measures on local cultures outside Europe.

Economic and political dimensions of international law are often overlain with a social identity dimension. While, in reality, these dimensions are inseparable, this chapter is devoted to a social identity analysis of the EU's employment of external trade instruments to promote human rights worldwide. This analysis sheds new light on the enactment of EU trade policies in this sphere, their employment and their potential to enhance compliance with international human rights law. These EU identity-driven trade measures present both benefits and limitations, and have different effects on in-group and out-group members. A social identity analysis of EU trade and human rights policy also offers some policy recommendations which may improve the prospects of EU measures in this field.

Section II briefly introduces some central tenets of social identity in sociological and social psychological literature. Section III succinctly discusses certain links between international institutions and collective identity, and elaborates on the EU's collective identity as a human rights promoter, primarily through the use of external trade instruments for the

---

Paper No. 16-06, available at http://ssrn.com/abstract=2722663 (accessed 9 January 2017); Marjan Ajevski, ed., *Fragmentation in International Human Rights Law: Beyond Conflict of Laws* (London: Routledge, 2015); Payandeh Mehrdad, "Fragmentation within International Human Rights Law" in Mads Andenas and Eirik Bjorge, eds, *A Farewell to Fragmentation: Reassertion and Convergence of International Law* (Cambridge: Cambridge University Press, 2015) 297.

enforcement of global human rights treaties in other localities. Section IV draws some conclusions regarding the prospects of compliance with global human rights law following the employment of the above trade measures by the EU, and offers some recommendations which may enhance the effectiveness of such identity-driven legal mechanisms. Section V briefly recaps the chapter's central themes and provides a summary of conclusions.

II. SOCIAL IDENTITY

Identity is a central concept in sociology's established conceptual toolbox.[2] Identity matters in our daily life and affects people's perceptions and attitudes towards other people, as well as their own behaviour. Social identity mediates the relationships between individuals and the social group.[3] Individuals hold multiple identities that vary in their relative overall importance and each one is represented in the individual's mind.[4] Prominent identities include ethnicity, nationality, gender, religion and commitment to fundamental norms.[5]

People have individual and collective identities and these aspects of social identity are tightly bound together within the embodied self.[6]

---

[2] Richard Jenkins, *Social Identity*, 3rd edn (London: Routledge, 2008) 14. See also Steph Lawler, *Identity: Sociological Perspectives*, 2nd edn (Cambridge: Polity, 2014) 3 et seq.

[3] Michael A. Hogg, Deborah J. Terry and Katherine M. White, "A Tale of Two Theories: A Critical Comparison of Identity Theory with Social Identity Theory" (1995) 58 Social Psychology Quarterly 255 at 257; Marilynn B. Brewer, "The Many Faces of Social Identity: Implications for Political Psychology" (2001) 22 Political Psychology 115.

[4] Hogg et al. (note 3 above) at 259; Sheldon Stryker and Peter J. Burke, "The Past, Present, and Future of an Identity Theory" (2000) 63 Social Psychology Quarterly 284 at 286; Walter G. Stephan and Cookie White Stephan, *Intergroup Relations* (Social Psychology Series Westview Press, 1996) 90; Richard J. Crisp, "Prejudice and Perceiving Multiple Identities" in John F. Dovidio, Miles Hewstone, Peter Glick and Victoria M. Esses, eds, *The SAGE Handbook of Prejudice, Stereotyping And Discrimination* (Los Angeles: Sage, 2010) 508.

[5] Jenkins (note 2 above) at 5 defines identity as follows: "As a very basic starting point, identity is the human capacity – rooted in language – to know 'who's and who' . . . This involves knowing who we are, knowing who others are, them knowing who we are, us knowing who they think we are, and so on: a multi-dimensional classification or mapping of the human world and our places in it, as individuals and as members of collectives".

[6] Anthony Giddens and Philip Sutton, *Sociology*, 7th edn (Cambridge: Polity, 2013) 257; John C. Turner and Rina S. Onorato, "Social Identity, Personality,

Personal identity differentiates one's self from other individuals and includes personal traits and the self's social categorization into social groups (for example, by membership in certain groups).[7] In addition to personal identity, people identify themselves collectively; *collective identification* evokes imagery of people who resemble one another and share inter-subjective characteristics.[8] Despite this analytical distinction between personal and collective identities, it is often impossible in reality to disentangle group identity from personal identity.[9] This chapter largely discusses collective identities.

Two dynamic elements stand at the heart of social identity (both personal and collective): similarity and difference. Individuals and groups need a certain level of both similarity to and differentiation from others; and social identity derives from the fundamental tension between the sense of belonging and the sense of distinctiveness.[10]

Generally, social psychological scholarship tends to emphasize that identity and its cognitive consequences derive from group membership. Sociological literature tends to underline the dynamic and interpretative aspects of identity, and particularly its link to the "social role", underscoring that having a particular identity often pressures individuals to behave according to social expectations related to the particular role (such as "parent", "teacher" or "leader").[11]

Social identity is formed in a dialectic process between internal (individual) and external (group) categorizations. Humans have the propensity

---

and the Self-Concept: A Self-Categorization Perspective" in Tom R. Tyler, Roderick M. Kramer and Oliver P. John Lawrence, eds, *The Psychology of the Social Self* (Cambridge: Polity, 1990) 11 at 38; see also Jenkins (note 2 above) at 37–9.

[7] Stephen Worchel, "A Developmental View of the Search for Group Identity" in Stephen Worchel, Francisco Morales, Dario Paez and Jean Claude Deschamps, eds, *Social Identity: International Perspectives* (Los Angeles: Sage, 1998) 53 at 55; Turner and Onorato (note 6 above) at 13; Jenkins (note 2 above) at 112–13; Marilynn B. Brewer, "The Social Self: On Being the Same and Different at the Same Time" (October 1991) 17 Personality and Social Psychology Bulletin 475 at 475–6.

[8] Jenkins (note 2 above) at 102.

[9] Jan E. Stets and Peter J. Burke, "Identity, Theory and Social Identity Theory" (2000) 63 Social Psychology Quarterly 224 at 228. On the relationships between personal and collective identity, see John C. Turner, Penelope Oaks, Alexander Haslam and Craig McGarty, eds, "Self and Collective: Cognition and Social Context" (1994) 20 Personality and Social Psychology Bulletin 454.

[10] Brewer (note 7 above) at 475–7.

[11] On the importance of "role" in sociological identity theory, see also Hogg et al. (note 4 above) at 264. See also Giddens and Sutton (note 6 above) at 256–7.

to categorize individuals into groups,[12] and social categorizations – both internal and external – are cognitive tools that segment, classify and order the social environment. These categorizations do not merely organize the social world; they also provide a system of orientation for self-reference: they define the individual's place in society.[13] Individuals define themselves as belonging to some social groups; and certain aspects of their self-image are derived from the social categories to which they perceive themselves as belonging. Individuals self-categorize themselves differently according to the contexts in which they find themselves and the contingencies with which they are faced.[14] Thus, individuals always act in the context of a complex social structure out of which multiple identities emerge.[15]

Social groups, like individuals, strive to establish their identity and this group identity often outlives its members.[16] Groups interact with other groups and their individual members to construct a group identity. This collective identity has two dimensions to it: the identity of the particular group vis-à-vis its members, and the group's identity as it relates to other groups.[17] Groups strive to establish an independent identity from other groups and also struggle with group members to maintain the group's identity as equal to, if not more important than, the individual members' identity.[18]

The identity formation process begins with categorization undertaken by an external collective group or categorization that is done internally by

---

[12] See, for example, Henri Tajfel, *Human Groups and Social Categories: Studies in Social Psychology* (Cambridge: Cambridge University Press, 1981) 255–9; Phyllis Anastasio, Betty Bachman, Samuel Gaertner and John Dovidio, "Categorization, Recategorization and Common Ingroup Identity" in Russell Spears, Penelope J. Oakes, Naomi Ellemers and S. Alexander Haslam, eds, *The Social Psychology of Stereotyping and Group Life* (Oxford: Blackwell, 1997) 236.

[13] Henri Tajfel and John C. Turner, "The Social Identity of Intergroup Behaviour" in Stephen Worchel and William G. Austin, eds, *Psychology of Intergroup Relations* (Chicago: Nelson Hall, 1986) 7.

[14] Ibid. at 12. See also Stets and Burke (note 9 above) at 225; Jenkins (note 2 above) at 112–13.

[15] Jan E. Stets and Peter J. Burke, "A Sociological Approach to Self and Identity" in Mark Leary and June Tangney, eds, *Handbook of Self and Identity* (New York: Guilford Press, 2002) 9–10.

[16] Worchel (note 7 above) at 65.

[17] Ibid. at 65, 72–3. See also Alberto Melucci, "The Process of Collective Identity" in Hank Johnston and Bert Klandermans, eds, *Social Movements and Culture*, vol. 4 (Minneapolis: University of Minnesota Press, 1995) 41 at 47–8.

[18] Worchel (note 7 above) at 65. See also at 56–62 on the various stages in the development of group identity.

the individual.[19] In both cases, identity emerges (and is maintained) within a two-way relationship between self-categorization and collective categorization. Thus, individuals present themselves in a particular way and that presentation is accepted or contested by significant others, and others' responses feed back to the presenter. Similarly, individuals may internalize collective identity into their self-identity and that internalization is likely to modify the way they present themselves to others.[20] Consequently, some scholars view the identity construction process as "negotiations" between individuals and the collective.[21] Internal or external aspects of identity may be dominant at different stages of identity formation and often interact simultaneously.[22]

As discussed above, identity consists of two core elements of similarity and difference. Some scholars emphasize the role of highlighting the *differences* ("boundaries") between social groups in the process of constructing and maintaining *collective identity*.[23] From this perspective, group identification is constructed "across the group boundary";[24] highlighting difference vis-à-vis other groups generates internal similarity among the group members.[25]

The concept of identity is closely associated with the symbolic-interactionist approach in sociological literature.[26] This "micro-sociological" approach analyses social behaviour in terms of daily interactions between people, as well as between the individual and the wider social structure.[27] Symbols and rituals are often part of the formation and maintenance of group identity.[28] Symbols and community rituals

---

19 Jenkins (note 2 above) at 12, 109.

20 Ibid. at 44, 71, 93.

21 See, for example, Stets and Burke (note 9 above) at 227.

22 Jenkins (note 2 above) at 71, 78, 81, 84, 111. See also Stets and Burke (note 15 above) at 225; Hogg et al. (note 3 above) at 257.

23 Fredrik Barth, "Introduction" in Fredrik Barth, ed., *Ethnic Groups and Boundaries: The Social Organization of Culture Difference* (New York: Little, Brown & Company, 1969) 9 at 10–12; Jenkins (note 2 above) at 121, 44.

24 Jenkins (note 2 above) at 44. See also Barth (note 23 above) at 16.

25 Jenkins (note 2 above) at 12.

26 On the symbolic-interactionist approach and international law, see Moshe Hirsch, "The Sociology of International Economic Law: Sociological Analysis of the Regulation of Regional Agreements in the World Trading System" (2008) 19 EJIL 277 at 291–4.

27 On the link between social identity and the symbolic-interactionist approach, see, for example, Hogg et al. (note 3 above) at 255–6.

28 Hodaka Morita and Maroš Servátka, "Symbols, Group Identity and the Hold-Up Problem" (30 November 2011), available at http://ssrn.com/abstract=1966354 (accessed 9 January 2017); Jenkins (note 2 above) at 144.

often generate or reinforce a sense of shared belonging.[29] These symbols spawn an image of group homogeneity and often mask diversity among members of the identity group.[30] Collective narratives often contribute to the emergence and maintenance of social identities.[31]

Institutions often reflect and reinforce identities.[32] Most collective identities are institutionalized to a certain degree; and the prominent examples are ethnic or gender identities.[33] Organizations (such as nation-states) are occasionally involved in shaping social identities, and particularly in collective identification. Organizational memberships are aspects of individual identity.[34] People join organizations, inter alia, to acquire a new identity or validate an existing one.[35] Some organizations (like criminal courts) possess the capacity to authoritatively identify people (individually or collectively) as belonging to a certain group; thus stigmatizing, potentially, their incumbents.[36]

Identities often generate significant practical consequences. Once identity is activated, the main impacts relate to people's perception (including self-perception), evaluations (including self-evaluation), and behaviour towards other people. It is noteworthy that the link between identity and behaviour is neither straightforward nor always predictable. Identity is likely to have certain impacts but does not determine everything.[37] The core process underlying many consequences relates to depersonalization, that is, viewing people as a function of their respective group membership, rather than in terms of their individual characteristics or interpersonal relationships.[38]

---

[29] Morita and Servátka (note 28 above) at 1; Randall Collins, *Interaction Ritual Chains* (Princeton: Princeton University Press, 2004) 95, 98; Jenkins (note 2 above) at 135–6.

[30] Jenkins (note 2 above) at 137, 143; Collins (note 29 above) at 81–3.

[31] See, for example, Lawler (note 2 above) at 23–44; Francesca Polletta, "'It Was like a Fever . . .'. Narrative and Identity in Social Protest" (1998) 45 Social Problems 137; Klaus Eder, "A Theory of Collective Identity" (2009) 12 European Journal of Social Theory 427; Kath Woodward, *Understanding Identity* (London: Hodder Education, 2002) 28.

[32] Jenkins (note 2 above) at 45, 163.

[33] Ibid. at 163.

[34] Michael A. Hogg and Deborah J. Terry, "Social Identity Theory and Organizational Processes" in Michael A. Hogg and Deborah J. Terry, eds, *Social Identity Processes in Organizational Contexts* (Hove: Psychology Press, 2001) 1.

[35] Jenkins (note 2 above) at 180.

[36] Ibid. at 185, 198, 45. On international institutions and stigmatization, see section IV.B below.

[37] Ibid. at 6–7, 9.

[38] On the interpersonal–intergroup continuum, see Tajfel and Turner (note 13 above) at 8–10. See also Hogg et al. (note 3 above) at 261; Stets and Burke (note 9 above) at 231–2; Turner et al. (note 9 above) at 455.

Perception: At the cognitive level, the activation of social identity leads individuals identified with a group to accentuate perceived similarities between the self and other in-group members, and people tend to perceive themselves as more similar to other group members.[39] Individuals also tend to emphasize perceived similarities among the group members[40] and this stereotyped perception enhances the sense of group homogeneity.[41] On the other side of the identity boundary, identification with a group tends to sharpen the perceived differences between group members and out-group members;[42] out-group members are more likely to be perceived as undifferentiated.[43]

Evaluation: Identification with a group tends to enhance self-evaluation which constitutes a motivation for social identification.[44] The enhanced self-worth that accompanies group identity does not regularly accompany unilateral identification with a group but it rather derives from the group's acceptance of the individual as a member.[45] People identified with a particular group tend to evaluate members of the group positively[46] and to evaluate people belonging to other groups negatively.[47] Perceived similarity within the group tends to promote greater liking, trust and solidarity with in-group members.[48] Group identity is often accompanied by

---

39 Stets and Burke (note 9 above) at 225, 233; Hogg et al. (note 3 above) at 260.

40 Jenkins (note 2 above) at 114–15; Hogg et al. (note 3 above) at 260.

41 Stets and Burke (note 9 above) at 226; Hogg et al. (note 3 above) at 260; Stephan and Stephan (note 4 above) at 100 explain that one way of increasing self-esteem is to exaggerate between-group differences and minimize within-group differences on positively evaluated dimensions.

42 Jenkins (note 2 above) at 154; Hogg et al. (note 3 above) at 260. See also Stets and Burke (note 9 above) at 225.

43 Stephan and Stephan (note 4 above) at 94.

44 Stets and Burke (note 9 above) at 232, 225; Hogg et al. (note 3 above) at 260; Barbara-Ann Mullin and Michael A. Hogg, "Motivations for Group Membership: The Role of Subjective Importance and Uncertainty Reduction" (1999) 21 Basic and Applied Social Psychology 91 at 91–92; Henri Tajfel, *Human Groups and Social Categories: Studies in Social Psychology* (Cambridge: Cambridge University Press, 1981) 254.

45 Stets and Burke (note 9 above) at 233.

46 Ibid. at 226; Tajfel and Turner (note 13 above) at 13.

47 Stets and Burke (note 9 above) at 232.

48 Dominic Abrams and Michael A. Hogg, "Social Identity and Self-Categorization" in Dovidio et al. (note 4 above) 179 at 182. The general tendency of in-group members to favour members of their own group over other groups has some exceptions. Charles Stangor and John T. Jost, "Commentary: Individual, Group and System Levels of Analysis and their Relevance for Stereotyping and Intergroup Relations" in Spears et al. (note 12 above) 336 at 346.

stereotyping, that is, attributing specific personal traits to people based on their membership in a social group.[49]

Behaviour: Identification with a group demands some loyalty and behavioural conformity; and group members orient their behaviour towards other members.[50] As discussed above, the sociological analysis of identity emphasizes the important function of "social role".[51] "Enacting" that role according to the group's expectations is likely to enhance self-esteem.[52] From a legal perspective, the most undesirable impacts of social identity relate to behaviour towards non-members. Identification with a group is very often accompanied by the tendency to provide in-group members better treatment ("favouritism") and discriminatory treatment towards out-group members.[53]

Collective entities (such as states and international institutions) hold multiple identities; some are institutionalized in various legal rules, while others are semi-institutionalized in diverse soft laws or informal international groups. These identities often affect the perception, judgment and behaviour of international actors, including their positions, and the behaviour they undertake regarding international legal rules and institutions.[54]

III. THE EU'S IDENTITY, TRADE POLICY AND THE PROMOTION OF HUMAN RIGHTS NORMS

A. International Institutions' Identity

The formation and activities of international institutions often reflect collective identities. Membership in these organizations often represents various identity ties, such as regional (for example, Organization for

---

[49] Stephen Worchel and Hank Rothgerber, "Changing the Stereotype of the Stereotype" in Spears et al. (note 48 above) 72 at 74–8.

[50] See for example, Jenkins (note 2 above) at 157–8.

[51] Giddens and Sutton (note 6 above) at 307–8; Stets and Burke (note 9 above) at 227.

[52] Hogg et al. (note 3 above) at 257–8.

[53] Ibid. at 260; Tajfel and Turner (note 13 above) at 13; Stets and Burke (note 9 above) at 232; Jenkins (note 2 above) at 7; Stephan and Stephan (note 4 above) at 92–3.

[54] On the mutual links between social identities and international law, see Moshe Hirsch, *Invitation to the Sociology of International Law* (Oxford: Oxford University Press, 2015) Ch 4 at 104–6, 116–26.

American States that also represent certain ideological traits);[55] religious (for example, Organization for the Islamic Conference);[56] historical (for example, the Commonwealth of Nations);[57] or ideological (for example, NATO).[58] The identity of an international institution[59] regularly coexists with (and is often related to) its members' national identities, as well as with the identities of other international institutions with whom it is affiliated. The latter identity link is prominent concerning the ties between the Islamic Conference, the Arab League and the African Union,[60] or between the European Union (EU) and the Council of Europe.[61]

Like other identity groups, international institutions often have symbols,[62] including flags, anthems,[63] a special memorial day (for example,

---

55 See, for example, the website of the Organization of American States, "Who We Are", http://www.oas.org/en/about/who_we_are.asp (accessed 9 January 2017).

56 Said Mahmoudi, "Organization of the Islamic Conference" in Rüdiger Wolfrum, ed., *Max Planck Encyclopaedia of Public International Law* (Oxford: Oxford University Press, 2009), available at opil.ouplaw.com/home/EPIL (accessed 9 January 2017).

57 On the Commonwealth of Nations and its links to the British Empire, see Laurie Fransman, "Commonwealth Subjects and Nationality Rules" in Wolfrum (note 56 above).

58 On the collective identity and the ideology of NATO, see, for example, Christopher Hemmer and Peter J. Katzenstein, "Why is There No NATO in Asia? Collective Identity, Regionalism, and the Origins of Multilateralism" (2002) 56 International Organization 575 at 587–8.

59 On the stages of development of international organizations' identity in light of developmental psychological literature, see Sungjoon Cho, "An International Organization's Identity Crisis" (2014) 34 Northwestern Journal of International Law and Business 359 at 373–83.

60 See for example, Mahmoudi (note 56 above) at para 5.

61 The Council of Europe quotes Juncker in its official website: "the Council of Europe and the European Union were products of the same idea, the same spirit and the same ambition. They mobilised the energy and commitment of the same founding fathers of Europe": *The Council of Europe's Relations with the European Union*, available at http://pjp-eu.coe.int/en/web/south-programme2/themes/-/asset_publisher/uy8MSISGcuDC/content/cepejcourtofappealfezoctober2015?redirect=%2Fen%2Fweb%2Fsouth-programme2%2Fthemes&inheritRedirect=true (accessed 9 January 2017).

62 The link between the symbol of the Organization of American States (OAS) and its identity is clarified by the organization's statement: "The logo of the Organization . . . is the central element of the institutional identity of the Organization". The official website of the OAS is http://www.oas.org/en/about/logo.asp (accessed 9 January 2016).

63 On the ASEAN's flag, see the Charter of the Association of Southeast Asian Nations (adopted 20 November 2007, entered into force 15 December 2008) 2624 UNTS 223 (ASEAN), art 37.

to celebrate the establishment of the organization)[64] and, occasionally, collective narratives as well.[65]

The identities of international organizations may be discerned from their constituent documents,[66] and particularly from provisions regarding the admission of new members and exclusion/suspension of existing members[67] which highlight the "boundaries" between them and other international groups. Similarly, the practice of international institutions in other spheres (such as sanctions imposed on non-members) and decisions adopted by their judicial organs, also contribute to the formation or change of their identity. Occasionally, the basic instruments of international institutions expressly aim to construct a common identity.[68] Thus, for example, the Constitutive Treaty of the Union of South American Nations affirms the members' "determination to build a South American identity".[69]

States occasionally join international institutions to reaffirm their identity, and many states are interested in admission to an organization like the Organisation for Economic Co-operation and Development (OECD) that projects an image of a "prestigious club"[70] or the "rich

---

64 On the Pan American Day and the Organization of American States, see Pan-American Day April 14, available at http://www.oas.org/columbus/PanAmericanDay.asp (accessed 9 January 2017); on the ASEAN Day, see ASEAN, art 39. See also Southern Africa Development Community (SADC) Anthem, available at http://www.sadc.int/files/5713/7883/0057/SADC_Anthem_Objectives.pdf (accessed 9 January 2017).

65 See also, OAS, "Our History", available at http://www.oas.org/en/about/our_history.asp (accessed 9 January 2017). On the EU's collective narrative, see further below.

66 Mahmoudi (note 56 above) at para 5 notes that the Charter of the 1972 Charter of the Organization of the Islamic Conference was inspired by the Charter of the Arab League and the Charter of the Organization of African Union.

67 See, for example, the 1992 OAS Protocol of Washington (which amended the OAS Charter by adding a new art 9) which stipulates the suspension of any member whose democratically elected government has been overthrown by force. On this amendment and the practice of OAS in that regard, see Konstantinos D. Magliveras, *Exclusion from Participation in International Organisations* (The Hague: Kluwer, 1999) 165, 171–4.

68 See, for example, ASEAN, arts 35 and 1(14).

69 Third recital of the Preamble to the South American Union of Nations Constitutive Treaty (signed 23 May 2008, entered into force 11 March 2011) 2742 UNTS.

70 See, for example, regarding South Korean membership in the OECD, Dong–Chon Suh, "Trade and Financial Liberalization in South Korea and Implications for Southeast Asia" in Daljit Singh and Reza Y Siregar, eds, *ASEAN and Korea* (Institute for Southeast Asian Studies, Singapore, 1997) 49 at 68.

man's club".[71] International institutions also affect the international identity of states (including non-members) by classifying them according to level of "development" (for example, "least developed states" or "developed states")[72] or the quality of their governance.[73] Decisions by international organizations (including their tribunals) labelling a particular state "aggressive"[74] or imposing sanctions on another, may contribute to the preservation or modification of state identity (for example, as a "pariah state").

B. The European Union's Identity as Human Rights Promoter Worldwide

1. EU identity

The topic of European identity and its links with the EU drew the attention of numerous scholars.[75] EU institutions are involved in the construction of European identity and they have constructed (occasionally together with the Council of Europe) various symbols of collective identity. As discussed above,[76] symbols and rituals are often involved in the formation and main-

---

71 On the OECD as the "rich man club", see, for example, Thalif Deen, "Chile to Join the 'Rich Man's Club'" *Inter Press Service* (21 December 2009), available at http://www.ipsnews.net/2009/12/development-chile-to-join-the-rich-mans-club/ (accessed 9 January 2017).

72 On the classification of states in accordance with their level of economic development, see, for example, the Human Development Index (HDI), developed by the UN Development Program (UNDP), available at http://hdr.undp.org/en/statistics/ (accessed 9 January 2017); The World Bank, Country and Lending Groups, available at http://data.worldbank.org/about/country-classifications (accessed 9 January 2017).

73 See the World Bank's *Worldwide Governance Indicators* (WGI), available at http://info.worldbank.org/governance/wgi/index.aspx#home (accessed 9 January 2017); Daniel Kaufmann, Aart Kraay and Massimo Mastruzzi, "The Worldwide Governance Indicators: Methodology and Analytical Issues" (2011) 3 Hague Journal on the Rule of Law 220.

74 See the UN Charter, art 39.

75 See, for example, Juan Diez Medrano, "The Public Sphere and the European Union's Political Identity" in Jeffrey T. Checkel and Peter J. Katzenstein, eds, *European Identity* (Cambridge: Cambridge University Press, 2009) 81 and the references therein. For a survey of political science literature on European identity and the European Union, see Erik Jones, "Identity and Solidarity" in Erik Jones, Anand Menon and Stephen Weatherill, eds, *The Oxford Handbook of the European Union* (Oxford: Oxford University Press, 2012) 690. See also Jeffrey Checkel and Peter Katzenstein, "The Politicization of European Identities" in Jeffrey T. Checkel and Peter J. Katzenstein, eds, *European Identity* (Cambridge: Cambridge University Press, 2009) 1.

76 See section II above.

tenance of group identity. Symbols and community rituals often generate or reinforce a sense of shared belonging. Thus, for example, the EU[77] Parliament adopted the European flag in 1983 (previously adopted by the Council of Europe);[78] the EU's leaders officially adopted the European anthem in 1985 (formerly adopted by the Council of Europe),[79] and the EU's institutions annually celebrate Europe Day (9 May) in which the collective memory of the 1950 Schuman Declaration and the ensuing moral lessons are reinforced.[80] As noted below, the EU's members also published a formal decision on the European Identity in 1973.

Additional practical frameworks implemented by the EU's institutions also project out the European identity,[81] including the common currency (adopted by most EU members),[82] vehicle registration plates (since 1998),[83] and the eu domain name extension (since 2006).[84]

---

[77] On the EU's "narratives of projection" (and specifically regarding the WTO), see Kalypso Nicolaidis and Robert Howse, "'This is my EUtopia' . . .: Narrative and Power" (2002) 40 Journal of Common Market Studies 767.

[78] European Union, *The European flag*, available at http://europa.eu/about-eu/basic-information/symbols/flag/index_en.htm (accessed 10 January 2017).

[79] European Union, *The European Anthem*, available at http://europa.eu/about-eu/basic-information/symbols/anthem/index_en.htm (accessed 10 January 2017).

[80] European Union, *Europe Day – EU Open Doors*, available at http://europa.eu/about-eu/basic-information/symbols/europe-day/index_en.htm#why_europe_day (accessed 10 January 2017); European Union, *The Schuman Declaration – 9 May 1950*, available at http://europa.eu/european-union/about-eu/symbols/europe-day/schuman-declaration_en (accessed 10 January 2017). On the commemorative rituals that have developed since 1957 to mark the anniversaries of the signing of the Rome Treaty, see Hannes Hansen-Magnusson and Jenny Wustenberg, "Forging European Memory: The Treaties of Rome as a Common Tradition in the Making?" (Paper prepared for the Biennial Conference of the European Union Studies Association, Boston, 3–5 March 2011).

[81] On the impacts of symbols on European identity, see Michael Bruter, "Winning Hearts and Minds for Europe: The Impact of News and Symbols on Civic and Cultural European Identity" (2003) 36 Comparative Political Studies 1148 at 1165–7.

[82] On the links between the common currency and European collective identity, see, for example, Jean Pisani-Ferry and Adam S. Posen, eds, *The Euro at Ten: The Next Global Currency?* (Washington: Peterson Institute for International Economics, 2009) 1; Giles Bootheway, "The Symbolic Value of the Euro in the Eurozone Crisis" (2012) 19 Proceedings of ASBBS 77 at 77 et seq., available at http://asbbs.org/files/ASBBS2012V1/PDF/B/BoothewayG.pdf (accessed 10 January 2017).

[83] Council Regulation (EC) No. 2411/98 of 3 November 1998 on the recognition in intra-Community traffic of the distinguishing sign of the Member State in which motor vehicles and their trailers are registered, [1998] OJ L299/1.

[84] European Union, "Top level domain .eu", available at http://ec.europa.eu/ipg/basics/urls/doteu_en.htm (accessed 10 January 2017).

2. EU identity and human rights

Norms often constitute a significant element of collective identity, and the social constructivist approach in international relations literature[85] emphasizes the link between social identity and "constitutive norms" defining group membership.[86] International human rights norms have a particular status in that regard and they occasionally play a significant role in defining the identity of organizations of democratic and liberal states.[87]

The founding treaties of the European Economic Community (EEC) were generally silent on the subject of human rights, reflecting primarily the EEC's economic nature.[88] As envisaged in 1957, human rights were to be protected by individual member states through their national constitutions and laws. In addition, since each original member of the EEC was also a party to the European Convention on Human Rights (ECHR) and subject to the jurisdiction of the European Court of Human Rights, the human rights of their residents were internationally protected by the Court.[89]

On the internal level, human rights have only gradually emerged in EU law through the case law of the European Court of Justice (since

---

[85] Collective identity is a core concept of the social constructivist approach in contemporary international relations literature. See, for example, Peter J. Katzenstein, Ronald L. Jepperson and Alexander Wendt, "Norms, Identity, and Culture in National Security" in Peter J. Katzenstein, ed., *The Culture of National Security: Norms and Identity in World Politics* (New York: Columbia University Press, 1996) 33 at 54.

[86] Rawi Abdelal, Yoshiko M. Herrera, Alastair Iain Johnston and Rose McDermott, eds, "Identity as a Variable" (2006) 4 Perspectives on Politics 695 at 697–8. For Reus-Smit, state societies have been based on fundamental moral purposes derived from their identity. Jack Donnelly, "The Ethics of Realism" in Christian Reus-Smit and Duncan Snidal, eds, *The Oxford Handbook of International Relations* (Oxford: Oxford University Press, 2008) 150 at 156.

[87] See, for example, Thomas Risse and Kathryn Sikkink, "The Socialization of International Human Rights Norms into Domestic Practices: Introduction" in Thomas Risse, Stephen C. Ropp and Kathryn Sikkink, eds, *The Power of Human Rights* (Cambridge: Cambridge University Press, 1999) 1 at 12.

[88] Gráinne De Búrca, "The Evolution of EU Human Rights Law" in Paul Craig and Gráinne De Búrca, eds, *The Evolution of EU Law*, 2nd edn (Oxford: Oxford University Press, 2011) 465 at 475; Giuseppe Balducci, "The Study of the EU Promotion of Human Rights" in Knud Erik Jørgensen and Katie Verlin Laatikainen, eds, *Routledge Handbook on the European Union and International Institutions* (London: Routledge, 2013) 185 at 193; Elizabeth F. Defeis, "Human Rights and the European Court of Justice: An Appraisal" (2007) 31 Fordham International Law Journal 1104 at 1106.

[89] Defeis (note 88 above) at 1107 (and see the references therein).

1969).[90] On the external level, human rights were initially promoted through the intergovernmental European Political Cooperation (EPC) in 1970.[91] The ECJ derived fundamental human rights from the common constitutional traditions and international human rights obligations of the member states.[92] Urged by the European Parliament (EP) and the growing concern with the external role and perception of the EU in the world at the time, the European Council issued a declaration on European identity in 1973.[93] The EP began, during the 1970s, to request the EEC to include human rights conditionality in its development aid programs;[94] however, the first multinational development agreement to include such a clear human rights clause was the 1989 Fourth Lomé Convention between the EEC and African-Caribbean-Pacific countries.[95]

Since the establishment of the EPC, and particularly after the end of the Cold War, EU bodies have repeatedly stated that human rights protection constitutes a *constitutive norm*.[96] Thus, for example, Article 2 of the Treaty on European Union (TEU) solemnly states that:

---

[90] See, for example, European Parliament, "A Comparative Study of EU and US Approaches to Human Rights in External Relations" (Directorate-General for External Policies, November 2014) at 18–19 and see the references therein, at http://www.europarl.europa.eu/RegData/etudes/STUD/2014/534981/EXPO_STU(2014)534981_EN.pdf (accessed 10 January 2017). See, for example, Defeis (note 88 above) at 1108 et seq.

[91] Stefan Kadelbach, "Charter of Fundamental Rights of the European Union" in Rüdiger Wolfrum, ed., *Max Planck Encyclopaedia of Public International Law* (Oxford: Oxford University Press, 2013), paras 1–6, available at opil.ouplaw.com/home/EPIL (accessed 10 January 2017) (and see the references therein); De Búrca (note 88 above) at 475; Balducci (note 88 above) at 193.

[92] Kadelbach (note 91 above) at para 6.

[93] De Burca (note 88 above) at 479; Balducci (note 88 above) at 193.

[94] Balducci (note 88 above) at 193.

[95] Article 5(1) of the Fourth Lomé Agreement provided as follows: "Cooperation shall be directed towards development centred on man, the main protagonist and beneficiary of development, which thus entails respect for and promotion of all human rights. Cooperation operations shall thus be conceived in accordance with the positive approach, where respect for human rights is recognized as a basic factor of real development and where cooperation is conceived as a contribution to the promotion of these rights." Fourth ACP – EEC Convention (signed 15 December 1989), available at http://www.epg.acp.int/fileadmin/user_upload/LomeIV1989.pdf (accessed 10 January 2017).

[96] On human rights as "core values" of the EU, see also European Union, *Human Rights and Democracy*, available at http://eeas.europa.eu/human_rights/index_en.htm (accessed 10 January 2017).

> The Union is founded on the values of respect for human dignity, freedom, democracy, equality, the rule of law and respect for human rights, including the rights of persons belonging to minorities. . . [97]

The Preamble to the Charter of Fundamental Rights of the European Union underlines this by stating that:

> The peoples of Europe . . . are resolved to share a peaceful future based on common values. Conscious of its spiritual and moral heritage, the Union is founded on the indivisible, universal values of human dignity, freedom, equality and solidarity; it is based on the principles of democracy and the rule of law. . . [98]

The central role of human rights protection in the *EU identity*[99] was explicitly emphasized by the EU's bodies. Thus, for example,[100] the EU Commission states that: "the European Union has gradually come to define itself in terms of the promotion of those [human] rights and democratic freedoms".[101] In the "Document on The European Identity" (1973), the EU's foreign ministers clarified that:

> . . . Sharing as they do the same attitudes to life, based on a determination to build a society which measures up to the needs of the individual, they are determined to defend the principles of representative democracy, of the rule of law, of social justice – which is the ultimate goal of economic progress – and of respect for human rights. All of these are *fundamental elements of the European Identity* . . . .[102] (emphasis added)

---

[97] Consolidated Version of the Treaty on European Union, OJ C83/13 EN.

[98] Charter of Fundamental Rights of the European Union, OJ C83/389 EN.

[99] On the central role of human rights in the EU's identity, see also Marise Cremona, "Values in the EU Foreign Policy" in Malcolm Evans and Panos Koutrakos, eds, *Beyond the Established Legal Orders: Policy Interconnections between the EU and the Rest of the World* (Oxford: Hart Publishing, 2011) 275 at 307. Bjorn Kleizen, "Externalizing EU Law, Policy and Values: Europe's Global Identity, Mechanisms of Rule Transfer and Case Studies on Illegal Logging and Bosnia and Herzegovina" (19 December 2015) 7, available at http://ssrn.com/abstract=2706564 (accessed 10 January 2017).

[100] See also, Commission Communication, *The European Union and the External Dimension of Human Rights Policy: From Rome to Maastricht and Beyond* COM(95) 567 final at 5.

[101] Ibid. at para 12. See also Marise Cremona, "Values in the EU Constitution: The External Dimension", Centre on Democracy, Development, and the Rule of Law (2004) 26 Stanford Institute for International Studies 2.

[102] Declaration on European Identity published by the Nine Foreign Ministers (Copenhagen, 14 December 1973), available at http://www.cvce.eu/content/

The EU's institutions are legally committed to comply with fundamental human rights[103] and they may suspend certain membership rights of member states which seriously and persistently breach these norms.[104] As noted above,[105] identities of international institutions may particularly be discerned from provisions regarding the admission of new members which highlight the "boundaries" between them and other international groups. Any European country that wishes to become a member of the EU must satisfy the existing members' and the EU institutions' provisions that it respects human rights and is committed to applying them.[106] In addition, accession to the ECHR constitutes a de facto condition for EU membership[107] and the EU itself shall accede to the Convention.[108]

The EU's human rights policies are particularly pronounced in its external relations with other international actors. The EU often presents itself as human rights promoter in the international arena.[109] This external

---

publication/1999/1/1/02798dc9-9c69-4b7d-b2c9-f03a8db7da32/publishable_en.pdf (accessed 10 January 2017).

103 See TEU, art 3(1); EU Charter of Fundamental Rights, art 51.

104 TEU, art 7. See also Manfred Nowak, "Human Rights 'Conditionality' in Relation to Entry to, and Full Participation in, the EU" in Philip Alston, ed., *The EU and Human Rights* (Oxford: Oxford University Press, 1999) 687 at 690. On the link between certain sanctions operated by the EU members against Austria in 2000 and the EU identity, see Stefan Seidendorf, "Defining Europe Against its Past? – Memory Politics and the Sanctions against Austria in France and Germany" (2005) 6 German Law Journal 439 at 443 et seq.

105 See section III.A above.

106 TEU, art 49; European Council in Copenhagen: Conclusions of the Presidency (22 June 1993) DOC/93/3 Date: 22/06/1993 ("Copenhagen Criteria"), art 7(A)(iii). On the link between this condition to become a member of the EU and the underlying identity of the EU, see Helene Sjursen, "Why Expand? The Question of Legitimacy and Justification in the EU's Enlargement Policy" (2002) 40 Journal of Common Market Studies 491 at 508.

107 See, for example, Gwendolyn Sasse, "EU Conditionality and Minority Rights: Translating the Copenhagen Criterion into Policy" (2005) EUI Working Papers RSCAS No. 2005/16 1, available at http://sar.org.ro/wp-content/uploads/2013/01/EU-conditionality-and-minority-rights-Translating-Copenhagen-criterion-into-policy.pdf (accessed 10 January 2017).

108 TEU, art 6.

109 See, for example, Giuseppe Balducci, "The study of the EU promotion of human rights: the importance of international and internal factors" (October 2008) GARNET Working Paper No. 61/08 3 at 16. See also Cremona (note 101 above) at 7 et seq. See also Gráinne de Búrca, "The European Courts and the Security Council: Between Dédoublement Fonctionnel and Balancing of Values: Three Replies to Pasquale De Sena and Maria Chiara Vitucci" (2009) 20 EJIL 853.

feature of EU identity arises, for example, from Articles 3(5)[110] and 21(1)[111] TEU,[112] as well as from diverse public documents published by EU bodies. Thus, for instance,[113] the EU Council stated in a "strategic" document in 2012 that:

> The European Union is founded on a shared determination to promote peace and stability *and to build a world founded on respect for human rights*, democracy and the rule of law. *These principles underpin all aspects of the internal and external policies of the European Union*. . .
>
> The EU will continue to throw its full weight behind advocates of liberty, democracy and human rights throughout the world. . . *The EU will speak out against any attempt to undermine respect for universality of human rights*.[114] (emphasis added)

This perceived role of the EU in the international community is also emphasized in the EU's official website: "The European Union sees human

---

110 TEU, art 3(5) provides as follows: "5. *In its relations with the wider world*, the Union shall uphold and promote its values and interests and contribute to the protection of its citizens. It shall contribute to peace, security, the sustainable development of the Earth, solidarity and mutual respect among peoples, free and fair trade, eradication of poverty and the *protection of human rights*, in particular the rights of the child, as well as to the strict observance and the development of international law, including respect for the principles of the United Nations Charter" (emphasis added).

111 TEU, art 21(1) provides that "1. *The Union's action on the international scene shall be guided by the principles* which have inspired its own creation, development and enlargement, and which it seeks to advance in the wider world: democracy, the rule of law, the universality and *indivisibility of human rights and fundamental freedoms*, respect for human dignity, the principles of equality and solidarity, and respect for the principles of the United Nations Charter and international law" (emphasis added).

112 On arts 3(5) and 21 of the TEU, see Lorand Bartels, "The EU's Human Rights Obligations in Relation to Policies with Extraterritorial Effects" (2014) 25 EJIL 1071 at 1073–5.

113 See also *Joint Communication to the European Parliament and the Council, Human Rights and Democracy at the Heart of EU external action – towards a more effective approach* (12 December 2011) COM(2011) 886 final at 4, available at http://eur-lex.europa.eu/LexUriServ/LexUriServ.do?uri=COM:2011:0886:FIN:EN:PDF (accessed 10 January 2017); Council of the European Union, *Council Conclusions on the Action Plan on Human Rights and Democracy 2015–2019* (20 July 2015), available at http://eeas.europa.eu/human_rights/docs/action-plan-on-human-rights-and-democracy-2015-2019_en.pdf (accessed 10 January 2017).

114 Council of the European Union, *EU Strategic Framework and Action Plan on Human Rights and Democracy* (25 June 2012) 11855/12 at 1–2, available at http://www.consilium.europa.eu/uedocs/cms_data/docs/pressdata/EN/foraff/131181.pdf (accessed 10 January 2017).

rights as universal and indivisible. It actively promotes and defends them both within its borders and when engaging in relations with non-EU countries".[115]

As previously noted, identity consists of two core elements of similarity (mainly on the internal level) and difference (mainly on the external level). Individuals and groups need a certain level of both similarity and differentiation from others, and social identity derives from the tension between the sense of belonging and the sense of distinctiveness.[116] An analysis of the EU's current constitutional framework for human rights protection reveals a clear difference between the importance accorded to human rights in EU external relations as compared with internal relations.[117] The existing constitutional framework (with the exception of anti-discrimination law) assigns a more circumscribed role to human rights within the context of internally focused EU policies, and the dominant focus is external, empowering and even obliging the EU to promote human rights actively in its international policies.[118]

This EU bifurcated approach may be explained by some sociological literature that emphasizes the role of highlighting social differences ("boundaries") between the social group and other groups in the process of constructing and maintaining collective identity. Emphasizing differences vis-à-vis other groups generates internal similarity among the group's members.[119] The EU's emphasis on external human rights policies underlines its identity as a liberal-democratic group[120] towards other international groups.

3. The EU's social role as a human rights promoter worldwide

Sociological literature underlines the link between social identity and social role; underscoring that, having a particular identity often pressures individuals and groups to behave according to social expectations related to their particular role.[121] Where people identify with a group or social role, they tend to adopt the meaning that accompanies that particular identity, and act accordingly to represent that meaning.[122] The above-discussed

---

115 European Union, *Human Rights and Democracy*, available at http://eeas.europa.eu/human_rights/index_en.htm (accessed 10 January 2017).

116 See section II above.

117 De Búrca (note 88 above) at 491, 492–4.

118 Ibid. at 467 and see the references therein; see also at 494.

119 See section II above.

120 On the role of human rights norms in defining identities of liberal states, see Risse and Sikkink (note 87 above) at 1–2.

121 See section II above.

122 Stets and Burke (note 9 above) at 227; see also Hogg et al. (note 3 above) at 256; Stets and Burke (note 15 above) at 11 et seq.

self-representation of the EU as a promoter of human rights worldwide[123] has been significantly accepted in the international community, and has led to the construction of a social role regarding the protection of human rights in the international system. Recognition of the EU's role is discernible, for instance, from literature,[124] statements of human rights organizations,[125] and the awarding of the Nobel Prize for contribution to the advancement of peace, democracy and human rights.[126]

This social role of the EU in the international community influences the behaviour of EU institutions and other international actors in this field. For example, if a certain state commits serious and extensive violations of human rights, expectations that the EU will react and adopt some measures against that state are likely to arise. Such expectations create social pressure on the EU and affect its behaviour in the international system.

---

[123] See, for example, the EU statements cited above in this section (such as the 2012 "strategic paper"). On the EU self-representation regarding the emphasis of values in its foreign policy, see also, Sonia Lucarelli, "Introduction: Values, Principles, Identity and European Union Foreign Policy" in Sonia Lucarelli and Ian Manners, eds, *Values and Principles in European Union Foreign Policy* (London: Routledge, 2006) 1 at 2–4.

[124] See, for example, Balducci (note 109 above) at 1–3, 16–21; Joseph S. Nye, *Soft Power* (New York: Public Affairs, 2004) at 76, 80; Richard Gowan and Franziska Brantner, "A Global Force for Human Rights? An Audit of European Power at the UN" (2008) European Council on Foreign Relations Policy Paper 1 at 8, available at http://www.ecfr.eu/page/-/ECFR-08_A_GLOBAL_FORCE_FOR_HUMAN_RIGHTS-_AN_AUDIT_OF_EUROPEAN_POWER_AT_THE_UN.pdf (accessed 10 January 2017).

[125] Thus, the Human Rights Watch's World Report (2015) states as follows: "The EU continued to play a leadership role on certain country resolutions at the UN Human Rights Council and UN General Assembly, including on Belarus, North Korea, and Burma, securing continuation of important UN reporting mechanisms for all three countries. But the EU failed to play a leading role in bringing new human rights crisis, such as the recent crackdown in Egypt or the situation in Uzbekistan, to the agenda of multilateral forums": Human Rights Watch, "World Report 2015: European Union" (2015), available at https://www.hrw.org/world-report/2015/country-chapters/croatia-european-union-france-germany-greece-hungary-italy (accessed 10 January 2017). See also OCHCR, "Migrant crisis: 'High time for Europe to reclaim a leading role in human rights' – UN experts", available at http://www.ohchr.org/EN/NewsEvents/Pages/DisplayNews.aspx?NewsID=16592&LangID=E (accessed 10 January 2017).

[126] Nobel Prize Committee Website, "European Union (EU) – Facts" (21 May 2014), available at http://www.nobelprize.org/nobel_prizes/peace/laureates/2012/eu-facts.html (accessed 10 January 2017).

C. External Trade Instruments and the Promotion of Human Rights

The EU's identity as a human rights promoter is projected outwards through a variety of frameworks[127] and this section focuses on trade measures. The two principal trade instruments in this sphere are conditioned preferences for developing countries[128] and human rights clauses in trade agreements with non-members. These trade instruments (elaborated below) illustrate the local (European) adaptation of global human rights standards.

Trade preferences granted to developing countries (in addition to those prescribed under WTO law) are regulated by the EU's "Generalized System of Preferences" (GSP) legislation, and such preferences are conditioned by compliance with certain requirements relating to human rights.[129] The 2012 GSP Regulation elaborates the conditions that beneficiary countries included in the "special incentive arrangement" (GSP+)[130] must comply with including: the ratification of a series of international human rights

---

[127] See, for example, European Commission, *Furthering Human Rights and Democracy Across the Globe* (2007), available at http://eeas.europa.eu/human_rights/docs/brochure07_en.pdf (accessed 10 January 2017); European Union, *EU Strategic Framework on Human Rights and Democracy* (25 June 2012), available at http://www.consilium.europa.eu/uedocs/cms_data/docs/pressdata/EN/foraff/131169.pdf (accessed 10 January 2017). On various policy strategies adopted by the Commission to integrate human rights in development cooperation, see David D'Hollander, Axel Marx and Jan Wouters, "Integrating Human Rights in EU Development Cooperation Policy: Achievements and Challenges" (April 2014) Leuven Centre for Global Governance Studies Working Paper No. 134 at 5–7, available at http://www.fp7-frame.eu/wp-content/materiale/w-papers/WP134-DHollander-Marx-Woutersx.pdf (accessed 10 January 2017).

[128] On the legality of conditioned trade preference to developing countries under the WTO law, see WTO, "European Communities – Conditions for the Granting of Tariff Preferences to Developing Countries – Report of the Appellate Body" (7 April 2004) WT/DS246/AB/R at paras 173–89; Peter Van den Bossche and Werner Zdouc, *The Law and Policy of the World Trade Organization: Text, Cases and Materials*, 3rd edn (Cambridge: Cambridge University Press, 2013) 330–5.

[129] Lorand Bartels, *Human Rights Conditionality in the EU's International Agreements* (Oxford: Oxford University Press, 2005) 7–12, 68–70.

[130] See art 1(2)(b) Council Regulation (EU) No 978/2012 of the European Parliament and Council of 25 October 2012, applying a scheme of generalised tariff preferences and repealing Council Regulation (EC) No 732/2008, [2012] OJ L303/1 (hereinafter, "EU GSP Regulation"). As of 28 January 2016, 14 countries are involved in the GSP+ program. See European Commission, "Trade policy promotes sustainability and human rights" (28 January 2016), available at http://europa.eu/rapid/press-release_IP-16-169_en.htm (accessed 10 January 2017).

conventions (listed in its Annex VIII);[131] the absence of unlawful reservations to these conventions;[132] and no identification of serious failure to effectively implement any of those conventions (as determined by the "relevant conventions monitoring bodies").[133] These tariff preferences are to be temporarily withdrawn if the beneficiary country does not fulfil the above requirements or fails to cooperate with the Union's monitoring procedures set out in this Regulation.[134]

Since 1992,[135] the EU's trade agreements with third parties have included a "human rights clause" requiring the parties to respect human rights and democratic principles.[136] In 1995 the EU Council adopted a formal policy of including such clauses in all future cooperation and trade agreements[137] and they are contained in agreements with over 120 countries.[138] The recent human rights provisions present a similar structure: (i) a basic obligation to comply with human rights; (ii) a provision allowing a party to undertake appropriate measures in case of breach of the above "essential clause"; and (iii) monitoring and implementation provisions.[139] Thus, for example, Article 2 of the EU–Jordan Association Agreement (2002) provides that:

> Relations between the Parties, as well as all the provisions of the Agreement itself, shall be based on respect of democratic principles and fundamental human rights as set out in the Universal Declaration on Human Rights, which

---

131 EU GSP Regulation, art 9(1)(b).

132 Ibid., art 9(1)(c).

133 Ibid., art 9(1)(b).

134 Ibid., Preamble.

135 On the evolution of such human rights provisions in the EU treaties, see Bartels (note 129 above) at 12 et seq.

136 Lorand Bartels, "Human Rights and Sustainable Development Obligations in EU Free Trade Agreements" (September 2012) Legal Studies Research Paper Series University of Cambridge Faculty of Law 1; Communication from the Commission to the Council and the European Parliament, *The European Union's role in promoting human rights and democratisation in third countries* COM/2001/0252 final; D. Sicurelli, "The EU as a Promoter of Human Rights in Bilateral Trade Agreements: The Case of the Negotiations with Vietnam" (2015) 11:2 Journal of Contemporary European Research 230 at 231, 235.

137 Bartels (note 136 above) at 3.

138 European Parliament, *The European Parliament's Role in Relation to Human Rights in Trade and Investment Agreements* (February 2014) at 6, available at http://www.europarl.europa.eu/RegData/etudes/etudes/join/2014/433751/EXPO-JOIN_ET(2014)433751_EN.pdf (accessed 10 January 2017).

139 Ibid. at 8. Regarding the above second element ("non-execution clause"), these measures must be taken in accordance with the relevant rules of international law: see Bartels (note 136 above) at 7.

guides their internal and international policy and constitutes an essential element of this Agreement.[140]

IV. APPRAISAL: SOCIAL IDENTITY AND COMPLIANCE WITH HUMAN RIGHTS LAW

The fact that the above trade instruments are significantly motivated by the EU's collective identity and its perceived role as a human rights promoter worldwide leads to several conclusions regarding compliance with international human rights legal rules in this context. As elaborated below, collective identities are involved in the operation of trade measures against human rights violators, as well as the reaction by states targeted by such measures.

A. In-group Identity and Compliance with Norms

Social identity often constitutes an influential factor that promotes compliance with group's norms. Sociological deviance literature discusses a variety of societal factors involved in compliance and breach of norms, including external motivations (such as "social control") and internal motivations (such as identity).[141] One of the consequences of the formation of group identity relates to compliance with the group's norms.[142] As discussed above, the link between identity and compliance with international norms is particularly significant as regards the "constitutive norms" defining group membership.[143] Compliance motivated by the sense of belonging to the group does not necessarily depend on social control mechanisms; and conformity with norms may take place where the actor's activity is invisible to other members of the group.

---

140 EURO-MEDITERRANEAN AGREEMENT establishing an Association between the European Communities and their Member States, of the one part, and the Hashemite Kingdom of Jordan, of the other part (15 May 2002) OJ L129/3, art 2.

141 See, for example, Hirsch (note 54 above) at 172–4 (and see the references therein).

142 Goodman and Jinks highlight the link between identity and acculturation: "The touchstone of this mechanism is that identification with a reference group generates varying degrees of cognitive and social pressures – real or imagined – to conform": Ryan Goodman and Derek Jinks, "How to Influence States: Socialization and International Human Rights Law" (2004) 54 Duke Law Journal 621 at 626. See also Ryan Goodman and Derek Jinks, "Incomplete Internalization and Compliance with Human Rights Law" (2008) 19 EJIL 725 at 726.

143 See section III.B above.

Since human rights are a constitutive element in the EU's identity as a Western-liberal community[144] and EU membership signals acquiring or validating existing international identity, these factors exert significant influence on the 28 members of this prestigious group (new and older ones) to comply with international human rights law. The above-discussed EU legal rules regarding conditioned accession to the EU and suspension of membership rights reflect and reinforce this important feature of EU group membership. The EU's identity, however, does not ensure that all members comply with its human rights norms. Generally, a member whose bond with the group is weak (or socially alienated from the group) is less likely to be committed to the group's norms.[145] From this perspective, if an EU member is significantly less identified with the group, or perceives itself as socially marginalized in the European Community, it is more likely to breach the group's norms, including those relating to human rights.

B. Trade Sanctions and International Social Labelling

As already noted, certain international institutions possess the capacity to authoritatively identify people or groups as belonging to a certain category and thus may affect the identity of and stigmatize their incumbents.[146] The suspension of trade benefits by the EU (for example, under the GSP program) carries not only certain economic consequences but also a signal by a significant human rights actor classifying that particular country as a violator of international human rights norms. This international social labelling is significant to the targeted states, occasionally more than the economic consequences of trade sanctions. From this perspective, the volume of trade flows affected by the EU's measures is not the crucial factor, but rather the accompanied social marker. Stigmatization effects influence the prospects of compliance with international human rights

---

[144] See, for example, Frank Schimmelfennig, "The Community Trap: Liberal Norms, Rhetorical Action, and the Eastern Enlargement of the European Union" (2001) 55 International Organization 47 at 59 (and see the references therein).

[145] On the link between weak bond to society and noncompliance, see Paul Rock, "Sociological Theories of Crime" in Mike Maguire, Rod Morgan and Robert Reiner, eds, *The Oxford Handbook of Criminology* (Oxford: Oxford University Press, 2012) 57; John J. Macionis, *Sociology*, 14th edn (Pearson, 2012) 202.

[146] On "labelling" by international institutions, see section II above. On the stigmatization effects of international travel bans, see Erica Cosgrove, "Examining Targeted Sanctions" in Peter Wallensteen and Carina Staibano, eds, *International Sanctions: Between Wars and Words* (London: Routledge, 2005) 207 at 226–7.

law. Social identity literature indicates that identity is formed in a dialectic process between a local actor and the international community; and local states are not passive objects in this process. Thus, the local targeted state may challenge and try to reject such stigmas relating to the breaching of human rights.[147]

C. Out-group Members and Compliance with the Group's Norms

While a group's constitutive norms are expected to significantly influence in-group members, they are not likely to have the same impact on out-group members. *Non-member states* targeted by EU trade measures relating to allegations of breach of human rights often experience a sense of social exclusion and discrimination. The suspension of trade benefits by the EU also conveys a moral judgement, often relating to the legitimacy of the particular government. The current conception of international human rights is closely linked with the international legitimacy of the particular government. [148]

Suspending trade benefits by the EU in this context often also means stigmatization of a local actor by a prestigious international institution. The latter effect exerts social pressure on the targeted state to comply but is also liable to entail local resentment. Thus, while the EU's employment of trade measures in this context may intensify external social pressure on the particular state (which is likely to promote compliance), it may also, at least in the short term, increase the sense of alienation[149] and exclusion within the local society (which tends to diminish the prospects of compliance).

---

[147] See, for example, with regard to the EU human rights policy, Rebecca Adler-Nissen, "Stigma Management in International Relations: Transgressive Identities, Norms, and Order in International Society" (2014) 68 International Organization 143 at 160–65.

[148] On the link between the conception of international human rights and international legitimacy, see, for example, Balducci (note 109 above) at 4; Michael Joseph Smith, "Sovereignty, Human Rights and Legitimacy in the Post-Cold War World" (2001), available at http://faculty.virginia.edu/irandhumanrights/mjsonsovty.htm (accessed 10 January 2017). On international human rights protection and standard of legitimacy (and "standard of civilization"), see Jack Donnelly, "Human Rights: A New Standard of Civilization?" (1998) 74 International Affairs 1 at 14.

[149] On the impact of animosity and strained relations on the prospects of the diffusion of norms between communities, see Moshe Hirsch, "The Interaction between International Investment Law & Human Rights Treaties: A Sociological Perspective" in Tomer Broude and Yuval Shany eds, *Multi-Sourced Equivalent Norms in International Law* (Oxford: Hart Publishing, 2011) 211 at 226–7.

D. Exclusionary Effects and Inclusive Frameworks

The above observations regarding the positive influence of in-group effect on compliance and the negative influence of out-group effect on local compliance, suggest that the employment of EU trade measures in this sphere should be undertaken in an inclusive context, which downplays the social boundaries between the EU and non-members. Thus, it is desirable that such an inclusive framework (which includes the link between trade measures and human rights performance) highlights features shared by both parties (such as common heritage, ideological ties and so on). A comprehensive framework that emphasizes common identity, if meaningful for the particular non-member state, is expected to decrease the sense of exclusion and enhance the prospects of compliance with specific human rights. If a non-member breaches human rights in this context, the social identity perspective does not suggest undertaking sweeping exclusionary measures. From this perspective, severing ties across the board domains (such as discontinuation of all economic, cultural and technical programs) is not desirable. Similarly, expulsion of the violator from major international socio-economic groups (which may push the banished state to bond with persistent violators) is also not recommended; but instead the particular trade sanctions are accompanied by signals regarding potential partnership in the future.

E. Incoherent Policy and Legitimacy

Identity-driven strategies influence the prospects for compliance with international human rights law, but identity is not the sole or determinative factor affecting compliance. The combination of social identity and other factors (such as economic interests or socio-cultural ties with the violator), seems to lead the EU occasionally to apply these trade measures towards non-members suspected of breaching human rights in an inconsistent manner.[150] Such an incoherent approach might be a realistic

---

[150] See, for example, Armin Paasch, "Human Rights in EU Trade Policy – Between Ambition and Reality" (December 2011), Ecofair Trade Dialogue Discussion Paper 3 at 12–13; Nivedita Sen and Balu G. Nair, "Human Rights Provisions in the Forthcoming India-EU Free Trade Agreement" (2011) 4 NUJS Law Review 417 at 423, 430; Guy Harpaz and Eyal Rubinson, "The Interface between Trade, Law and Politics and the Erosion of Normative Power Europe" (2010) 35 European Law Review 551 at 566–70; Laura Beke and Nicolas Hachez, "The EU GSP: A Preference for Human Rights and Good Governance? The Case of Myanmar" (March 2015) Leuven Centre for Global Governance Studies

response to the tension between global human rights standards and local multiple factors involved in foreign policy; yet it erodes the legitimacy of the EU's human rights policy towards non-member states.

F. Identity-driven Measures and Considerations of Efficiency

The above EU trade provisions have been implemented in only a small subset of potential cases,[151] and their effect on compliance with international human rights law is generally uncertain or limited.[152] These facts should not lead to the conclusion that the EU is likely to discard the inclusion of such provisions in its GSP programme and trade agreements, or not apply such trade measures following a significant breach of human rights. Considerations of efficiency do not constitute the crucial factor in this sphere. The "logic of identity" is different from (and occasionally

---

Working Paper No. 155 12, available at https://ghum.kuleuven.be/ggs/publications/working_papers/new_series/wp151-160/wp155-beke-hachez.pdf (accessed 10 January 2017); Fabienne Zwagemakers, "The EU's Conditionality Policy: A New Strategy to Achieve Compliance" (January 2012) IAI Working Papers 12/03 at 5–6, available at http://www.iadb.org/intal/intalcdi/PE/2012/09808.pdf (accessed 10 January 2017); Daniela Donno, "Legalization and Leverage: Human Rights Conditionality in the European Union's Economic Agreements" (American Political Science Association Annual Meeting, New Orleans, September 2012) 7–9, 19–24, and see the references therein; Bartels (note 136 above) at 17–19; Paasch (above) at 14–15. See also Hadewych Hazelzet, "Suspension of Development Cooperation: An Instrument to Promote Human Rights and Democracy?" (August 2005) European Centre for Development Policy Management at 12–13; Michael Ewing-Chow, "First Do No Harm: Myanmar Trade Sanctions and Human Rights" (2007) 5 NW Journal of International Human Rights 153 at 156–61, 179.

[151] Lorand Bartels, "A Model Human Rights Clause for the EU's International Trade Agreements" (February 2014) German Institute for Human Rights and MISEREOR 17 at 18, available at http://ssrn.com/abstract=2405852 (accessed 10 January 2017); European Parliament (note 138 above) at 12; Bartels (note 136 above) at 9; Sen and Nair (note 150 above) at 427. See also Beke and Hachez (note 150 above) at 11.

[152] On the effectiveness of these EU trade measures, see, for example, CARIS (Centre for the Analysis of Regional Integration at Sussex), "Mid-term Evaluation of the EU's Generalised System of Preferences: Final Report" 161, available at http://trade.ec.europa.eu/doclib/docs/2010/may/tradoc_146196.pdf (accessed 10 January 2017); Meredith Kolsky Lewis, "Human Rights Provisions in Free Trade Agreements: Do the Ends Justify the Means?' (2014) 12 Loyola University Chicago International Law Review 6 at 9–10, 21, available at http://ssrn.com/abstract=2633540 (accessed 10 January 2017); Yaraslau Kryvoi, "Why European Union Trade Sanctions Do Not Work" (3 February 2012) Harvard European Law Working Paper No. 04/2007 at 42–6.

inconsistent with) the "logic of efficiency". The central motivation leading to the adoption of these legal provisions and trade measures relates to the self-image of the EU and its aspiration to project its identity as a human rights promoter worldwide. Considerations of efficiency apparently affect this EU policy; however, they do not constitute the predominant factor in this sphere. The underlying link between the EU's trade-human rights policy and its collective identity indicates that this policy is relatively durable.

V. CONCLUDING REMARKS

Unlike the well-known processes of fragmentation in international human rights law, the employment of EU trade instruments to enforce human rights treaties operates to enhance global legal integration through regional mechanisms. The EU activities in this sphere illustrate some tensions between global human rights law and local standards of compliance. Informed by social identity literature, the above sections highlight the role of identity ties involved in the establishment of these EU trade instruments as well as their effects on the identity of the other local actors outside Europe. This analysis also leads to certain policy recommendations regarding the enhancement of compliance with international human rights law in such context.

The use of these trade mechanisms for improving compliance with global human rights law is significantly motivated by the collective identity and perceived social role of the EU in the international community as a promoter of human rights worldwide. The central role of human rights protection in the EU's identity is particularly discerned from legal provisions included in the EU's fundamental treaties (including those relating to the admission of new members), as well as in a series of public statements issued by its central organs. The EU's social role as a human rights promoter has been significantly recognized in the international society; and it generates social expectations (and pressure) regarding future activities by EU institutions in this field.

The EU's identity as a human rights promoter is also projected outwards through trade measures, prominently conditional preferences to developing countries and human rights clauses in trade agreements with non-members. These identity-driven strategies may affect the identity of other local actors targeted by such measures. The suspension of trade benefits by the EU in this context carries with it not only economic consequences but also the labelling of the targeted country as a human rights violator. Such stigmatization effects may improve the prospects for local compliance with international human rights law. On the other hand, local actors targeted by trade measures relating to allegations of breach of human rights often experience a sense of social exclusion and discrimination. Thus, while the EU's employment of trade measures in this context may often enhance the prospects for local compliance, it may also (at least in the short term) entail resentment within the particular local society, which tends to diminish the likelihood of compliance.

The latter undesirable social effects of trade exclusionary measures suggest that the operation of EU trade measures in this sphere should be undertaken in an inclusive context which downplays the social boundaries between the EU and the particular targeted local actor (for example, by highlighting the common heritage, ideological ties, and so on). Such shared ties, if meaningful to the non-EU country, are likely to decrease the sense of exclusion and enhance the prospects for local compliance with the global human rights standards. From this perspective, undertaking sweeping exclusionary measures (such as severing ties in across the board domains or expulsion from international groups) is not desirable.

The use of the above trade measures against states suspected of violating human rights is affected by additional factors (such as local economic interests or political ties with the suspected country) which apparently lead to the inconsistent application of these measures. Such inconsistency erodes the legitimacy of the employment of trade measures towards non-member states. These trade mechanisms attract a lot of attention but have been implemented in a small subset of potential cases, and their effect on local compliance with global human rights treaties is generally uncertain or limited. The latter assessments are not likely to lead the EU to discard the inclusion of human rights provisions in trade agreements with non-member states or preference programs for developing countries. The "logic of identity" is different from the "logic of efficiency"; while considerations of efficiency apparently affect this EU policy, they do not constitute the predominant factor in this sphere. The underlying link between the EU trade-human rights policy and its collective identity also indicates that this policy is relatively durable.

9. Observing the small gestures: human rights vectors in the Vietnamese trade law environment*

Lisa Toohey

I. INTRODUCTION

Eleanor Roosevelt famously believed that universal human rights begin "in small places, close to home".[1] She reminds us that it is not just the grand flourishes that represent the work of human rights, but that this work is also in the incremental improvements that can, and must, take place when an opportunity arises. Without upholding rights in everyday life, Roosevelt concludes, "we shall look in vain for progress in the larger world".[2] This chapter, inspired by Roosevelt's words, examines a typically overlooked nexus between trade law and human rights – that of the regulatory aspects of trade law as a vector or conduit for human rights discourse. Human rights lawyers have many well-founded critiques of trade law as a domain that impedes the fulfillment of human rights. I nonetheless argue that human rights-supporting dimensions of trade law do exist, and should be given attention and acknowledgment within the human rights literature as part of a broader mapping exercise of the interaction between the two fields. This is particularly important in the Asian region, which has been by far the most dynamic in terms of international economic integration but one of the least responsive in engaging with international human rights regimes.

* This chapter is based on a paper presented to the workshop on "Mapping the Impact of International Trade and Human Rights on Local Practice", held in July 2014 at the International Institute for the Sociology of Law in Oñati, Spain. I gratefully acknowledge the support and inspiration of my colleague Gillian Moon and my Vietnamese friends for their assistance with language and cultural context.

[1] Eleanor Roosevelt, "In Our Hands", speech delivered at the United Nations, on the 10th anniversary of the Universal Declaration of Human Rights, New York, 1958.

[2] Ibid.

Focusing on Vietnam as a case study, this chapter argues that trade law is a vital and important site of "small place" human rights discourse. Vietnam's complex and multi-layered engagement with human rights concepts is a product of the many cultural influences on contemporary Vietnamese law. There is no doubt that Vietnam's treatment of particular individuals and groups remains of concern, and any perceived dissent towards the Communist Party is likely to be swiftly and harshly managed. Even if the instruments of control over Vietnamese society wielded by the government and the Party are hard for Westerners – used to rights such as freedom of expression – to understand or accept, many human rights criticisms of Vietnam are at least partly deserved.

However, this chapter argues that insufficient attention is paid to the emergence of threads of human rights discourse within the economic sphere in Vietnam. To this end, this chapter first outlines the mainstream debate on trade and human rights, before explaining the emergence of human rights discourses in Vietnam. The chapter then focuses on three ways in which trade law positively impacts a human rights discourse in Vietnam – as a conduit for procedural reforms that support human rights; through incorporation of specific human rights obligations in "new generation" trade agreements; and by developing a cohort of internationally-oriented lawyers who act as domestic 'change agents'.

II. THE TRADE AND HUMAN RIGHTS DEBATE

As has been acknowledged elsewhere in this volume, there is an extensive body of literature that engages with the interaction of trade and human rights. There has been extensive critique made of the negative impacts produced by globalization on human rights, as well as critiques of the impact of trade rules themselves on the promotion of human rights.[3] There have also been analyses of the human rights potential of the existing trade rules, with Cassimatis offering a comprehensive survey of the trade law mechanisms that demonstrates their limitations and potential as human rights mechanisms,[4] and Moon's analysis offering ways in which space for human rights can be accommodated within the World Trade

[3] Ernst-Ulrich Petersmann, "Human Rights and International Economic Law in the 21st Century: The Need to Clarify their Interrelationships" (2001) 4:1 J Int'l Econ L 3.

[4] Anthony Cassimatis, *Human Rights Related Trade Measures under International Law* (Leiden: Martinus Nijhoff Publishers, 2007).

Organization (WTO) treaty regime.[5] The majority of literature focuses on the analysis of legal rules, and the reasons why policy space should be created for the better integration of the trade and human rights regimes. There is considerably less attention focused on ways in which trade regimes do actually create human rights-facilitating changes, and still less attention on the actors (individuals, organizations) and their roles. The methodological basis for this chapter is based strongly on the constructivist approach of Finnemore.[6] The focus of attention for the constructivist is how understandings about an international regime are constructed, created and negotiated, and constructivist analyses of the international trade regime have offered unique insights into the nature of rule-making and rule-taking in trade law.[7] This chapter builds on those approaches, while specifically looking at a different question of how concepts from one field of international integration – human rights – find expression in another – international trade law.

Critical to this approach is an awareness of language and modes of discourse, especially in the complex political and cultural context of Vietnam. Language already represents a significant issue in the trade and human rights debate. The idea of different languages spoken by two separate groups is common. John Jackson once observed, "The language in the literature regarding human rights on the one hand, and trade on the other presents a dichotomy of discourses, like ships passing in the night".[8] Helfer's project on intellectual property and human rights presents a rigorous analysis of the interaction between two modes of discourse – "actors who are habituated to the discourse of one complex legal and political system but not the other . . . two communities [that] speak very differ-

---

[5] See, for example, Gillian Moon, "Fair in Form, But Discriminatory in Operation – WTO Law's Discriminatory Effects on Human Rights in Developing Countries" (2011) 14:3 J Int'l Econ L 553.

[6] Martha Finnemore and Stephen J. Toope. "Alternatives to 'Legalization': Richer Views of Law and Politics" (2001) 55:3 Int'l Org 743.

[7] Robert Wolfe, "See You in Geneva? Legal (Mis)Representations of the Trading System" (2005) 11:3 Eur J Int'l Relations 339; Sungjoon Cho, "Beyond Rationality: A Sociological Construction of the World Trade Organization" (2012) 52:2 Va J Int'l L 321; Andrew T.F. Lang, "Reconstructing Embedded Liberalism: John Gerard Ruggie and Constructivist Approaches to the Study of the International Trade Regime" (2006) 9:1 J Int'l Econ L 81.

[8] John H. Jackson, "Reflections on the Possible Research Agenda for Exploring the Relationship between Human Rights Norms and International Trade Rules" in Frederick M. Abbott, Christine Breining-Kaufmann and Thomas Cottier, eds, *International Trade and Human Rights: Foundations and Conceptual Issues* (Ann Arbor: University of Michigan Press, 2006) 19.

ent languages".[9] However, as this chapter discusses below, there can be advantages to this dichotomy, especially in places where human rights discussion is politically very sensitive.

III. HUMAN RIGHTS IN VIETNAM: HISTORY AND LANGUAGE

Vietnam has had a complicated engagement with human rights throughout its history. Authors such as Nghia have highlighted the centrality of pre-colonial legal history to an understanding of Vietnam's transitional legal system.[10] Centuries of repeated attempts to incorporate and retain Vietnam as part of successive Chinese Empires from 111 BCE until the mid-1400s[11] profoundly shaped the Vietnamese system of government and led to a Confucian influence on the Vietnamese approach to law. Many argue that Confucianism's focus on obligation and group harmony is at the expense of pursuing individual rights, and that the heart of Confucianism is the harmonious existence of the society. This is even more complicated in Vietnam, where Confucian and Chinese legalist principles were overlaid with indigenous, broadly Buddhist and Daoist Vietnamese values. These are identified and illustrated by Van Tai, who explains that Vietnam adopted Confucian precepts in the law, as well as Chinese legalist principles such as criminal liability of the family for the acts of an individual and the application of Confucian ethics, resulting in different legal rights for individuals of higher status. However, he also notes the indigenous Vietnamese principles in the legal code of the Lê Dynasty (1428–1788) that is not found in Confucian codes, such as higher standards of behaviour for officials.[12]

Nghia argues that another important overlay to the reception of Western human rights is the concept of Vietnamese collectivism, which emphasizes the role of the individual in a family, village or society. He

---

[9] Laurence R. Helfer and Graeme W. Austin, *Human Rights and Intellectual Property: Mapping the Global Interface* (Cambridge: Cambridge University Press, 2011) 504.

[10] Truong Trong Nghia, "The Rule of Law in Vietnam: Theory and Practice" in L. Gordon Flake, ed., *The Rule of Law: Perspectives from the Pacific Rim* (Missoula: The Mansfield Centre for Pacific Affairs, 2000) 123.

[11] See Nicholas Tarling, *The Cambridge History of Southeast Asia* (Cambridge: Cambridge University Press, 1992) 97.

[12] Ta Van Tai, "The Vietnamese Tradition of Human Rights" (1990) 38:3 Am J Comp L 717.

believes that this concept has profound consequences for a culture of human rights, because "[u]nder such a system, the collective interest of society is supreme over individual interests; people who fight for their own interests are often viewed as selfish and egotistical".[13] A similar view is held by Phan Nhat Thanh, who argues that "while Easterners hear human rights as individual rights, these rights must be a part of the whole society, and are unable to be separated from issues of state, state power and national sovereignty".[14] These cultural dimensions translate into the attitude of lawmakers and bureaucrats, who are "trained to administer a socialist legal system . . . [and often] have neither an academic nor a cultural understanding of the concepts of natural rights, liberalism, and the sharing of legal rights between the individual and the state that exists in Western democracies".[15]

The Vietnamese words given to express human rights are also equivocal – while the term *nhân quyền* is more direct and was originally brought into Vietnamese in the 1800s, the term *quyền lợi* is used more commonly but actually connotes interests, power or benefit.[16] Van Tai focuses on the first two of these meanings, observing that:

> The term [*quyền lợi*] means both "power" and "interest", the very two concepts the Confucians despised and avoided because their value system emphasized personal virtues and the sense of duty. . ..The idea expressed in the German word Recht and the French word droit is not expressed or implied in either the Sino-Vietnamese or Chinese terms.[17]

History too shows a very mixed pattern of invocation of human rights concepts in Vietnam. From the beginning of the 1940s, the country was engaged in the fight against French colonialism and subsequent Japanese invasion, and by 1945 Japanese surrender allowed the Vietminh to take

---

13 Pham Duy Nghia, "Confucianism and the Conception of the Law in Vietnam" in John Gillespie and Penelope Nicholson, eds, *Asian Socialism and Legal Change: The Dynamics of Vietnamese and Chinese Reform* (Canberra: Australian National University, 2005) 76 at 81.

14 Phan Nhat Thanh, *Recognising Customary Law in Vietnam: Legal Pluralism and Human Rights* (Doctor of Philosophy in Law, University of Wollongong, 2011) (unpublished) 127.

15 John Gillespie, "Private Commercial Rights in Vietnam: A Comparative Analysis" (1994) 30 Stan J Int'l L 325 at 327.

16 Alexander Woodside, "An Enlightenment for Outcasts: Some Vietnamese Stories" in Jeffrey N. Wasserstrom, Greg Grandin, Lynn Hunt and Marilyn B. Young, eds, *Human Rights and Revolutions* (Lanham: Rowman & Littlefield, 2007).

17 Tai (note 12 above) at 2.

control of the country and force the abdication of the Emperor. At that time, Ho Chi Minh made a Declaration of Independence that referenced both the American Declaration of Independence and the French Declaration of the Rights of Man to support his claim for independence.[18] Following the end of armed conflict and the reunification of the country in 1976, the Communist Party of Vietnam completed substantial land reforms and instituted a political system based on central planning and socialist values, including a classically communist antipathy to human rights discourse. As Ai observes, this is one of many symptoms of the "contradictory and paradoxical" relationship with human rights in Vietnam.[19] The state management model to which Vietnam aspired was modelled along orthodox communist principles, including those from the Soviet and Chinese experience, and included a retreat from engagement with the international community outside the Communist sphere,[20] although Vietnam nonetheless became a signatory to the International Covenant on Civil and Political Rights in 1982. By 1986, it was recognized that broader international integration was necessary for the economic future of the country, and the *đổimới* (renovation) of the country commenced.[21] At the same time, Vietnam entered into the "Asian values" debate, becoming a signatory to the 1993 Bangkok Declaration on Human Rights, a declaration that included an assertion of the importance of "non-interference in the internal affairs of States, and the non-use of human rights as an instrument of political pressure".[22]

More recently, with Vietnam's full integration into the international economic system, there has remained a paradoxical engagement with human rights – there is an increase in official rhetoric supporting certain types of human rights, and even increased interest in the historical context, with some scholars arguing that the Lê Codes "prescribed" human rights in Vietnam,[23] and others tracing liberal political rights in the work of

---

[18] Ho Chi Minh, speech in Ba Dinh Square, Hanoi, Vietnam on 2 September 1945.

[19] Vo Van Ai, "Human Rights and Asian Values in Vietnam" in Ole Bruun and Michael Jacobsen, eds, *Human Rights and Asian Values: Contesting National Identities and Cultural Representations in Asia* (London: Routledge, 2003).

[20] See the description of early land reforms earlier in this section.

[21] Communist Party of Vietnam, *Political Report Presented by the Seventh CPV Central Committee to the Eighth National Party Congress in Hanoi* (28 June to 1 July 1996).

[22] Final Declaration of the Regional Meeting for Asia of the World Conference on Human Rights, Bangkok (2 April 1993), art 5.

[23] Do Danh Huan, "Human Rights in Vietnam's Ancient Feudal Law", Vietnam L & Legal Forum (20 November 2014).

anti-colonial nationalist Phan Bội Chau.[24] It can be difficult to unravel the motivation behind these assertions. On the one hand, they could suggest a wish to legitimize human rights as part of Vietnamese legal culture, something to be rediscovered and developed upon, or a way of justifying that adequate human rights principles already exist, and resisting external pressures for change. The latter explanation may find some resonance with international human rights activists, who express concern that freedom of expression in Vietnam has recently become more restricted, and dissent ever more severely repressed. Similarly, the United Nations Special Rapporteur has expressed concern about the treatment of religious freedoms on the ground of national security and public morals.[25] At the same time, the 2013 revisions to the Vietnamese Constitution incorporated Chapter II, entitled "Human Rights and Citizen's Fundamental Rights and Duties", with extensive recitations of most international human rights standards. Commentators such as Kinley and Nguyen identify areas in which improvements have been made on human rights in Vietnam – education, gender equality and the rights of minorities – before also observing that "there remains a sizeable gap between the rights provided in law and the mechanism for their actual implementation".[26]

Perhaps the most that can be said by way of summary is that the historical-cultural and political contexts of contemporary Vietnamese life push and pull in confusing and inconsistent directions in relation to human rights, and this is, first, because the socialist system overlays rather than replaces pre-socialist approaches[27] and, second, because the Vietnamese government does not accept the concept of human rights as monolithic. This becomes increasingly obvious when examining the comparatively straightforward integration of certain rights-language into Vietnamese law reform in the trade law context. The following section seeks to explain why certain types of human rights seem to be easily assimilated within Vietnam's trade law reforms.

---

24 Bui Ngoc Son, "The Introduction of Modern Constitutionalism in East Asian Confucian Context: The Case of Vietnam in the Early Twentieth Century" (2011) 7:2 Nat'l Taiwan Univ L Rev 423.

25 Heiner Bielefeldt, "Report of the Special Rapporteur on Freedom of Religion or Belief, Mission to Viet Nam", United Nations Human Rights Council, A/HRC/28/66 (30 January 2015).

26 David Kinley and Hai Nguyen, "Viet Nam, Human Rights and Trade: Implications of Viet Nam's Accession to the WTO", *Dialogue on Globalization* Occasional Paper No 39/2008, 14, available at http://library.fes.de/pdf-files/iez/global/05359.pdf (accessed 10 January 2017).

27 Ai (note 19 above).

IV. THREE VECTORS OF HUMAN RIGHTS WITHIN THE TRADE LAW SPHERE

Economic life in Vietnam is a dynamic and changing area, at least partly due to the dual concerns of the Communist Party to create economic growth but maintain strict political controls. As the remainder of this chapter explains, the trade realm is a site in which international norms can permeate domestic reform efforts in a comparatively uncontroversial manner, even against the backdrop of Vietnam's ambivalence towards human rights as an indivisible set of enforceable personal entitlements. Furthermore, a discourse of human rights is occurring that is not reflective of mainstream human rights discourse, but is significant and worthy of closer attention. This is, what Roosevelt reminds us, the small places within the bigger focus of economic reform. It is also "close to home" in the sense that the economic development of Vietnam is close to the heart of every Vietnamese person, as well as to its leaders.

In Vietnam, like in many of its regional neighbors, international economic law represents an important site of international law discourse, and a realm in which debate about domestic law reform is less politically risky. The following section sets out three, often overlooked ways in which trade law in Vietnam has been a subtle but significant conduit for human rights-supportive reform.

A. Trade Reform as a Conduit for Procedural Human Rights Improvements

There is a considerable body of literature on how international norms are created and disseminated at a local level, the way in which the norms underpinning international law are transplanted into recipient states, and the tensions of resistance and adaptation that occur.[28] However, the focus tends to be on the reception of norms within a discrete subject matter, rather than between and across regimes.

The process of international economic integration has forced Vietnam to open its laws to external criticism. As I have explored in previous work, trade reforms can be used as leverage to lock in a wide range of liberalizing legal and economic reforms. The reform efforts that accompany processes

---

[28] See, for an overview, John Gillespie, "Developing a Decentred Analysis of Legal Transfers" in Sarah Biddulph and Pip Nicholson, eds, *Examining Practice, Interrogating Theory: Comparative Legal Studies in Asia* (Leiden: Brill, 2008); Sarah Biddulph, *Legal Reform and Administrative Detention Powers in China* (Cambridge: Cambridge University Press, 2007).

such as WTO accession are typically led by foreign technical assistance projects that take a broad view of the legal and economic changes that will be required to support compliance with trade law rules.[29] An example is domestic reforms focused upon the enhancement of judicial independence, undertaking "reform of the courts and the judiciary to establish their independence from the executive".[30] Those domestic reforms as part of the WTO accession were occurring at a time when international human rights advocacy was looking at how domestic procedural mechanisms could be deployed for the enforcement of human rights.

This is the first of three ways in which trade can and does support human rights – by opening a space for foreign law reform input. The benefits of these reform projects flow beyond merely the trade space. For example, Vietnam launched a National Administrative Reform Project ("Project 30") in 2007, which was funded by international donors and the Vietnamese government, and was a project that implemented WTO standards but also had substantial benefits for citizens by tackling the complex business permit system and corruption as well as reforming the administrative law, clarifying grounds for review of administrative actions, and providing for regulatory impact assessments.[31]

These are reforms, initiated in response to WTO imperatives, which have direct implications for good governance and a very practical means of containing and tempering bureaucratic discretion at central and provincial levels. Similarly, it was trade-focused technical assistance projects that undertook the work that led to the 2009 Law on the Promulgation of Normative Instruments and articulated a strategy of publishing court decisions. Once again, the purpose of reforms was to implement WTO obligations on transparency in relation to draft laws, but human rights activists have praised this publication strategy as an important step for the protection of universal human rights.[32] These kinds of universal transfers

---

[29] Lisa Toohey, "Accession as Dialogue: Epistemic Communities and the World Trade Organization" (2014) 27:2 Leiden J Int'l L 397.

[30] United Nations, "Resolution of the United Nations General Assembly 48/134 on National institutions for the promotion and protection of human rights", A/RES/48/134 (20 December 1993), available at http://www.un.org/documents/ga/res/48/a48r134.htm (accessed 10 January 2017).

[31] World Trade Organization, "Trade Policy Review: Report by the Secretariat – Vietnam" WT/TPR/S/287 (13 August 2013) 42–3, available at https://www.wto.org/english/tratop_e/tpr_e/s287_e.pdf (accessed 10 January 2017).

[32] Vu Cing Guai and Joel Ng, *Vietnam: Rule of Law for Human Right in the ASEAN Region: A Baseline Study* (Depok: Human Rights Resource Centre, 2011) 291, available at http://hrrca.org/rule-law-human-rights-asean-region-baseline-study/ (accessed 10 January 2017).

of procedural reform support human rights practices even if they are labelled as trade-related reform.

B. Human Rights Obligations in "New Generation" Trade Agreements

The second way in which trade can and does support human rights is more overt, achieved through substantive rules of trade that benefit procedural human rights. While the WTO rules are typically criticized for their negative impact upon access to medicines, essential services and impact upon cultural diversity, there has been little attention paid to their positive impacts upon procedural human rights. Successive generations of trade agreements have also more overtly addressed "non-mainstream" issues that directly benefit human rights, with the Trans-Pacific Partnership (TPP) providing a classic example.[33] The TPP, a 30-chapter agreement, represents a new era in the linkages for human rights and trade for Vietnam in several respects, but most notably for its inclusion of labour rights in Chapter 19, "regulatory coherence" requirements in Chapter 25, and commitments to combat corruption and facilitate transparency in Chapter 26.

The side letter between Vietnam and the United States provides a bilateral modification to Chapter 19 of the TPP that demonstrates an unprecedented linkage of trade and human rights issues.[34] In this side letter, Vietnam guarantees to make substantial changes to the operation of grassroots labour unions and change the role of the Vietnam General Confederation of Labour, the umbrella union that has constitutional power to represent all Vietnamese workers.[35] Vietnam has also committed in the side letter to changes to the right to strike, bringing its currently complex legislation into line with the International Labour Organization provisions. This may transform the nature of workers' strikes, as currently

---

33 As of May 2016, the TPP has not yet entered into force as it is in the process of being ratified by its signatories.

34 United States–Viet Nam Plan for the Enhancement of Trade and Labour Relations, 4 February 2016, available at https://ustr.gov/sites/default/files/TPP-Final-Text-Labour-US-VN-Plan-for-Enhancement-of-Trade-and-Labour-Relations.pdf (accessed 10 January 2017).

35 The International Trade Union Confederation (ITUC) is one of the most vocal critics of the role of the General Confederation of Labour, arguing that it fails adequately to represent workers in negotiations, and instead that it "mainly takes the interests of the government and the enterprise into account during negotiations". The ITUC Global Rights Index, Survey of Violations of Trade Union Rights, available at http://survey.ituc-csi.org/Vietnam.html?lang=en#tabs-3 (accessed 10 January 2017).

the complex laws for legal strikes make them unfeasible.[36] Hence, it would be foreign intervention in the TPP that increases the rights of Vietnamese workers. Finally, the side letter requires that Vietnam expand the prohibitions on forced labour to eliminate debt bondage and forced labour in drug rehabilitation centres – a human rights issue that has long been an area of concern for NGOs. Compliance with the side letter is subject to the general dispute-settlement mechanism in the TPP in Chapter 28, and Article VIII.3 also specifically allows the US to suspend future tariff concessions for non-compliance by Vietnam.

The transparency and enforcement mechanisms of the TPP side agreement are also noteworthy, as they extend WTO-style obligations to the labour chapter. There is an obligation to open draft legislation for public comment; an obligation to release statistical data on compliance; and an obligation to develop education programs to support the reforms. These are clear ways in which the TPP, while firmly a product of international trade law, is also serving as a vector for human rights development.

C. Agents of Change – the Role of Individuals

The recurring theme in this chapter is the unexpected and often invisible ways in which the international trade regime positively interacts with human rights development. The third vector of change is that of individuals involved in the trade regime, as through their interactions they can and often do create changes of discourse within Vietnam about expectations of rights and approaches to governance.

International trade obligations can create more liberal law reforms by shifting the locus of law reform discussions. Political economists have long been aware of the role of trade agreements as a means to "lock in" domestic reforms;[37] however, the external scrutiny of trade law reforms by international bodies such as the WTO creates a shift of power within domestic governments towards those government departments that defend the country against trade disputes. In the case of Vietnam, as in China, the imperative of economic integration and development has placed the Ministry of Commerce in a more powerful position than ever before. At the same time, foreign-trained lawyers are in demand in government positions in trade roles, and there is considerable movement and overlap

---

[36] Mark Anner, "Worker Resistance in Global Supply Chains: Wildcat Strikes, International Accords and Transnational Campaigns" (2015) 7:1–2 Int'l J Lab Research 17.

[37] John Ravenhill, "Regionalism" in J. Ravenhill, ed., *Global Political Economy* (Oxford: Oxford University Press, 2005) 116 at 120–4.

between their positions in Vietnamese universities, local consultancy roles and government positions.

As elsewhere, these trade communities function as an epistemic or interpretive community, using a common language that is imbued with concepts from Western legal education.[38] The effect of international education is substantial; as Watson observes:

> if borrowing is the main way law develops, and if the lawmaking elite is bound by its legal culture, and if this culture is restricted by what the elite does not know, then it follows that the quality of legal education, including exposure to Comparative Law (where that occurs), plays a powerful role in law reform.[39]

Increasing numbers of Vietnamese lawyers, mostly from the public sector, are travelling abroad to complete higher education in law, particularly to the United States, Australia and the United Kingdom, with both Vietnamese and foreign governments offering scholarships.[40] A common course of study for these students includes a range of international law courses, encompassing not just trade but other subjects that impart the Western legal tradition of rights and their enforcement, as well as courses on international organizations, environmental law, human rights and public international law. A substantial number of Vietnamese students go on to complete human rights-related PhDs in Australia, the United States and elsewhere.[41] While many of these actually return to commercial jobs, and are in demand because of their advanced English and analytical skills, they carry the ideas they learned overseas with them. Currently, the most articulate and capable lawyers in Vietnam are almost uniformly graduates of foreign universities, and Nicholson and Hinderling document the emergence of this new legal elite in Vietnam, who were not educated in China or Russia as in the pre-reform years, but instead in Europe, the United States, Australia and Japan.[42] Mosse's anthropological work on

---

38 For more detailed development of this theory, see Toohey (note 29 above).

39 Alan Watson, *Legal Transplants: An Approach to Comparative Law* (Atlanta: University of Georgia Press, 1974) 118.

40 Bui Thi Bich Lien, "Legal Education and the Legal Profession in Contemporary Vietnam – To Change or not to Change" in John Gillespie and Albert Chen, eds, *Legal Reforms in China and Vietnam: A Comparison of Asian Communist Regimes* (Abington; New York: Routledge, 2010).

41 See *Index of Vietnamese Law-Related Theses*, available at http://law.unimelb.edu.au/centres/alc/research/research-programs/vietnam/vlrn/index-of-vietnamese-law-related-theses (accessed 10 January 2017).

42 Pip Nicholson and Samantha Hinderling, "Effectiveness of Donor-funded Legal Education: A Vietnamese Retrospective" in S. Steele and K. Taylor, eds,

international development professionals is an illustration of "the many and unpredictable ways in which development's travelling rationalities get translated (back) into local social and political arrangements"[43] and, in the same vein, the new liberal rationalities learned by foreign graduates are translated back into their work. The postgraduate overseas legal education of elite Vietnamese lawyers has given rise to commercially oriented lawyers who perform human rights work in a diverse variety of ways, often not visible to human rights activists but nonetheless conducive to the development of a law-based state in Vietnam.

Vietnamese lawyer Le Cong Dinh is an unusually prominent example. As a Fulbright Scholar, Le Cong Dinh studied postgraduate law in the United States, before returning to Vietnam and working on the high profile catfish case against the United States in 2003.[44] As Gillespie observes, it was Dinh's foreign education that inspired his interest in cause lawyering, and provided him with interactions with foreign lawyers, and from these experiences he developed an interest in human rights advocacy. Dinh gained local prominence as a human rights and constitutional lawyer, and international prominence after being arrested in 2009 and charged with sedition.[45] Many other internationally trained lawyers work much more conservatively to promote legal change, and are cautious of the risks that broader advocacy entails. Even without advocating politically risky reforms, these foreign-trained lawyers act as agents of adaptation of international norms, and in turn they impact upon the way their local communities engage with law-based rights and the rule of law. Their mode of discourse, while influenced by liberal ideas, is explicitly one of trade and economic development. The role of these local vectors of legal change is an ideal subject for future study, although sensitivity needs to be had to the ethical dimensions of such research.

Legal Education in Asia: Globalization, Change and Contexts (Abington; New York: Routledge, 2010) 241.

43 David Mosse, "The Anthropology of Expertise and Professionals in International Development" in David Mosse, ed., *Adventures in Aidland: The Anthropology of Expertise and Professionals in International Development* (New York: Berghahn Books, 2013) 3–4.

44 N.T. Tung, N.V. Thanh and M.J. Phillips, "Policy Research – Implications of Liberalization of Fish Trade for Developing Countries: A Case Study of Vietnam", GTZ and ODI, Project PR 26109, available at http://projects.nri.org/fishtrade/vietnam.pdf (accessed 25 January 2017).

45 John Gillespie, "The Juridification of Cause Advocacy in Socialist Asia: Vietnam as a Case Study" (2013) 31 Wis Int'l L J 672.

V. CONCLUSION

As Eslava notes, "The sites where we can observe the international normative order operating through and within the nation-state proliferate tremendously once we shift our gaze to the market place".[46] Vietnam makes a fascinating case study of the ways in which international human rights norms filter through the marketplace, while being adapted, incorporated and requisitioned in culturally specific ways. Both Roosevelt and Eslava prompt us to think about the less obvious sites of human rights activity in daily life, to examine the less visible or micro-levels where human rights discourse is created. In the case of Vietnam, trade integration has been an impetus and a politically appropriate forum for reforms that have the ability to greatly facilitate the tempering of government power and the promotion of a more rule of law-based approach to rights.

It is not the objective of this chapter to make an ambit claim that trade has an overwhelmingly positive impact upon human rights (for it does not), nor to claim that trade rights will automatically engender a transition towards a liberal human rights agenda (for it will not). However, the purpose of the chapter is to simply explore some of the less-visible dimensions of human rights discourse occurring within the field of trade law. In doing so, it has highlighted three ways, or vectors, in which trade law facilitates the development of a rights-based approach to law. This has included the conduits that are created between the two fields, as part of general economic integration and more overt human rights obligations in "new generation" trade agreements, as well as through attitudes of foreign-trained trade law officials, practitioners and academics, themselves conduits for new ideas about the relationship between law, rights and development.

One of the most fruitful areas for furthering the work on the engagement of trade law with human rights (and vice versa) is to recognize that practices exist to support the development of human rights even where they are not labeled as such. Mapping of these practices could usefully form part of a broader exercise of more fully mapping the engagement between trade law and human rights, for the interactions between these two fields are far more extensive than is often visible from a distance.

---

[46] Luis Eslava, "Istanbul Vignettes: Observing the Everyday Operation of International Law" (2014) 2:1 Lon Rev Int'l L 3 at 11.

PART IV

Dilemmas of local performance: the case of China

10. Coordinating human rights and trade policy in China: the case of environmental protection*

Pitman B. Potter

I. INTRODUCTION

International, regional, and subnational disputes over issues of trade and human rights have become increasingly serious obstacles to international cooperation. Coordinating local performance of international standards on trade and human rights can be an important step towards preventing and resolving these disputes. As discussed in the introduction to this volume, coordination of trade and human rights compliance has been difficult due to normative and operational obstacles. Nonetheless, coordinating trade and human rights performance remains a useful approach to upholding human rights standards even while promoting trade performance. Coordinated compliance discourse offers the possibility for overcoming the conflicts between trade and human rights, by "bundling" normative and institutional dimensions of trade and human rights performance. This chapter examines China's efforts to manage its environmental challenges in the context of performance of international trade standards associated with the General Agreement on Tariffs and Trade (GATT) and the World Trade Organization (WTO). In addition, this case study will examine alternative approaches to strengthening environmental protection, and the possible implications for trade policy.

---

* This chapter is based on a paper presented to the workshop on "Mapping the Impact of International Trade and Human Rights on Local Practice", held in July 2014 at the International Institute for the Sociology of Law in Oñati, Spain.

II. COORDINATING PERFORMANCE OF INTERNATIONAL TRADE AND HUMAN RIGHTS STANDARDS

Despite the challenges discussed above, coordination of trade and human rights performance remains a compelling goal. Policy efforts to strengthen local coordination of international trade and human rights performance in Asia will be essential to strengthening both the international trade system and international human rights.[1] Coordination of trade and human rights performance involves values and organizations, and thus depends on the normative and operational paradigms of "selective adaptation" and "institutional capacity".[2] Selective adaptation focuses on normative conditions for local implementation of international trade and human rights standards. Selective adaptation of international trade and human rights standards involves both conscious and unconscious processes and is revealed through the component elements of perception about standards and norms, complementarity between local and non-local standards and norms, and legitimacy of both international standards and local implementation.

Organizational dimensions involve the paradigm of institutional capacity, which examines the ability of implementing agencies to perform their assigned tasks in the context of local socio-economic and political conditions. Building on existing approaches to institutional capacity focused on internal structures, resources and processes,[3] we also focus on relational questions of institutional purpose, bureaucratic and geographic location, regulatory orientation towards formality and/or discretion, and

---

[1] See, for example, Asia Pacific Foundation, "Advancing Canada's Engagement with Asia on Human Rights: Integrating Business and Human Rights" (25 September 2013), available at http://www.asiapacific.ca/sites/default/files/filefield/human_rights_taskforce_v3.pdf (accessed 10 January 2017).

[2] Pitman B Potter, "Chapter One" in *Assessing Treaty Performance in China: Trade and Human Rights* (Vancouver: UBC Press, 2014).

[3] HV Savitch, "Global Challenge and Institutional Capacity: Or How We Can Refit Local Administration for the Next Century" (1998) 30:3 Admin & Soc'y 248; William Blomquist and Elinor Ostrom, "Institutional Capacity and the Resolution of the Commons Dilemma" in Michael D McGinnis, ed., *Polycentric Governance and Development: Readings from the Workshop in Political Theory and Policy Analysis* (Ann Arbor: University of Michigan Press, 1999) 60; Patsy Healey, "Building Institutional Capacity through Collaborative Approaches to Urban Planning" (1998) 30:9 Environment & Planning A 1531; Stéphane Willems and Kevin Baumert, *Institutional Capacity and Climate Actions* (Paris: OECD Environmental Directorate; International Energy Agency, 2003).

staff cohesion and discipline. Taken together, the paradigms of selective adaptation and institutional capacity offer important tools for understanding normative and operational conditions affecting coordination of trade and human rights performance.

As a key element of human rights,[4] the right to a safe, clean, healthy and sustainable environment offers an important challenge for trade policy. International trade policy standards focused on production, such as anti-dumping and subsidies, and on local regulation and governance, such as national treatment and transparency, potentially inhibit effective environmental protection efforts. China's environmental protection project offers a compelling case study of coordination of trade and human rights performance, due to factors of growth-centred economic policy; imperatives of poverty reduction; and widening environmental degradation – challenges that are shared with much of the developing world.

III. ENVIRONMENTAL PROTECTION AND TRADE POLICY IN CHINA

China today faces an unprecedented environmental crisis, despite many decades of legislation and policymaking.[5] The horrific chemical explo-

---

[4] UN Human Rights Council, *Report of the Independent Expert on the issue of human rights obligations relating to the enjoyment of a safe, clean, healthy and sustainable environment, John H Knox*, A/HRC/22/43 (24 December 2012), available at http://www.ohchr.org/Documents/HRBodies/HRCouncil/RegularSession/Session22/A-HRC-22-43_en.pdf (accessed 10 January 2017). See also John H Knox, *United Nations Mandate on Human Rights and the Environment*, available at http://srenvironment.org/annual-reports/ (accessed 10 January 2017); United Nations Environment Program, *High Level Expert Meeting on the Future of Human Rights and Environment: Moving the Global Agenda Forward*, available at http://www.unep.org/ecalendar/contents/details_view.asp?EventID=2104 (events detailed main page) (accessed 10 January 2017); Alan Boyle, "Human Rights and the Environment: Where Next?" (2012) 23:3 Eur J Int'l L 613; Henry J Steiner, Philip Alston and Ryan Goodman, "Environment, Development and Human Rights" in *International Human Rights in Context: Law, Politics, Morals* (Oxford: Oxford University Press, 2008) 1153.

[5] Chai Jing, *Qiongding zhixia* (*Under the dome*) (film) (2015); Xu Beina, "China's Environmental Crisis", Council on Foreign Relations (25 April 2014), available at http://www.cfr.org/china/chinas-environmental-crisis/p12608 (accessed 10 January 2017); Alex L Wang, "China's Environmental Tipping Point" in Timothy Weston and Lionel Jensen, *China In and Beyond the Headlines* (Lanham: Rowman and Littlefield, 2012) 112; Joel Jay Kassiola and Sujian Guo, eds, *China's Environmental Crisis: Domestic and Global Political Impacts and Responses* (New York: Palgrave MacMillan, 2010).

sion and fire in Tianjin in August 2015 seemed to exemplify the overlapping problems of lax regulation, corruption and lack of transparency in China's environmental protection challenge.[6] China's legal regimes for environmental protection and trade policy are key domains upon which the possibilities of coordinating trade and environmental performance depend.

A. Legal Dimensions of China's Environmental Challenge

China's environmental challenge presents important issues for the development of China's socialist legal system. The effectiveness of Chinese law and regulation in supporting environmental protection reflects the broader question of the authority and capacity of law to regulate vested interests in socialist China.

PRC laws and regulations on environmental protection emerge from Article 9 of the PRC Constitution specifying state ownership over natural resources, and so depend upon on the regulatory and supervisory authority of the Party/state. China's first Environmental Protection Law of the PRC (1990) (EPL) asserted administrative authority of governmental agencies to oversee environment protection efforts.[7] In addition, provinces and localities have come to emphasize environmental protection locally.[8] Nonetheless, legal and regulatory enforcement on environmental protection has been inconsistent.[9]

---

[6] *BBC News*, "China explosions: What we know about what happened in Tianjin" (17 August 2015), available at http://www.bbc.com/news/world-asia-china-33844084 (accessed 10 January 2017); Jun Mai, "Tianjin warehouse blasts: Evidence of corruption, says Chinese premier as he vows nobody will be exempt from punishment", *South China Morning Post* (24 September 2015), available at http://www.scmp.com/news/china/policies-politics/article/1860908/tianjin-warehouse-blasts-evidence-corruption-says (accessed 10 January 2017).

[7] Environmental Protection Law of the People's Republic of China, 26 December 1989 (entered into force 1 April 1990), available at http://www.china.org.cn/english/environment/34356.htm (accessed 10 January 2017).

[8] See e.g, Government of Hong Kong Environmental Protection Department, "Provincial and Local Environmental Protection Bureaux/Environmental Information Centres," http://www.epd.gov.hk/epd/english/links/mainchina/link_pro_lepb.html (accessed 15 February 2017); Lingyi Wang, ed., *Jieyuexing shehui zhong de Shanghai zhihui* (*Shanghai wisdom on the resources saving type society*) (Beijing: Social Science Academic Press, 2006).

[9] "13 shengji zhengfu xiang wei yifa anshi baogao niandu huanbao qingkuang" (Thirteen provincial governments have not yet provided timely reports on yearly environmental conditions), Renda xinwen wang (NPC news net), (Dec. 17, 2016), http://npc.people.com.cn/n1/2016/1207/c14576-28932679.html (accessed 15

While extending to government agencies primary if not exclusive authority to monitor and enforce environmental protection efforts, the EPL initially acknowledged state development plans to be the central policy priority, qualified when possible by environmental considerations. The EPL emphasized the overall authority of state agencies (now primarily the Ministry of Environmental Protection) over environmental regulation while still allocating jurisdiction to local governments to oversee regulation and protection efforts. The EPL also provided that environmental protection measures should be incorporated into economic development policies, setting up the possibility of cooperation or competition between environmental agencies and those responsible for economic development policy, such as the National Development and Reform Commission. The EPL specified the responsibilities and potential civil and criminal liabilities for enterprises found in violation of the pollution and environmental protection provisions in the law and associated regulations, although to a great extent this resulted simply in a system of "pollution licenses" which added to the cost of doing business but did little to deter pollution. Centralization of authority combined with deference to economic development undermined the effectiveness of the original EPL in monitoring and enforcing environmental protection.

In response to rising public awareness of pollution problems and criticism of governments' seeming inability to manage them, the EPL was revised in 2014.[10] The revised EPL came into effect on 1 January 2015 and provides for more integrated approaches to environmental protection – permitting broader involvement from non-government actors albeit still subject to overall authority and control by the Party/state:

> Article 4: The protection of environment is a basic national policy for China. The state shall adopt economic and technological policies and measures favorable for conservation and circulatory use of resources, protection and improvement of environment and harmony between human and nature, so as to coordinate economic and social development with the work of environmental protection.

February 2017); Bo Zhang and Cong Cao, "Policy: Four Gaps in China's New Environmental Law", *Nature* (21 January 2015), available at http://www.nature.com/news/policy-four-gaps-in-china-s-new-environmental-law-1.16736 (accessed 10 January 2017); Erin Ryan, "The Elaborate Paper Tiger: Environmental Enforcement and the Rule of Law in China" (2013) XXIV Duke Envir L & Pol'y Forum 183.

[10] Environmental Protection Law of the People's Republic of China, 24 April 2014 (entered into force 1 January 2015), available at https://www.chinadialogue.net/Environmental-Protection-Law-2014-eversion.pdf (accessed 10 January 2017).

> . . .
>
> Article 6: All units and individuals shall have the obligation to protect the environment.
>
> Local people's governments at various levels shall be responsible for the environment quality within areas under their jurisdiction.
>
> Enterprises, public institutions and any other producers/business operators shall prevent and reduce environmental pollution and ecological destruction, and shall bear the liability for their damage caused by them in accordance with the law.
>
> Citizens shall enhance environmental protection awareness, adopt low-carbon and energy-saving lifestyles, and conscientiously fulfill the obligation of environmental protection.
>
> . . .
>
> Article 9: The people's governments at various levels shall strengthen environmental protection publicity and dissemination, encourage self-governing grassroots organizations, social organizations and environmental protection volunteers to carry out the publicity of environmental protection laws, regulations and knowledge, so as to facilitate a favorable atmosphere for environmental protection.
>
> Educational departments and schools shall incorporate environmental protection knowledge into the curriculum of school education so as to cultivate the environmental protection awareness among students.
>
> News media shall carry out the publicity of environmental protection laws, regulations and knowledge, and facilitate the exercise of public supervision on environmental violation activities.
>
> Article 10: The competent department of environmental protection administration under the State Council shall conduct unified supervision and management of the environmental protection work throughout the country.
>
> The competent departments of environmental protection administration of the local people's governments at or above the county level shall conduct unified supervision and management of the environmental protection work within areas under their jurisdiction.
>
> Other relevant administrative departments of the people's governments at or above the county level and the environmental protection departments of military units shall conduct supervision and administration over resources conservation and environmental pollution prevention and control in accordance with applicable laws.

Thus, the EPL reiterates the principle of central control (Article 10) even while imposing on local people's governments responsibility for environmental quality in the areas under their jurisdiction, and responsibility to take measures to improve environment conditions. This extends to prevention and control of pollution and other environment hazards. In an important development, the revised EPL permits non-state actors under limited circumstances to launch civil actions for compensation for environmental harm:

> Article 58. For activities that cause environmental pollution, ecological damage and public interest harm, social organizations that meet the following conditions may file litigation to the people's courts:

(1) Have their registration at the civil affair departments of people's governments at or above municipal level with sub-districts in accordance with the law;
(2) Specialize in environmental protection public interest activities for five consecutive years or more, and have no law violation records. Courts shall accept the litigations filed by social organizations that meet the above criteria. The social organizations that file the litigation shall not seek economic benefits from the litigation.

The provision for civil society actors to pursue environmental litigation in the People's Courts may encourage stronger efforts at environmental monitoring and enforcement particularly at the local level, although questions of implementation remain. Resort to the PRC court system to seek redress for government inaction or ineffective regulation on environmental matters calls to mind the experience of the Administrative Litigation Law (ALL), enacted in 1989.[11] Aimed at curtailing the power of bureaucratic agencies, the ALL formalized the authority of the People's Courts to review administrative agency decisions: imposing fines; restricting or infringing on property rights; intervening in business operations; denying licenses; and a number of other matters. While the potential for greater civil society initiative in seeking judicial remedies for government mismanagement and corruption seemed promising,[12] the pattern of ALL litigation suggested that its effects were limited.[13] Political intervention to thwart the application of the law – particularly in cases reviewing police misconduct – as well as efforts to secure exceptions from judicial review through legislation have combined to weaken the ALL's potential impact. This experience needs to be borne in mind when assessing the potential effects of EPL provisions on public interest environmental litigation.

One potential role for public interest environmental litigation would be to encourage enforcement of the 2003 PRC Environmental Impact Assessment Law (EIAL).[14] The EIAL was enacted "in order to implement the sustainable development strategy, to take precautions against adverse

---

[11] Pitman B Potter, "The Administrative Litigation Law of the PRC: The Changing Relationship between the Courts and Administrative Agencies in China" in *Chinese Law and Government* (Fall 1991).

[12] Neil J Diamant, Stanley B Lubman and Kevin J O'Brien, *Engaging the Law in China: State, Society, and Possibilities for Justice* (Stanford: Stanford University Press, 2005); George J Gilboy and Benjamin L Read, "Political and Social Reform in China: Alive and Walking" (2008) 3 Wash Q 143.

[13] Kevin J O'Brien and Lianjiang Li, "Suing the Local State: Administrative Litigation in Rural China" (2004) 51 The China J 75; Minxin Pei, "Citizens v. Mandarins: Administrative Litigation in China" (1997) 152 The China Q 832.

[14] Environmental Impact Assessment Law of the People's Republic of China, 28 October 2002 (entered into force 1 September 2003), available at http://www.

effects on the environment after implementation of plans and completion of construction projects, and to promote the coordinated development of the economy, society and environment" (Article 1). The law requires relevant departments of the State Council as well as local people's governments at the prefecture and provincial level to develop plans on land-use that incorporate environmental impact assessments:

> Article 2: Evaluation of environmental effects mentioned in this Law consists of the analysis, prediction and assessment made of the possible environmental effects after implementation of plans and completion of construction projects, ways put forth and measures for preventing or mitigating the adverse effects on the environment, and the methods and systems applied for follow-up monitoring.
>
> Article 3: When plans within the scope . . . of this Law are formulated, the environmental effects produced by the projects to be constructed within the territory of the People's Republic of China or within the sea areas under the jurisdiction of the People's Republic of China shall be evaluated in accordance with this Law.
>
> Article 4: The environmental effects shall be evaluated in an objective, open and impartial manner, with an all-round consideration given to the possible effects on the various environmental factors and on the ecological system, which is composed of the factors, after a plan is implemented or a project is constructed, providing a scientific basis for decision-making.

The EIAL requires environmental impact assessments to be made for "special programs" in industry, agriculture, forestry, energy, and a range of other sectors, which must include analysis, countermeasures and a conclusion on environmental impacts. Environmental assessments must be consulted in the course of project approval. While initial reports were disappointing (calling to mind the ALL experience),[15] public interest environmental litigation may potentially become more effective in inducing local officials to intensify enforcement of EIAL requirements.

General provisions of the EPL and EIAL are augmented by a range of laws and regulations on specific issues such as conservation, water protection and pollution control. China's Air Pollution Law (rev. 2015)[16]

---

npc.gov.cn/englishnpc/Law/2007-12/06/content_1382122.htm (accessed 13 April 2016).

[15] Worldwatch Institute, "China to Strengthen Public Participation in Environmental Impact Assessments", available at http://www.worldwatch.org/china-strengthen-public-participation-environmental-impact-assessments (accessed 10 January 2017).

[16] Clean Air Alliance of China, "Final New PRC Air Law on Air Pollution Prevention and Control" (September 2015), available at http://en.cleanairchina.org/product/7332.html (accessed 10 January 2017); Xinhua News, "Xinhua Insight:

aims to address the increasingly deadly air pollution problems in virtually all China's cities.[17] The Water Pollution Control Law (rev. 2008)[18] and the 2015 "Action Plan for Water Pollution Prevention"[19] express state policy goals to resolve China's burgeoning water pollution problem.[20] Yet China has enacted a wealth of environmental protection laws and regulations over the past 30 years, but with limited effect in constraining ever-worsening pollution.[21]

To the extent that the PRC legal system is primarily an instrument of policy enforcement,[22] enforcement of the formal legal standards on environmental protection remains subject to the processes of balancing policy priorities. Economic growth priorities are evident in state economic plans. The 12th Five Year Plan (FYP) (2011–2015) cited economic growth as the primary objective, while the 13th FYP continues this emphasis, noting for example the goal to double China's 2010 GDP level by 2020.[23] Economic growth imperatives are also evident in the foreign investment

---

China passes law to control air pollution", Xinhuanet (29 August 2015), available at http://news.xinhuanet.com/english/2015-08/29/c_134568483.htm (accessed 10 January 2017).

[17] Justin Worland, "China Issues 'Red Alert' Over Devastating Air Pollution", *Time* (19 December 2015), available at http://time.com/4155365/china-red-alert-smog/ (accessed 10 January 2017); "What is China doing to tackle its air pollution", *BBC News* (20 January 2016), available at http://www.bbc.com/news/world-asia-china-35351597 (accessed 10 January 2017).

[18] Law of the PRC on Prevention and Control of Water Pollution, 28 February 2008 (entered into force 1 June 2008), available at http://www.npc.gov.cn/englishnpc/Law/2011-02/14/content_1620412.htm (accessed 10 January 2017).

[19] EU-China Environmental Governance Programme, *Action Plan for Water Prevention* (May 2015), available at http://www.china.org.cn/government/laws/2007-04/17/content_1207459.htm (accessed 10 January 2017).

[20] Morgan Winsor, "China's Pollution Crisis: Nearly Two-Thirds of Underground Water is Graded Unfit for Human Contact, Report Says", *International Business Times* (4 June 2015), available at http://www.ibtimes.com/chinas-pollution-crisis-nearly-two-thirds-underground-water-graded-unfit-human-1953442 (accessed 10 January 2017); Avraham Ebenstein, "The Consequences of Industrialization: Evidence from Water Pollution and Digestive Cancers in China", *Review of Economics and Statistics* (2010), available at http://www.mitpressjournals.org/doi/abs/10.1162/REST_a_00150 (accessed 10 January 2017).

[21] See China.org.cn, at http://www.china.org.cn/english/environment/34152.htm (accessed 10 January 2017).

[22] Pitman B Potter, *China's Legal System* (Cambridge: Polity Press, 2013).

[23] Jianfeng Zhang, "Xi expounds on guideline for 13th Five-year Plan", *CCTV.com* (11 March 2016), available at http://english.cntv.cn/2015/11/03/ARTI1446559744633822.shtml (accessed 10 January 2017); Jon Taylor, "Growth, livelihoods to be focused at plenum", *Beijing Review* (28 October 2015), available at

guide and catalogue of 2011 and 2015,[24] and the State Council's 2010 opinion on foreign investment.[25] While these measures also contain references to the need to build sustainability into China's economic development program, the growth agenda remains primary.

The dominant influence of the National Development and Reform Commission's (NDRC's) economic growth priorities often works to marginalize the influence of government ministries and agencies charged with public interest imperatives such as environmental protection.[26] While some have suggested the NDRC's influence has faded of late, increasingly public opposition to Xi Jinping's economic reforms suggests otherwise.[27] In addition, local cadre evaluation systems are often unable to change behavior of local officials to attend to environmental conditions over economic indicators such as employment, capital investment and economic

---

http://www.china.org.cn/opinion/2015-10/28/content_36913499_2.htm (accessed 10 January 2017).

[24] Rainy Yao, "Update: Latest Guidance Catalogue for Foreign Investment Industries Released", *China Briefing* (20 March 2015), available at http://www.china-briefing.com/news/2015/03/20/breaking-news-updated-guidance-catalogue-foreign-investment-industries-released.html (accessed 10 January 2017); Ministry of Commerce, People's Republic of China, "Catalogue for the Guidance of Foreign Investment Industries" (21 February 2012), available at http://english.mofcom.gov.cn/article/policyrelease/aaa/201203/20120308027837.shtml (accessed 10 January 2017).

[25] Fa Guo, "Several Opinions of the State Council on Further Utilizing Foreign Investment", *Invest in China* (2010), available at http://www.fdi.gov.cn/1800000121_39_2583_0_7.html (accessed 10 January 2017).

[26] Dexter Roberts, "China's Economic Policy Factory: The NDRC", *Bloomberg* (30 June 2013), available at http://www.bloomberg.com/news/articles/2013-06-20/chinas-economic-policy-factory-the-ndrc (accessed 17 January 2017). While some have suggested that the NDRC's influence has faded of late, increasingly public opposition to Xi Jinping's economic reforms suggests otherwise.

[27] Compare Peter Martin, "The Humbling of the NDRC: China's National Development and Reform Commission Searches for a New Role Amid Restructuring", 14:5 China Brief (6 March 2014), available at http://www.jamestown.org/programs/chinabrief/single/?tx_ttnews%5Btt_news%5D=42057&cHash=8866680e4f4e57e8997beb2cfbaa7aaa#.VxUvPWNN38s with Elizabeth Economy, "The Fits and Starts of China's Economic Reforms", *Forbes Asia* (25 January 2016), available at http://www.forbes.com/sites/elizabetheconomy/2016/01/25/the-fits-and-starts-of-chinas-economic-reforms/#42d3ee3522f6 and William Ide and Salbal Dasgupta, "Worries About China's Economic Reform Progress Grow", *Voice of America* (10 March 2016), available at http://www.voanews.com/content/china-economy-reforms/3228862.html. All websites accessed 10 January 2017.

growth rates.[28] Local governments and officials are often complicit in environmental destruction, as economic indicators are often given priority over conservation and environmental protection. These policy distortions, combined with underlying socio-cultural and political obstacles to enforcement of formal law and regulation, have contributed to the generally weak state of legal performance in environmental protection.

In response, the government has expressed increased awareness of the importance of protecting the natural environment. The 12th FYP gave specific preference to sustainable development goals linked with environmental protection, while the State Council's 2010 opinion on utilizing foreign investment and the 2011 and 2015 Guiding Catalogues for foreign investment offer incentives for environmentally sustainable projects.[29] The recently announced 13th FYP contains specific provisions for reducing pollution and protecting the environment.[30] The potential involvement of local community groups and semi-autonomous NGOs under the new EPL may bring additional voices to the table and challenge the government's long-standing monopoly on environmental protection discourse. This has the implications for other policy sectors where primary authority for policy enforcement remains with the Party/state.

B. Environmental Protection and China's Trade Relations

China's regulatory regime for environmental protection has implications for trade policy positions in a variety of areas, including subsidies. The general lack of environmental enforcement has been identified as a significant contributor to low-cost exports, upon which 22 percent of China's economy depends.[31] Non-enforcement of environmental standards in

---

[28] Alex L Wang, "The Search for Sustainable Legitimacy: Environmental Law and Bureaucracy in China" (2013) 37 Harv Envir L Rev 365; Carl F Minzner, "Riots and Cover-ups: Counterproductive Control of Local Agents in China" (2009) 31:1 U Pa J Int'l L 53.

[29] Joseph Casey and Katherine Koleski, "Backgrounder: China's 12th Five Year Plan", *U.S.-China Economic & Security Review Commission* (24 June 2011), available at http://origin.www.uscc.gov/sites/default/files/Research/12th-FiveYearPlan_062811.pdf (accessed 10 January 2017).

[30] Deborah Seligsohn and Angel Hsu, "How China's 13th Five-Year Plan Addresses Energy and the Environment", *China File* (10 March 2016), available at https://www.chinafile.com/reporting-opinion/environment/how-chinas-13th-five-year-plan-addresses-energy-and-environment (accessed 10 January 2017).

[31] World Bank, "Exports of goods and services (% of GDP)", available at http://data.worldbank.org/indicator/NE.EXP.GNFS.ZS (accessed 10 February 2017).

effect underwrites the lowering of production costs by exporting firms. Even if these arrangements do not constitute subsidies under the GATT/WTO Subsidies Agreement,[32] the link between trade performance and the government's environmental policy and practice is clear.

The GATT/WTO trade regime does permit government supports for environmental compliance. Under the GATT Agreement on Subsidies and Countervailing Measures ("Subsidies Agreement"), support for environmental compliance is generally excluded from the category of prohibited (actionable) subsidies, subject to a range of exceptions, such as:

> 8.2 (c) assistance to promote adaptation of existing facilities to new environmental requirements imposed by law and/or regulations which result in greater constraints and financial burden on firms, provided that the assistance:
> (i) is a one-time non-recurring measure; and
> (ii) is limited to 20 percent of the cost of adaptation; and
> (iii) does not cover the cost of replacing and operating the assisted investment, which must be fully borne by firms; and
> (iv) is directly linked to and proportionate to a firm's planned reduction of nuisances and pollution, and does not cover any manufacturing cost savings which may be achieved; and
> (v) is available to all firms which can adopt the new equipment and/or production processes.[33]

Thus, subject to compliance with the limitations provided, the PRC government assistance to firms supporting investment in environmental compliance is generally acceptable under the Subsidies Agreement.

Aside from subsidies questions, issues arise around issues of selective enforcement of environmental protection rules.[34] When selective enforce-

---

[32] Agreement on Subsidies and Countervailing Measures, art 1, available at https://www.wto.org/english/docs_e/legal_e/24-scm.pdf (accessed 10 January 2017) defines subsidies largely in terms of government provision of funds or goods or the foregoing of revenue. Since failures of compliance with environmental laws and regulations are generally viewed as systemic issues of institutional capacity and corruption rather than deliberate acts of government, they generally do not qualify as subsidies. While government decisions on matters such as funding for environmental protection or design of cadre evaluations that do not provide adequate incentives for environmental enforcement may appear as deliberate foregoing of enforcement and the revenues that stem from it, such decisions are generally considered as too indirect to be classified as subsidies.

[33] Agreement on Subsidies and Countervailing Measures (note 32 above).

[34] On the general practice of selective enforcement of law and regulation in China, see Donghua Chen, Dequan Jiang, Shangkun Liang, Fangping Wang, "Selective Enforcement of Regulation" (2011) 4:1–2 Chinese J Accounting Research 9.

ment targets foreign companies, questions arise concerning the national treatment provisions of the GATT.[35] Concerns over inadequate and selective enforcement and potential conflicts with international trade rules were evident in the WTO Committee on Regional Trade Agreements in its discussion of the China-Switzerland Free Trade Agreement:[36]

> Chapter 12 addresses trade-related environmental issues between the Parties. The Parties . . . strive to improve the level of environmental protection by all means, including by effective implementation of their environmental laws and regulations. They further recognize that it is inappropriate to encourage trade or investment by weakening or reducing the protections afforded in domestic environmental laws, regulations, policies and practices. The Parties agree that environmental standards shall not be used for protectionist trade purposes (Article 12.2).

China's use of environmental protection measures in trade matters also involves issues of discrimination. China's imposition of restrictions on exports of various rare earth elements along with exports of Tungsten and Molybdenum was deemed discriminatory despite China's claim that the restrictions were necessary for reasons of resource conservation and environmental protection.[37] The WTO Appellate Body concluded that the restrictions were aimed at achieving industrial policy goals of supporting

---

[35] Bloomberg News, "China Targeting Foreign Companies, American Chamber Says" (2 September 2014), available at http://www.bloomberg.com/news/articles/2014-09-02/u-s-companies-say-china-subjectively-enforcing-laws (accessed 10 January 2017); IHS, "China's implementation of expanded environmental regulation is variable but foreign firms face only moderate selective enforcement" (7 May 2015), available at https://www.ihs.com/country-industry-forecasting.html?ID=1065998990 (accessed 15 February 2017); Ma Xiaoying and Leonard Ortolano, *Environmental Regulation in China: Institutions, Enforcement and Compliance* (Lanham: Rowman & Littlefield, 2000).

[36] WTO Committee on Regional Trade Agreement, "Factual Presentation: Free Trade Agreement between Switzerland and China (Goods and Services)" WT/REG351/1 (18 June 2015) 36–7.

[37] World Trade Organization, "China – Measures Related to the Exportation of Rare Earths, Tungsten and Molybdenum", DS 431 (2014), available at https://www.wto.org/english/tratop_e/dispu_e/cases_e/ds431_e.htm (accessed 10 January 2017). See generally, Markus Wagner, "WTO Law and the Right to Regulate: China – Rare Earths" (2014) 18:10 ASIL Insights, available at https://www.asil.org/insights/volume/18/issue/10/wto-law-and-right-regulate-china-–-rare-earths (accessed 10 January 2017); Bill Butcher, "WTO Open Trade Rules and Domestic Environmental Protection Policies: A Balancing Approach" in Larry Kreiser, Soocheol Lee, Kazuhiro Ueta, Janet E. Milne and Hope Ashiabor *Environmental Taxation and Green Fiscal Reform* (London: Edward Elgar, 2014), 69–81 at 72–8.

Chinese producers of electronic components and were not justified under GATT Article XX general exceptions.

China's environmental challenges have also given rise to trade issues concerning food production and supply systems.[38] As a result, China faces challenges over the safety of its exports.[39] GATT Article XX(b) (General Exceptions) permits signatory parties to impose import restrictions "necessary to protect human, animal or plant life or health, provided these are non-discriminatory and do not constitute a disguised restriction on trade".[40] In the "Shrimp/Turtle Case" brought by India, Malaysia, Pakistan and Thailand against the US, the WTO Appellate Body confirmed that countries have a right under GATT Article XX to take trade action to protect the environment provided non-discrimination criteria are met.[41]

However, measures limiting imports, whether under GATT/WTO,

---

[38] See, for example, Guangwei He, "China's Dirty Pollution Secret: The Boom Poisoned Its Soil and Crops", *Tainted Harvest: Environment 360 Special Report Part I* (30 June 2014), available at http://e360.yale.edu/feature/chinas_dirty_pollution_secret_the_boom_poisoned_its_soil_and_crops/2782/ and Guangwei He, "In China's Heartland, A Toxic Trail Leads from Factories to Fields to Food", *Tainted Harvest: Environment 360 Special Report Part II* (7 July 2014), available at http://e360.yale.edu/feature/chinas_toxic_trail_leads_from_factories_to_food/2784/; Rob Schmitz, "China's toxic harvest: growing tainted food in 'cancer villages'", *Marketplace World* (16 April 2013), available at http://www.marketplace.org/topics/world/chinas-toxic-harvest-growing-tainted-food-cancer-villages; Charles W Freeman III and Xiaoqing Lu, *Assessing Chinese Government Response to the Challenge of Environment and Health* (Washington: Centre for Strategic and International Studies, 2008). All websites accessed 10 January 2017.

[39] Stanley Lubman, "Why Americans Should Worry About China's Food Safety Problems", *China Real Time* (21 May 2013), available at http://blogs.wsj.com/chinarealtime/2013/05/21/why-americans-should-worry-about-chinas-food-safety-problems/ (accessed 10 January 2017); Jenifer Huang McBeath and Jerry McBeath, *Environmental Change and Food Security in China* (Dordrecht: Springer, 2010) 230–1; Nicholas Zamiska, "Who's Monitoring Chinese Food Exports?" *Wall Street Journal* (9 April 2007), available at http://www.wsj.com/articles/SB117608207682763704 (accessed 10 January 2017).

[40] General Agreement on Tariffs and Trade (GATT: Geneva 1986), art XX, available at https://www.wto.org/english/docs_e/legal_e/gatt47_e.pdf (accessed 10 January 2017).

[41] World Trade Organization, "United States – Import Prohibition of Certain Shrimp and Shrimp Products – Report of the Appellate Body" (AB-1998-4), WT/DS58/AB/R (12 October 1998), available at https://www.wto.org/english/tratop_e/dispu_e/58abr.pdf (accessed 10 January 2017). For discussion, see World Trade Organization, "The environment: a specific concern", available at https://www.wto.org/english/thewto_e/whatis_e/tif_e/bey2_e.htm#dolphin (accessed 10 January 2017).

Article XX ("General Exceptions") or under the Sanitary and Phytosanitary Measures (SPS) Agreement, must focus on the health aspects of the imported product and cannot impose a signatory party's environmental regulatory standards on the regulatory regimes or production methods of other parties. This distinction between the imported product and the process for its production was addressed in the Tuna/Dolphin disputes (I: Mexico–US // II: EEC, Netherlands–US), in which GATT panels held that the US was not permitted to embargo tuna products from producing states such as Mexico or from intermediary countries on grounds that local regulations on production of tuna did not satisfy US regulatory requirements, but could impose trade measures on the quality or content of the tuna imported.[42] Trade measures restricting imports from China on health grounds must still meet the non-discrimination standards of GATT and WTO. Hence, a US measure restricting poultry imports from China was rejected by a WTO Dispute Resolution Panel on grounds that it was did not satisfy the procedural, evidentiary and non-discrimination requirements of the SPS Agreement, and was not justified under GATT, Article XX.[43]

Nonetheless, from 2002 to 2012, China's agricultural exports to the US faced some 19,401 import refusals on SPS Agreement grounds, second only to India among the BRIICS economies (Brazil, Russia, Indonesia, India, China, South Africa).[44] China's other trade partners have also relied on the SPS Agreement to restrict imports from China.[45] On the

---

42 World Trade Organization, "United States – Restrictions on Imports of Tuna: Report of the Panel" (DS21/6 – 39S/155) (2 September 1991), available at http://www.worldtradelaw.net/document.php?id=reports/gattpanels/tunadolphinI.pdf and "United States – Restrictions on Imports of Tuna: Report of the Panel" (DS/29R) (16 June 1994), available at http://www.worldtradelaw.net/document.php?id=reports/gattpanels/tunadolphinII.pdf. For discussion, see World Trade Organization, "The environment a specific concern", available at https://www.wto.org/english/thewto_e/whatis_e/tif_e/bey2_e.htm#dolphin. All websites accessed 10 January 2017.

43 World Trade Organization, "United States – Certain Measures Affecting Imports of Poultry from China", WT/DS392/R (29 September 2010), available at https://www.wto.org/english/tratop_e/dispu_e/cases_e/ds392_e.htm (accessed 10 January 2017).

44 Murali Kallummal and Hari Maya Gurung, "Agricultural Products Imported by United States and SPS Measures Based Refusals: Impact of Refusals by the FDA of United States on BRIICS Countries", 26–7, available at http://www.academia.edu/7430130/Agriculture_Products_Imported_by_United_States_and_SPS_Measures_based_Refusals_Impact_of_Refusals_by_the_FDA_of_United_States_on_BRIICS_Countries (accessed 10 January 2017).

45 Fengxia Dong and Helen H Jensen, "China's Challenge: Conforming to Sanitary and Phytosanitary Measures for Agricultural Exports" (2004) 10:2

other hand, China itself has often relied on the SPS Agreement as grounds for restricting agricultural imports,[46] despite complaints that regulatory conditions in China are inconsistent with the transparency requirements of the SPS Agreement.[47]

In sum, China environmental challenges have significant implications for its compliance with international trade policy standards. China's environmental challenges, and the regulatory system developed to manage them, give rise to trade policy issues around subsidies, selective enforcement and national treatment, as well as health-based restrictions. The potential conflicts between China's environmental protection regime and its obligations under international trade law invite consideration of alternative ways to manage China's environmental challenges.

IV. COORDINATING ENVIRONMENTAL PERFORMANCE: THE POTENTIAL FOR CORPORATE SOCIAL RESPONSIBILITY

We have used the concept of "coordinated compliance" to explore challenges and opportunities for more fulsome performance on international trade and human rights standards.[48] Applying this approach to China's environmental challenge, we move from the question of national performance of international standards to the issue of local performance of national standards.[49] A key element in building coordinated compliance in China's environmental protection involves bridging the gaps between formal accountability to the state under the EPL regime and informal

---

Iowa Ag Rev, available at http://www.card.iastate.edu/iowa_ag_review/spring_04/article4.aspx (accessed 10 January 2017).

[46] US International Trade Commission, *China's Agricultural Trade: Competitive Conditions and Effects of U.S. Exports* (Investigation No. 332-518, Publication 4219) (March 2011) 9 et seq.

[47] European Commission, "China–SPS–Import conditions related to milk and dairy products" (12 December 2014), available at http://madb.europa.eu/madb/sps_barriers_details.htm?barrier_id=10881 (accessed 10 January 2017).

[48] Asia Pacific Foundation of Canada, "Advancing Canada's Engagement with Asia on Human Rights: Integrating Business and Human Rights" (2013), available at https://www.asiapacific.ca/sites/default/files/filefield/human_rights_taskforce_v3.pdf (accessed 10 January 2017).

[49] Pitman B Potter, "International and Domestic Selective Adaptation: The Case of Charter 08" in John Gillespie and Pip Nicholson, eds, *Law and Development and the Global Discourses of Legal Transfers* (Cambridge: Cambridge University Press, 2012) 56.

accountability to society under emerging standards of corporate social responsibility (CSR).

China has given significant attention to CSR, primarily through establishment of central and local organizations aimed at publicizing best practices of business behavior.[50] China's CSR priorities emerged from the discourses of "harmonious society" (和谐社会) and "scientific development"（科学发展）through which the Hu Jintao leadership (2002–2012) attempted to balance economic growth imperatives. Xi Jinping's government, after focusing on anti-corruption and consolidation of political power during its early years in power, has focused more recently on issues of quality of life.[51] CSR offers potential for strengthening environmental protection in pursuit of these goals.

In the environmental context, CSR stands as an alternative to formal legal and regulatory enforcement.[52] Chinese regulatory authorities are increasingly suggesting that commitments to CSR principles be included as conditions for business license approval. Civil awareness campaigns on CSR are also aimed at building environmental compliance. CSR has the potential to augment provisions under the new EPL for public interest environmental litigation. In contrast to the dynamic of formal accountability that characterizes environmental protection law and regulation, CSR may be appreciated as an exercise in informal accountability. Whereas compliance with formal legal requirements on environmental protection involves relations between business firms and the state, CSR involves relations with society more broadly.

The emergence of CSR initiatives and campaigns reflects the government's dilemma of securing social development conditions in the face of policy priorities of economic growth. Environmental protection is a compelling example of conditions where inadequate enforcement and performance of formal laws and regulations has mandated consideration of alternatives. China's CSR efforts represent an ironic return to the campaign-style measures of earlier years, which the formal legal

---

[50] Embassy of Sweden in Beijing, "A Study on Corporate Social Responsibility Development and Trends in China", available at http://www.csr-asia.com/report/CSR-development-and-trends-in-China-FINAL-hires.pdf (accessed 10 January 2017). See also China's Corporate Social Responsibility website, *China CSR*, available at http://www.chinacsr.com/en/, which extols the virtues of CSR and publicizes efforts by government agencies and business groups to encourage voluntary support (accessed 10 January 2017).

[51] Xinhua News, "Xinhua Insight: China to start reform focused on quality of life", Xinhuanet (11 December 2015), available at http://news.xinhuanet.com/english/2015-12/11/c_134907652.htm (accessed 10 January 2017).

[52] See generally, *China CSR* (note 50 above).

system was intended to replace. In an effort to secure better environmental enforcement in the face of indifferent performance by the engines of economic growth and the continued limits on effective legal regulation, CSR has become a necessary response. Nonetheless, many lawyers and law professors in China wonder whether the campaign-style rhetoric of China's CSR programs will undermine formal and consistent enforcement of China's laws and regulations. In the context of local political and policy competition over normative and institutional frameworks for environmental protection, CSR activities invite questions as to whether CSR is a substitute for legal compliance under the EPL regime, or a supplement.

On the one hand, the EPL is predicated on principles of socialist governance that emphasize the processes of local accountability to higher levels of government. The norms of "patrimonial sovereignty" are paramount as the EPL focuses on subordination of local economic actors to the policy dictates of the state while ensuring that local regulatory agencies remain subordinate to higher levels in the Party/state system. The importance of environmental protection centres on the goals of Party/state to deliver conditions of economic and social development. Thus, interpretation and application of environmental protection standards become simply a variant on the theme that law and policy is the exclusive purview of the Party/state. In many ways this follows the dynamic of internal accountability exemplified by corporate governance doctrines.[53] Thus, provisions on environmental protection focus primarily on accountability of polluters and regulators to other Party/state actors within the regulatory ambit of the Party/state. The focus of the EPL regime on internal accountability is aimed at protecting the integrity and governance authority of the Party/state. Even under the EPL's new provisions for public interest "social organizations" (EPL, Article 58), these non-governmental plaintiffs must still be formally recognized, approved and registered by the government. Recent efforts to require the establishment of CPC (Communist Party of China) units (*dangzu*) in all non-government organizations[54] suggest that the reach of the Party/

---

53 Pitman B Potter, "Coordinating Corporate Governance and Corporate Social Responsibility" (2009) HKU LJ 675. Reprinted in (2011) 1 Tsinghua LJ (15 January 2011) 43 (in Chinese). Reprinted as Pitman B Potter, "Coordinating Corporate Governance and Corporate Social Responsibility" in Wesley Cragg, ed., *Business and Human Rights* (Cheltenham: Edward Elgar, 2012).

54 Beijing News, "Shehui zuzhi lingdao jiguan yao sheli dangzu" (Leadership organs in social organizations must establish Party organs) (30 May 2015), available at http://www.bjnews.com.cn/news/2015/05/30/365259.html (accessed 10 January 2017).

state and the imposition of its policy and political interests will extend to public interest environmental litigation.

CSR regimes, on the other hand, tend to focus on informal accountability to society. Thus CSR approaches to environmental protection emphasize community input and engagement with economic and regulatory actors involved in environmental protection efforts. Use of "model company" benchmarks to encourage stronger compliance with environmental standards, application of a "regulation *plus*" model of governance whereby legal and regulatory standards are augmented by assessment and remediation of community impacts of pollution, and the use of community consultation mechanisms to solicit popular input on environmental questions, all reflect the external accountability dynamics of CSR.

Bridging the gaps between the formal regulatory standards of the EPL and the more informal processes of CSR regimes requires an effort at coordination much like that applied to coordinated performance of trade and human rights standards. Paradigms of selective adaptation and institutional capacity are useful to explain the potential for coordinated compliance in China's environmental protection regime. Component factors of perception, complementarity and legitimacy that inform selective adaptation can help identify elements of complementarity between the regulatory standards of the EPL and various CSR norms. *Perceptions* about the purposes and function of formal law and regulation in maintaining the authority of the Party/state may conflict with perceptions about CSR as a mechanism for protecting local community interests. Dynamics of *complementarity* invite consideration of the potential for harmonizing EPL doctrine and practice with the requirements of CSR. Questions about *legitimacy* emerge as the effectiveness of EPL measures are inseparable from questions about the authority of the Party/state, while the legitimacy of CSR efforts may be coloured by the competing legitimacy of local community relationships and interests. In light of new attention paid by the CPC to controlling NGOs and other civil society organizations,[55] legitimacy of environmental protection efforts emerging from civil society may lose autonomy and the legitimacy that goes with it.

Similarly, challenges of institutional capacity invite attention to operational questions of institutional purpose, location, orientation and

---

[55] "Zhongguo Gongchandang dangzu gongzuo tiaoli (shixing)" (CPC provisional regulations on the work of Party units) (16 June 2015), available at http://politics.people.com.cn/n/2015/0617/c1001-27166019.html (accessed 10 January 2017). An English translation is available at "Party Group Work Regulations (Provisional)", *China Law Translate*, available at http://chinalawtranslate.com/partygroupregs/?lang=en (accessed 10 January 2017).

cohesion as between EPL regulation and CSR approaches. Questions of *institutional purpose* emerge in the tension between upholding the authority of the Party/state under EPL doctrine and protecting the interests of local communities under CSR ideals. CPC dominance in the legal and regulatory system coupled with increased CPC involvement in civil society organizations allows CPC dictates to prevail, which often reflect priorities around economic growth and business development rather than community interests in environmental safety. Questions about *institutional location* draw attention to variation among China's geographic regions, but also to the locus of regulation and authority within the bureaucratic regulatory system. Thus EPL enforcement tends to be constrained by bureaucratic competition with development-oriented agencies such as the NDRC, while CSR initiatives appear somewhat freer from such bureaucratic political limitations.

Questions about *institutional orientation* also emerge as the formal orientation of the EPL regime may conflict with the more informal character of CSR programming. Here again the expansion of CPC involvement from the formal legal and regulatory system to the less formal NGO arena where CSR might be expected to predominate suggests a possible reduction in the diversity of institutional approaches to managing the environment and may well exacerbate existing issues of institutional orientation. Finally, institutional capacity in environmental protection depends on issues of *institutional cohesion*, involving the willingness of individuals within institutions to comply with edicts from organizational and extra-organizational leaders, and to enforce institutional goals. While challenges of institutional cohesion may arise in any organizational context, the institutional settings for EPL enforcement invite closer scrutiny of institutional cohesion than in the CSR context, where the relative lack of formal institutionalization may remove many of the conflicts of interest that lead to cohesion problems in more bureaucratic agencies.

CSR approaches also have application in China's international trade relationships. To the extent that CSR standards augment formal regulatory rules and processes, they may provide expanded incentives for compliance by Chinese and foreign companies.[56] The possibility that CSR efforts may reflect social concerns rather than bureaucratic interests may help to reduce problems of selective enforcement against foreign inves-

[56] Lanlin Bu and Michael Bloomfield, with Jiali An, "CSR Guide for Multinational Corporations in China: Prosperity with Integrity", *Harmony Foundation* (2013), available at http://harmonyfdn.ca/wp-content/uploads/2013/04/CSR-Guide-for-MNCs-in-China.pdf (accessed 10 January 2017).

tors – communities may care less about the nationality of polluters than government agencies with personal and financial links to local firms. Coordinating formal legal environmental performance with informal CSR standards may help address compliance questions in area of food safety that have contributed to application of General Exceptions (GATT, Article XX) and SPS safeguards against Chinese products. While uncertainties remain as to whether reported compliance with CSR standards reflects genuine changes in business behavior or is simply public relations reporting by another name,[57] the public attention paid to CSR behavior nonetheless operates as an important input to corporate conduct. This, combined with the public interest environmental litigation regime enshrined in the revised EPL, suggests hopeful possibilities for the future.

V. CONCLUSION

Just as the forces of globalization have challenged conventional expectations about the nation-state and its regulatory reach, so too has the importance of coordinating environmental protection and trade performance challenged conventional boundaries of law and policy. China's challenges in environmental protection have persisted despite decades of formal law and regulation, with multiple impacts on trade policy and performance. While human rights in environmental protection have often been seen as conflicting with trade policy priorities of efficiency and development, coordinated performance offers a promising middle ground. The potential for CSR efforts to improve the effectiveness of formal legal regimes for environmental protection suggests possible hopeful futures for China's environmental protection challenge.

---

[57] Christina Larson, "'Corporate Social Responsibility' Reports in China: Progress or Greenwashing?", Bloomberg (12 December 2013), available at http://www.bloomberg.com/news/articles/2013-12-12/corporate-social-responsibility-reports-in-china-progress-or-greenwashing (accessed 10 January 2017); Liwen Lin, "Corporate Social Responsibility in China: Window Dressing or Structure Change?" (2010) 28:1 Berkeley J Int'l L 64.

11. Structuring China's engagement with international human rights: the case of wage protection law and practice*

Sarah Biddulph

I. INTRODUCTION

The relationship between international trade and human rights and its local implementation, the theme of this book, is nowhere more apparent than in the area of labour. Decent work has been identified by many agencies including the International Labour Organisation (ILO) and the United Nations Development Program (UNDP) as core to human development, and key to enabling people to lead dignified, socially engaged lives.[1] But the international trade regime has not clearly contributed to improving the lives and livelihoods of all workers, especially those whose conditions of work are harsh, who receive little or no pay, whose health is harmed and whose working conditions deprive them of personal autonomy and dignity.[2]

China has been identified as one of the major threats to international labour standards (through competition for a larger share of low cost exports);[3] at the same time as it has been praised for lifting over 800

* This chapter is based on a paper presented to the workshop on "Mapping the Impact of International Trade and Human Rights on Local Practice", held in July 2014 at the International Institute for the Sociology of Law in Oñati, Spain. This research was supported by a grant from the Australian Research Council FT130100412.

[1] Selim Jahan, "Human Development Report 2015: Work for Human Development" in *Human Development Report* (Geneva: United Nations Development Programme, 2016).

[2] Ibid.

[3] Anita Chan and Robert Ross, "Racing to the Bottom: International Trade without a Social Clause" (2003) 24:6 Third World Q 1011; Gunseli Berik and Yana van der Meulen Rodgers, "The Debate on Labour Standards and International

million people out of poverty since commencing economic reforms in 1978.[4] As a large, powerful country, China's approach to labour regulation is significant. Domestic regulation of labour directly affects multiples of millions of people both in China and (indirectly) overseas. China is also a powerful international player, actively engaged in influencing the development of international trade and human rights rules.[5] Participation in bilateral and multilateral treaties has increasingly enabled China to export its vision of the relationship between law, business and labour, a trend which is only likely to accelerate. The most recent statement of this resolve was in the 13th Five Year Plan (2016–2020) on National Social and Economic Development, approved at the National People's Congress annual meeting in March 2016. It sets as a priority active participation in global governance through participation in rule setting, promoting multilateral conventions and entering into regional and bilateral trade agreements (Chapter 52). Therefore, an examination of labour protection in China is not only significant in terms of exploring how international principles are given effect domestically, but also in terms of how domestic law and policy might be influential in international rule-setting negotiations.

This chapter pursues an inquiry about international rules and their relationship to labour rights in China with a particular focus on the protection of wages, which is the core right of workers to be paid for their work.[6] While Chinese law makes clear provision that a person must be paid for their work, in many sectors non- or delayed payment of wages remains a systemic and severe problem. In this respect China is not unique, especially with the proliferation of non-standard forms of work throughout the world. Nevertheless the domestic regulatory environment remains implicated in these ongoing failures. What features of the Chinese regulatory environment have contributed to this problem? The central argument is that two factors combine to shape the regulatory environment in which ongoing problems of wages insecurity persist. The first is the substantive law itself. This analysis reveals that substantive law is generally moving

---

Trade: Lessons from Cambodia and Bangladesh" (2008) *Department of Economics Working Paper Series University of Utah* Working No. 2007-03.

4 The World Bank, *China: Overview* (Washington DC: The World Bank, 6 April 2016), available at http://www.worldbank.org/en/country/china/overview (accessed 11 January 2017).

5 In relation to human rights, see Katrin Kinzelbach, "Will China's Rise Lead to a New Normative Order? An Analysis of China's Statements on Human Rights at the United Nations (2000–2010)" (2012) 30:3 Nethl QHR 299.

6 The discussion in this chapter primarily relates to regulation and enforcement of labour rights (being paid) and not negotiation of labour interests, such as increasing pay and conditions of work, which the law regulates poorly.

closer to international wage conventions, but an increasingly wide range of working people (particularly those in non-standard work who suffer a high degree of wage insecurity) do not fall within the reach of the legal regime to protect wages. The second is poor enforcement of the law, which remains a core weakness of the labour law regime and the system of wages regulation in particular. These features of the domestic regulation of wages together constitute the local legal environment that is one basis for an evaluation of China's engagement with international treaties and norms (others being policy and politics). It is also the place from which China proceeds when engaging in international treaty and rule-setting negotiations.

After providing a brief background to the role of economic reform in producing problems with wages, the chapter examines the key features of substantive regulation of wage protection with reference to the main elements of major ILO Wages Conventions, in particular the Minimum Wage-Fixing Machinery Convention (No. 26) and the Wage Protection Convention (No. 95) covering legal regulation of the minimum wage, wage payment and wage protection. In the literature on workers' rights and work law, greater attention has been paid to the problem of the gap between law and practice than to the substantive law, possibly because the failure to enforce the law has been such a glaring problem. So, this chapter places some emphasis on an analysis of the substantive law, particularly on the ways in which the law excludes certain categories of workers from the scope of legal protections, or limits the scope of those protections. It finds that the focus of wage protection law on the existence of a "labour relationship" provides the legal basis for exclusion of a wide range of workers who are either outside the scope of a labour relationship or cannot prove that one exists. Fragmentation of the workforce contributes significantly to the problem. Fragmentation of work law, with its many periodic, local and sectoral regulatory responses to wage insecurity, is also a feature of substantive law on wages and contributes to the unevenness of regulation to protect wages.

The chapter then examines (more briefly) law enforcement and dispute resolution. The weakness of enforcement of labour laws, and wages protection in particular, is well understood. A number of factors combine to weaken enforcement of the law: the legal prescription of predominately state-led enforcement of the labour law, the weakness of collective labour power, and the costs and delays associated with pursuing individual dispute resolution through mediation, labour arbitration and litigation.[7]

---

[7] Sean Cooney, "Making Chinese Labor Law Work: The Prospects for Regulatory Innovation in the People's Republic of China" (2006) 30:4 Fordham

The law itself is also weakened by the willingness of the Party-state to circumvent legal rules and dispute-resolution procedures and the preference for administrative mechanisms to resolve problems that it fears will exacerbate social instability.[8] The substantial gap between law and practice in this area has not only led to serious breaches of workers' rights in respect of wages, but has also been the cause of widespread labour unrest. Throughout, it becomes apparent that the modes of enforcement of wages law are not only influenced by economic and rights considerations but are also deeply concerned with protecting social stability.[9] This preoccupation with stability, together with an instinct to centralize (in the Chinese Communist Party ("Party") and state organs) both enactment and implementation of laws, plays a significant role in shaping enforcement of wages regulation in China.

The chapter returns finally to evaluate these particular characteristics of domestic law and practice as an instance of local engagement with international norms (in this case on wage protection).

II. BACKGROUND

As China embraced economic reform, a key element of market reform was to create a labour market. By 1994, with the passage of the Labour

---

Int'l LJ 1050; Sean Cooney, Sarah Biddulph and Ying Zhu, *Law and Fair Work in China* (London: Routledge, 2013); Virginia Harper Ho, "From Contracts to Compliance? An Early Look at Implementation under China's New Labor Legislation" (2009) 23:1 Colum J Asian L 35; Aaron Halegua, "Getting Paid: Processing the Labor Disputes of China's Migrant Workers" (2008) 26:1 Berkeley J Int'l L 254; Mary Gallagher, "Mobilizing the Law in China: 'Informed Disenchantment' and the Development of Legal Consciousness" (2006) 40:4 Law & Soc'y Rev 783; Chang Hee Lee, *Industrial Relations and Collective Bargaining in China* Working paper no. 7 (Geneva: International Labour Office, Industrial and Employment Relations Department, 2009).

[8] Yang Su and Xin He, "Street as Courtroom: State Accommodation of Labour Protest in South China" (2010) 44:1 Law & Soc'y Rev 157; Ching Kwan Lee and Yonghong Zhang, "The Power of Instability: Unravelling the Microfoundations of Bargained Authoritarianism in China" (2013) 118:6 Am J Sociology 1475; Sarah Biddulph, "Responding to Industrial Unrest in China: Prospects for Strengthening the Role of Collective Bargaining" (2012) 34:1 Sydney L Rev 35; Yongshun Cai, *State and Laid-off Workers in Reform China: the Silence and Collective Action of the Retrenched, Routledge Studies of China in Transition* (Abingdon: Routledge, 2006).

[9] Sarah Biddulph, *The Stability Imperative: Human Rights and Law in China* (Vancouver: UBC Press, 2015).

Law, urban employment had successfully been transformed from a model of lifetime, administratively allocated work to a system based on labour contracts. The Labour Law was intended to increase both management flexibility and worker protection, but while it realized the first goal, it was not successful in achieving the second.[10] A model of labour relations based on written individual labour contracts (supplemented with collective contracts) effectively individualized labour relations.[11] The collective labour voice was to be exercised in theory through the officially sanctioned union movement (the All-China Federation of Trade Unions, ACFTU) and workers congresses in enterprises. But these organizations were and continue to be weak and are poor advocates for workers' interests. Further, poor enforcement of labour laws has led to the labour law regime being characterized as one of "strong law and weak enforcement".[12]

The logic of market reforms, coupled with weak legal protections for workers and poor law enforcement, has seen a growing disparity in both wage level and wage security between different sectors of the labour market, creating a "dual economy".[13] One fault line in wage levels and wage security in urban areas is between urban residents and rural migrants. The number of rural migrants moving to cities in search of work (and staying there for more than six months) increased from 80 million in 2001 to 150 million in 2009.[14] In 2012 the estimated number of migrant workers in cities was 250 million.[15] Rural migrant workers continue to be disproportionately concentrated in sectors of low and insecure wages such as construction, infrastructure engineering, labour intensive production and service sectors including hospitality and retail.[16]

Another fault line has emerged between highly skilled workers and

---

[10] Mary Gallagher and Baohua Dong, "Legislating Harmony: Labor Law Reform in Contemporary China" in Sarosh Kuruvilla, Ching Kwan Lee and Mary Gallagher, eds, *From Iron Rice Bowl to Informalization: Markets, Workers and the State in a Changing China* (Ithaca: Cornell University Press, 2011) 36 at 44.

[11] Eli Friedman and Ching Kwan Lee, "Remaking the World of Chinese Labour: A 30-Year Retrospective" (2010) 48:3 BJIR 507 at 507–9.

[12] Mary Gallagher, "China's Workers Movement & the End of the Rapid-Growth Era" (2014) 143:2 Daedalus: J American Academy of Arts & Sciences 81 at 83.

[13] Fang Cai and Meiyan Wang, "Growth and Structural Changes in Employment in Transition in China" (2010) 38:1 J Comp Econ 71 at 71.

[14] Ibid. at 74.

[15] Zhiming Cheng, Ingrid Nielsen and Russell Smyth, "Determinants of Wage Arrears and Their Implications for the Socioeconomic Wellbeing of China's Migrant Workers: Evidence from Guangdong Province" (2013) 50:13 Monash U Department of Econ Discussion Papers 1 at 2.

[16] General Office of the State Council, *Opinion on Comprehensively Managing*

workers in sectors of strategic importance, and those in failing state-owned enterprises, private and informal sectors. Economic transformation from the mid-1990s resulted in a transfer of urban employment from the relative security and prosperity of state-owned and collectively owned enterprises to the private and informal sector. As a result of these changes, the proportion of urban workers employed in state-owned and collectively owned enterprises fell from 76 percent in 1995 to 27 percent in 2005.[17] By 2005, 46 percent of the workforce were employed informally – that is they were self-employed or lacked a formal labour contract.[18] As workers in unprofitable state-owned enterprises were laid off or stood down, many of these people also joined the ranks of the urban poor, either under-employed or unemployed.[19]

The disparity in wage levels is often accompanied by wage insecurity for those at the bottom, which is a serious and systemic problem. While wage arrears occur in all sectors of the economy, this problem is particularly acute in private enterprises and rural migrant workers suffer disproportionately.[20] A recent report on wages and employment by *China Labour Bulletin* indicates that in Beijing only 5.5 percent of construction workers get paid on a monthly basis as required by law (with around 20 percent getting paid monthly on a survey of five cities).[21] It is not surprising then that disputes over wages have risen continuously since market reforms began and have been the cause of a large proportion of all mass disturbances and protests. The strike map compiled by *China Labour Bulletin* (which likely underestimates the total number of strikes) shows an increase in construction worker protests, most of which are related to wage arrears: 473 protests were recorded between August 2014 and the Lunar New Year holiday in February 2015 (with 128 of those in February 2015).

---

the Problem of Non-payment of Migrant Workers' Wages (Beijing: General Office of the State Council, January 2016).

[17] Albert Park and Fang Cai, "The Informalization of the Chinese Labor Market" in Sarosh Kuruvilla, Ching Kwan Lee and Mary Gallagher, eds, *From Iron Rice Bowl to Informalization: Markets, Workers and the State in a Changing China* (Ithaca: Cornell University Press) 17 at 17.

[18] Ibid. at 18.

[19] Sarah Biddulph, *The Stability Imperative: Human Rights and Law in China* (Vancouver: UBC Press, 2015) 33–4.

[20] Cooney (note 7 above) at 1053; Gerard Greenfield and Tim Pringle, "The Challenge of Wage Arrears in China" in Manuel Simón Velasco, ed., *Paying Attention to Wages* (Geneva: International Labour Organisation, 2002).

[21] China Labour Bulletin, *Wages and employment* (Hong Kong: China Labour Bulletin, 22 February 2016), available at http://www.clb.org.hk/content/wages-and-employment (accessed 11 January 2017).

The number of strikes and protests increased further in 2015 (to 2700) and in January 2016 alone there were 500.[22] There are also many similar reports from local areas. Each tells a similar story of arrears of wages and wage-related disputes being an acute, ongoing problem. In Guangdong province for example, in the first nine months of 2015 there were over 13 300 complaints about wages to the labour administrative departments accounting for 59.6 percent of the total number of complaints. Over 74 percent (398 in total) of mass protests province-wide over that period, involving in excess of 30 people, related to wages disputes, with a significant proportion of those being construction related.[23]

Wage disparity and wage insecurity, in terms of both inequality and social instability, are sensitive political issues. There is renewed high level concern that the economic downturn from the mid-2010s will further exacerbate already serious labour unrest.[24] For a Party-state that has promised its people that they would benefit from economic reform and development through creation of a "moderately prosperous society" and which, at the same time, is particularly sensitive to social instability, employment, wage determination and wage protection can be nothing if not central policy issues. The 13th Five Year Plan both reaffirms the commitment to realizing a "moderately prosperous society" and recognizes the challenges faced by the rise in factors that contribute to social instability. In the area of wages policy, the 13th Five Year Plan specifies expanding employment as a priority and within that comprehensively dealing with problems of wages arrears suffered by migrant workers (Chapter 62), promoting collective salary negotiation (Chapter 63) and improving the mechanism for increasing the minimum wage (Chapter 63). As Greenfield and Pringle pointed out in their 2001 discussion of the problem of wage arrears, the sense of urgency expressed by central authorities in dealing with the problem of wage arrears was driven by the fear of social instability, not a concern for the protection of the rights and interests of workers.[25] This priority focus on social stability has arguably not changed since then.[26]

---

22 Ibid.

23 Ningdan Zhang, "Hopes for resolving the problem of wages arrears in the construction industry in Guangdong: draft amendment to the Wages Payment Provisions has been submitted for deliberation", *Legal Daily* (23 February 2016).

24 Javier Hernandez, "Labor Protests Multiply in China as Economy Slows, Worrying Leaders", *New York Times* (14 March 2016), available at http://www.nytimes.com/2016/03/15/world/asia/china-labor-strike-protest.html?_r=0 (accessed 11 January 2017).

25 Greenfield and Pringle (note 20 above) at 39.

26 Biddulph (note 19 above).

III. REGULATION OF WAGES

A. International Obligations on Wages

Among the earliest and ongoing concerns of the ILO have been "decent wage levels" and "fair remuneration practices".[27] Part XIII of the Treaty of Versailles articulated the "provision of an adequate living wage" as a core measure required to promote the social justice necessary to underpin universal peace and as a fundamental principle underpinning establishment of the ILO.[28] Item three of the General Principles for regulating labour conditions specifies the centrality of a decent wage: "The payment to the employed of a wage adequate to maintain a reasonable standard of life as this is understood in their time and country".[29]

Initially, the ILO was concerned with fixing a minimum living wage through the Minimum Wage-Fixing Machinery Convention No. 26 (1928), which China has ratified. Later, it turned to establishing standards to establish wage payment practices which ensured that workers were paid directly, at regular intervals, without unjustified or arbitrary deductions, restrictions or bonds, in a currency that could be freely spent, and that wages received reasonable protection in corporate winding-up and insolvency proceedings (primarily set out in the Wage Protection Convention No. 95 and Recommendation No. 85).[30]

China has ratified the Minimum Wage-Fixing Machinery Convention (No. 26) and the Equal Remuneration Convention (No. 100), but not the

---

27 The 91st International Labour Conference, General Survey of the Reports Concerning the Protection of Wages Convention (No. 95) and the Protection of Wages Recommendation (No. 85), 1949. 1 (Geneva: International Labour Organization, 2003).

28 Treaty of Versailles, 28 June 1919 (entered into force 10 January 1920) Pt XIII.

29 Ibid., Article 427.

30 Other relevant wage-related conventions include: Equal Remuneration Convention (1951) No. 100 (ratified 1990); Minimum Wage Fixing Machinery (Agriculture) Convention, 1951 (No. 99) (not ratified); Minimum Wage Fixing Convention, 1970 (No. 131) (not ratified); Labour Clauses (Public Contracts) Convention, 1949 (No. 94) (not ratified); Protection of Workers' Claims (Employer's Insolvency) Convention, 1992 (No. 173) (not ratified); Contracts of Employment (Indigenous Workers) Convention, 1939 (No. 64) (not ratified); Social Policy (Non-Metropolitan Territories) Convention, 1947 (No. 82) (not ratified); Migration for Employment Convention (Revised), 1949 (No. 97) (not ratified); Plantations Convention, 1958 (No. 110) (not ratified); Social Policy (Basic Aims and Standards) Convention, 1962 (No. 117) (not ratified); 91st International Labour Conference (note 27 above) at 5.

other main wages conventions including the Wage Protection Convention No. 95. Despite not having ratified the Wage Protection Convention (No. 95), from the mid-1990s reforms made to Chinese wages legislation have brought Chinese regulation of wages closer to the provisions of these ILO wages conventions.[31] However, as the discussion below demonstrates, a substantial number of workers are excluded from the scope of these substantive protections. The analysis below of legal regulation of wages is organized to reflect the main provisions in the Minimum Wage-Fixing Machinery Convention and the Wage Protection Convention.[32] These include: minimum wage; period for payment of wages; non-discrimination principles and equal pay for equal work; prohibition of unlawful and inappropriate deductions from wages; priority to payment of employees' wages and other entitlements in corporate insolvency proceedings; and sanctions for failure to pay on time or in full.[33]

B. Minimum Wage Regulation

China recognized the Minimum Wage-Fixing Machinery Convention (No. 26) in 1984[34] but did not put legal provisions in place until 1993 and 1994.[35] It was not until passage of the Minimum Wage Regulations in 2003 (with effect from 1 January 2004, the "2004 Regulations") that the minimum wage system was fully implemented nationwide.[36] The 2004 Regulations expanded coverage of the minimum wage provisions to all wage earners within Chinese territory and expanded modes of calculation to include wages calculated on an hourly as well as monthly basis (articles 2, 5). The Labour Contract Law provides that the minimum wage acts as the base line for payment of workers on probation (article 20), temporary agency workers (article 58), and part-time or casual workers (article 72). The law now specifies punishments for employers found by the local

---

31 Cooney, Biddulph and Zhu (note 7 above) at 105.

32 The 91st International Labour Conference (note 27 above) at 8.

33 Liulu Zhang, "Study on Protection of Wages on Insolvency in Shanghai" (2010) 4:5 J China Executive Leadership Academy Pudong 73.

34 Yong Xie and Liyan Wang, "China's Minimum Wage: Development, Structure and Standard"(2015) 181:6 Research on Development 144.

35 In 1993 the Ministry of Labour (now the Ministry of Human Resources and Social Security, MoHRSS) passed the Enterprise Minimum Wage Regulations. The 1994 Labour Law also included a single provision on establishment of a minimum wage system: article 48.

36 Yang Du and Weiguang Pan, "Minimum Wage Regulation in China and Its Applications to Migrant Workers in the Urban Labor Market" (2009) 17:2 China & World Economy 79 at 80.

labour administration to be paying below the minimum wage of an order to make up the shortfall and/or a penalty of between 50 and 100 percent of the shortfall (article 85).

The 2004 Regulations specify that the minimum wage be adjusted at least every two years and be between 40 and 60 percent of the average monthly wage in that area.[37] Since then, the minimum wage has increased considerably across China. Though increases in the minimum wage were temporarily suspended in November 2008 as a result of the Global Financial Crisis,[38] minimum wage adjustments resumed in 2010.[39] During the period of the 12th Five Year Plan (2011–2015) the minimum wage increased significantly in response to the ambitious targets it set for increases of 13 percent on average each year.[40] This policy has not been continued into the 13th Five Year Plan (2016–2020) which merely articulates the need for rational determination of the minimum wage standards (Chapter 22.6) and improving the minimum wage mechanism (Chapter 63.1).

The minimum wage is set at (urban) prefectural city level with reference to the average local wage, productivity, unemployment rate, economic development and minimum living expenses (Labour Law, article 49).[41] As a consequence, rates vary significantly across the country. For example, at the end of 2015, Shenzhen's minimum wage was the highest in China at RMB 2030 per month and an hourly rate of RMB 18.7.[42] The lowest rate of RMB 850 per month was in Yichun, Heilongjiang Province.[43]

Some argue that the minimum wage is currently too high as it fails to take adequate account of wage levels of rural migrant workers and wage

---

[37] Xie and Wang (note 34 above) at 145–6.

[38] Friedman and Lee (note 11 above) at 528; Cooney, Biddulph and Zhu (note 7 above) at 117.

[39] Xie and Wang (note 34 above) at 146. In 2010, 30 regions increased the minimum wage by on average 22.78 percent; in 2012, 24 regions increased the minimum wage by on average 21.6 percent; in 2012, 25 regions increased the minimum wage by on average 20.2 percent; and in 2013, 27 regions increased the minimum wage by on average 17 percent.

[40] Xinhua News, "Key targets of China's 12th five-year plan", *Xinhuanet* (5 March 2011), available at http://news.xinhuanet.com/english2010/china/2011-03/05/c_13762230.htm (accessed 11 January 2017).

[41] Peng Jia, "Employment and Working Hour Effects of Minimum Wage Increase: Evidence from China" (2014) 22:1 China & World Economy 61 at 63; Du and Pan (note 36 above) at 81.

[42] Tangning Li, "28 Regions Raise the Minimum Wage", *Economic Information Daily* 3 (29 December 2015), available at http://news.xinhuanet.com/fortune/2015-12/29/c_128576033.htm (accessed 11 January 2017).

[43] China Labour Bulletin (note 21 above).

rates in the informal sector.[44] But for those for whom the minimum wage provides a floor, such as workers in export-oriented, labour-intensive industries in the Pearl River Delta, the minimum wage rate and policies for its increase matter greatly. Certainly, increases in the minimum wage have pushed up the cost of labour-intensive manufacturing in China (which typically pays workers the minimum wage) to the point that many of these industries have relocated their businesses to lower cost countries such as Vietnam, Cambodia and Bangladesh.[45] But with a doubling of the average wage between 2004 and 2014,[46] the minimum wage has steadily decreased as a proportion of the average wage. In 2004 the minimum wage exceeded 40 percent of the average wage in six provinces (Hebei, Shanxi, Jiangsu, Guangxi, Hubei and Hainan), but by 2013 it did so in none.[47] In 2013, for example, the minimum wage in Shanghai was 21.25 percent of the average wage. In Beijing it was 17.87 percent.[48] Judged against average local consumption, in 2013 the minimum wage exceeded average consumption in only nine (relatively less prosperous) provinces and fell far short of that in the more economically developed areas such as Beijing, Shanghai, Tianjin, Guangdong, Zhejiang and Chongqing.[49]

IV. WAGE PROTECTION

A. Basic Provisions on Wages: Periodicity, Deductions, Payment Method and Information on Wages

The 1994 Labour Law requires that there be equal pay for equal work (article 46), that wages be paid to the employee monthly in currency (article 50), that there can be no deductions or delays without reason (article 50) and that wages must be paid during legally designated holidays and periods of special leave for marriage and funerals, or legally specified public activities (article 51). However, these provisions were stated as general principles only and, coupled with imperfect implementation, left much space for systematic abuses of wages provisions, including: failure to pay wages, mandatory social insurance payments and overtime; taking bonds or guarantees at the commencement of employment; confiscation

44 Du and Pan (note 36 above) at 85.
45 China Labour Bulletin (note 21 above).
46 Ibid.
47 Du and Pan (note 36 above) at 84.
48 Xie and Wang (note 34 above) at 146.
49 Ibid. at 147.

of identity documents; taking significant deductions from wages for a wide range of reasons; and imposing penalties on employees terminating employment without permission.[50]

The Labour Contract Law was passed in 2007 in an attempt to address many of the problems that had emerged since 1994. One of the priorities of the Labour Contract Law (2007) was to increase incentives to raise the proportion of people employed with formal written contracts. It did so by prescribing penalties of double wages for the period of employment without a written labour contract (article 82). The Labour Contract Law also imposed penalties for failure to pay, or delayed payment of wages (article 85). Article 9 prohibits an employer from withholding identity cards and documentation and taking a bond or guaranty from employees, a practice that had become common in some sectors after the passage of the Labour Law. A fine of between RMB 500 and 2000 may be imposed by the local labour bureau for each breach of this prohibition (article 84). It also made some provision for protection of people employed without a written contract.

The rationale for increasing the proportion of workers with formal written contracts was not only to specify for both parties the specific terms of employment (including remuneration), but also to ensure basic conformity with the mandatory legal terms of the labour relationship, including pay and calculation of overtime, supplements and social security payments. The Labour Contract Law, article 30, for example, requires that wages are paid directly to the worker and that they be paid in full and on time. Overtime must be paid if it is worked (Labour Contract Law, article 31). The Labour Contract Law also restricts the circumstances in which penalties may be levied for breach of contract (article 25), to reimburse special training costs as agreed between the parties (article 25) and for breach of non-competition clauses for senior executives (articles 23, 24).

There is some evidence that since passage of the Labour Contract Law the rate of formal contracting has increased and there have been improvements in compliance with wages provisions for migrant workers, the group worst affected by wage insecurity. A survey in cities in the Pearl River Delta in 2006, 2008 and 2009 found that the proportion of migrant workers with written labour contracts increased after passage of the Labour Contract Law. It also found that workers with written labour contracts were more likely to be in a unionized workplace which paid mandatory social insurance contributions and that these workers suffered wage arrears at a reduced rate. Wage arrears were found to be less

---

[50] Cooney, Biddulph and Zhu (note 7 above) at 60–1.

prevalent in large, foreign or state-owned enterprises and enterprises with a union.[51] Another survey at a similar time and location confirmed these conclusions.[52]

Wage Protection Convention No. 95 requires information to be provided on how wages are calculated (article 14) and maintenance of wage records (article 15(d)). The Labour Law (article 16) and the Labour Contract Law (articles 17, 18) contain only general provisions on the items that are to be included in the labour contract, including a general category of "labour remuneration". Provisions for detailed regulation on the calculation and payment of wages were intended to be included in a separate Wages Law. While this law has been under consideration from the mid-1990s, it has not yet been enacted.[53] To date, only subordinate regulations have been passed in some sectors and in some localities to regulate these aspects of wages.[54]

For example, in 2016 Guangdong released a draft amendment to its Regulations on the Payment of Wages to strengthen regulatory controls on the payment of wages, with a particular focus on the construction industry.[55] It places a number of enforceable obligations on corporations by requiring establishment of a specialist wages account for the payment of wages and requires establishment of the real identity of employees to be paid from this account (article 33). Proof of establishment and payments

---

[51] Richard Freeman and Xiaoying Li, "How Does China's New Labor Contract Law Affect Floating Workers?" (2015) 53:4 British Journal of Industrial Relations 711.

[52] Cheng, Nielsen and Smyth (note 15 above) at 13–14.

[53] Greenfield and Pringle (note 20 above) at 35; Cooney, Biddulph and Zhu (note 7 above) at 72, 106.

[54] An example of sectoral regulation is the 2004 Provisional Measures on the Management of Payment of Wages to Migrant Workers in the Construction Sector (Cooney, Biddulph and Zhu (note 7 above) at 79). Examples of regional regulations include the 2005 Guangdong Province Regulations on the Payment of Wages (discussed in Cooney (note 7 above)); the Shenzhen Regulations on Payment of Employee Wages (2004 as amended in 2009), available at http://www.szhrss.gov.cn/ztfw/qybz/zcfg/201408/t20140804_2540914.htm; the Shanghai Municipal Measures on Enterprise Wages Payment 2003, available at http://www.12333sh.gov.cn/201412333/xxgk/flfg/gfxwj/ldbc/gzzl/201405/t20140506_1182111.shtml, and the Beijing Municipal Regulations on Wages Payment (2003 as amended in 2009), available at http://zhengwu.beijing.gov.cn/fggz/zfgz/t890715.htm. All websites accessed 11 January 2017.

[55] Legislative Affairs Office of the Guangdong Provincial People's Government, "Decision to Amend Regulations on the Payment of Wages" (3 November 2015), available at http://www.fzb.gd.gov.cn/publicfiles/business/htmlfiles/gdsfzb/lfyjzj/201511/13044.html (accessed 11 January 2017).

into a wages account are specified as an item required in the examination and approval of construction projects. These draft regulations strengthen the penalties that may be imposed on employers who delay or fail to pay wages by imposing a penalty of between 50 and 100 percent of the outstanding wages when payment is delayed by more than 15 days. Fines of up to RMB 200 000 may be imposed where there are repeated or large scale delinquencies in wage payments (article 10). They also provide for circumstances where the owner of the property (where construction is taking place) will be made directly liable to meet wage payment obligations if the property owner has failed to make payments to the construction contractor in accordance with the agreement between them.

In addition to some regulatory reform of wage payment systems, there has been an escalation in punitive responses for serious breaches of wage payment obligations. In 2011 the Criminal Law was amended to add the criminal offence of maliciously failing to pay wages. Article 276A provides for a term of up to three years' fixed-term imprisonment, criminal detention and/or a fine for refusing to pay a "relatively large amount" of labour remuneration. Where the consequences are serious, punishment of between three and seven years' imprisonment and a fine may be imposed.

While no data on the number of prosecutions and convictions is available prior to 2014, a flurry of activity in 2014 indicates that criminal prosecutions are now being used to name, shame and punish recalcitrant employers. The Supreme People's Court (SPC) Work Report stated that in 2014 there had been 753 convictions for this offence. On 23 December 2014, the SPC, Supreme People's Procuratorate (SPP), Ministry of Public Security (MPS) and Ministry of Human Resources and Social Security (MoHRSS) issued a notice calling for tougher handling of this crime in the Notice on Strengthening Coordinated Investigation of the Crime of Refusing to Pay Wages. Shortly after this notice was issued, the MoHRSS released details of cases where convicted employers had been imprisoned for periods of between 6 and 21 months and/or fined up to RMB 200 000.

B. Wage Protection for People Employed in Non-standard Forms of Employment: Agency Workers and the Principle of Equal Pay for Equal Work

In China, as everywhere, employment in non-standard forms of employment has expanded dramatically.[56] As China's market reforms have

[56] The ILO has defined this category to include: (1) temporary; (2) temporary agency work and other contractual arrangements involving multiple parties; (3)

deepened and with resultant pluralization of economic activity and work, there has been an explosion in the number of people employed as temporary agency workers, on a part-time and casual basis, project based, or on vocational internships. The premise of the regulatory regime adopted in the 1994 Labour Law was a model of regular, full-time work in a fixed workplace (based on a model of state-owned or foreign investment manufacturing enterprise).[57] Although the labour market had transformed dramatically by 2007, the Labour Contract Law continued to imagine a standard worker in those terms. While the Labour Contract Law makes provision in respect of the pay of casual or part-time workers who are employed on an hourly basis (Chapter 5, section 3)[58] and probationary workers (article 20),[59] these categories of worker do not receive the same protections as regular workers with fixed-term or open-ended contracts.[60] The Labour Contract Law did, however, include special provisions on one of the most prevalent forms of non-standard forms of employment: temporary agency work (also known as labour hire or dispatch workers: *laowu paiqian*). Agency workers are commonly employed alongside regular workers and perform identical tasks, but are often (though not inevitably) paid significantly less.[61]

The Labour Contract Law sought to address systemic abuse of agency workers, a form of employment that had previously been unregulated, by setting a range of restrictive conditions on the employment of agency workers (including wages) and establishment of labour hire companies.[62]

---

ambiguous employment relationships; and (4) part-time employment. It excludes independent, self-employed workers. International Labour Office, *Conditions of Work and Equality Department 2015. Non-standard forms of employment: Report for discussion at the Meeting of Experts on Non-Standard forms of Employment* (Geneva: International Labour Office, 2015) 1–2.

57 Cooney, Biddulph and Zhu (note 7 above) at 58.

58 Labour Contract Law, article 68 provides that a part-time worker is one employed for no more than four hours per day and 24 hours per week. They may be terminated at will without compensation.

59 During the probation period probationary workers must be paid not lower than the lowest wage for the same position or 80 percent of the wage specified in the labour contract, and not lower than the minimum wage (Labour Contract Law, article 20)

60 See the discussion of the "hierarchy of protection" in Cooney, Biddulph and Zhu (note 7 above) at 96–9.

61 Wenzhuo Peng, "Why it is so difficult to fundamentally deal with the abuse of temporary agency workers", *Workers Daily* (5 January 2016), available at http://media.workercn.cn/sites/media/grrb/2016_01/05/GR0502.htm (accessed 11 January 2017).

62 The minimum registered capital requirements for labour hire companies was set at RMB 500000 (Labour Contract Law, article 57).

It requires agency workers be paid the same as regular employees for the same work and that they be informed of the work they are to perform, as well as their pay and conditions (article 62). When a person employed by a labour hire company is not dispatched, the law requires they be paid not less than the minimum wage (article 58). Both the labour hire company (the employer) and end-user enterprise are prohibited from collecting fees from agency workers and from making deductions from their wages (article 60).

However, perversely, including specific regulation about these categories of worker in the law created incentives to expand these categories of non-standard employment throughout the entire labour market. An ILO report in 2015 stated that in 2011, 60 million (20 percent) of the urban workforce were temporary agency workers, compared to 27 million in 2007 (International Labour Office 2015, 13).[63] This expansion led to further rounds of regulation (2012 amendments to the Labour Contract Law and the 2014 MoHRSS Interim Provisions on Labour Hire) to strengthen restrictions on the use of agency workers and to reiterate the requirement of equal pay for equal work (Labour Contract Law, article 63). After some prevarication, the Interim Regulations on Labour Hire ultimately specified that the non-discrimination principle applies not only to wages but also to welfare and social security payments (article 9).[64]

However, these legislative reforms remain largely unsuccessful in changing practice. Restrictive provisions on labour hire arrangements continue to be subverted in a range of ways, such as through fake outsourcing to hide the number of agency workers actually employed.[65] In other areas of non-standard work, such as vocational internships, similar abusive practices are also common.[66] The legal promise of equal pay for equal work is also far from being realized.[67]

---

63 ILO (note 56 above) 13.

64 A September 2013 draft of the interim provisions provided that the protection of equal pay did not extend to welfare and social security payments: see http://www.scio.gov.cn/zhzc/8/4/document/1345141/1345141.htm (accessed 11 January 2017). Draft available at http://www.mohrss.gov.cn/SYrlzyhshbzb/zxhd/SYzhengqiuyijian/201308/t20130807_109508.htm (accessed 11 January 2017). The January 2014 Regulations, article 9 provided otherwise.

65 Peng (note 61 above).

66 Earl Jr Brown and Kyle deCant, "Exploiting Chinese Interns as Unprotected Industrial Labor" (2014)15:2 Asia PacL & Pol'y J 149.

67 Wenming Yang, "The new regulations on labour hire have been in force for four months: equal pay for equal work has encountered difficulties", *People's Daily* (15 July 2014), available at http://finance.sina.com.cn/china/20140715/045719702786.shtml (accessed 11 January 2017).

C. Preferential Payment of Wages in Employer Insolvency

Workers' wages and entitlements rank behind secured creditors and costs of insolvency administration and before tax and other unsecured creditors in the liquidation of an insolvent company (Enterprise Insolvency Law, articles 82 and 113). But the legally prescribed priority given to wages upon insolvency is undermined by the limited number of insolvent companies being dealt with through formal legal processes. Despite the dramatic increase in the number of enterprises established, since the Enterprise Insolvency Law came into effect in 2007 the number of insolvency cases accepted by the courts has declined from 4755 in 2006 to only 2100 in 2012.[68] Stigma attached to insolvency and concerns about the implications for social stability from non-payment of wages have combined to suppress the number of enterprises going through formal insolvency and reorganization proceedings. Courts also use a range of excuses to refuse to accept insolvency applications.[69] Therefore, many insolvent companies are either reorganized administratively, outside the legally prescribed priorities, or remain inactive as so-called "zombie companies". Many lack faith in judicial mechanisms to ensure payment of wages in insolvency proceedings and instead propose transferring this responsibility to local governments.[70]

D. Wage Guarantee Funds

Wage guarantee funds are another administrative mechanism to enable recovery of wage arrears both within and beyond the confines of insolvency proceedings. Wage guarantee funds are established in a limited number of sectors and localities, with no nationwide wage guarantee mechanism in existence. Each of these wage guarantee mechanisms limits both eligibility and the amount of wage arrears that can be paid from the fund. In the construction industry, where the problem of wage arrears has been particularly enduring and acute, in 2006 the State Council passed the Several Opinions on Resolving the Problems of Migrant Workers mandating nationwide establishment of a wages payment supervision and control

---

[68] Jian Ma, "An Analysis of the Statistics on Insolvency Cases Handled by the People's Courts 2003–12 (2003–2012)" (2014) 3 Legal Information 23.

[69] Shengfeng Xu and Sheng Zhang, "Empirical Analysis of the Inadequacies in Effectively Applying Bankruptcy Proceedings and Countermeasures" (2015) 1:400 L System & Economy 16 at 16, 18.

[70] Ibid. at 20.

system and establishment of a wages guarantee mechanism.[71] Cities and provinces with wage guarantee funds include Shenzhen, Shanghai, Zhejiang, Jiangsu and Hubei.[72] Two of the earliest and most developed are Shenzhen and Shanghai. As they are similar (but not identical) in scope and operation, the Shenzhen model (the first established and most recently revised) is examined in detail below.

The first wage guarantee fund was established in Shenzhen in 1996 under the Shenzhen Special Economic Zone Enterprise Wages Guarantee Rules.[73] These provisions were revised in 2008 (as the Shenzhen Special Economic Zone Enterprise Wage Protection Rules) ("Shenzhen Rules") and were interpreted in 2014 by the Shenzhen Special Economic Zone Detailed Implementing Provisions for the Enterprise Wages Protection Rules ("Detailed Implementing Provisions"). The wage guarantee fund is a dedicated fund administered by the Shenzhen Wages Guarantee Fund Committee, which is responsible for overseeing the collection and payment of monies into the fund. Funds are raised by an annual levy on employers (RMB 400 per annum) and payments from government subsidies as well as donations. Each year amounts are appropriated to the local Department of Human Resources and Social Security, which is responsible for making payments to workers in respect of unpaid wages. Employers covered by the fund include enterprise and non-enterprise employers and economic entities including social organizations, but exclude the self-employed (Shenzhen Rules, article 3), state-owned enterprises and government bodies (Detailed Implementing Provisions, article 2).

Workers with wage arrears may apply for payment from the fund where a court has accepted an insolvency application in respect of the employing unit, or where the legal representative or senior management of the employing unit has disappeared or absconded (Shenzhen Rules, article 14). Hence, the scope of eligibility to apply for payment from the fund extends beyond formal insolvency proceedings to include the not-uncommon circumstance where the management shut the door and disappear. Workers who have unpaid wages may receive payments from the fund for up to a total of six months of wage arrears and up to a maximum of 60 percent of the previous year's average wage. Where it is not possible to determine the amount of unpaid wages, the minimum wage is to be paid (Shenzhen Rules, articles 20, 33). The Shenzhen fund thus is available

---

71 Ibid.

72 Xianri Zhou, "A Comparative Study on the Wage Protection Fund System in Shenzhen and Shanghai" (2011) 1 JCUPL 64.

73 Ibid.

to meet only a portion of unpaid wages. It applies only to workers in a "labour relationship", which, as discussed in more detail below, operates to exclude a wide range of workers.[74]

Despite the comparatively limited scope of workers eligible to apply for payments from the wage guarantee fund, continuing high demand reveals the extent of wage arrears. In Shanghai, for example, in 2005 the Labour Inspectorate investigated and discovered 4000 enterprises in breach of their wage payment obligations and made payments from the fund of RMB 490 million to 600 000 workers. In 2007 it found 4100 enterprises in breach owing RMB 540 million to 750 000 workers.[75] These figures rose again in 2008, due to the impact of the Global Financial Crisis.[76] The report identified enterprises in breach of wages regulations as being concentrated in labour-intensive industries such as manufacturing, wholesale and retail trade, hotel, catering and hospitality sectors. Employers in these sectors also overwhelmingly evaded making payment into labour and social insurance funds.[77]

V. WHO IS COVERED BY THE WAGES PROVISIONS?

The question concerning who is covered by the wages provisions is of critical importance, as it determines how many and what types of workers in China are covered by the legal provisions for wage protection and the minimum wage. Chinese law draws a distinction between a labour relationship (*laodong guanxi*) where a person is employed by an employing unit under a labour contract (Labour Law, article 2) and a labour service relationship (*laowu guanxi*). The Labour Law regime and its wage protection mechanisms do not apply to the labour service relationship, which is treated as an ordinary commercial agreement regulated by the civil law. Minimum wage provisions and wage guarantee funds cover those in a "labour relationship", but not those in a civil employment relationship. Two issues are relevant in drawing the distinction: the formal manner in which a labour relationship is established and the substantive categories

---

[74] Workers are defined in the Shenzhen Rules as those who are in an "employment relationship". The Labour Contract Law provides that a labour relationship is established by conclusion of a written labour contract (article10) which the law contemplates is from the date of employment (article 7).

[75] Zhou (note 72 above).

[76] Ibid. at 75.

[77] Ibid. at 74.

of people who are considered to be in a labour service relationship. Both are addressed in turn.

The primary mechanism for establishing a labour relationship is by means of a written labour contract (Labour Law, article 16; Labour Contract Law, article 10). The Labour Contract Law provides the primary documentation necessary both to establish and to prove the existence and contents of a labour relationship (including pay, at article 17). Several problems have arisen because of this reliance on formal written contracts. One is that the rate at which enterprises entered into written contracts, particularly in the private sector, was historically very low. Migrant workers have borne the brunt of working in the informal workforce without a labour contract. Many are employed by individuals who do not have the necessary legal status (as an "employing unit" in Labour Law, article 2) to employ workers under a labour contract. In 2002 a survey of five large and five small cities found that 62 percent of permanent urban residents and 13 percent of migrant workers had written labour contracts. In the private sector, that fell to 27 and 7 percent respectively.[78] As a result, many workers without written contracts have difficulty proving that they are employed in a labour relationship (Halegua 2008) and so may be denied access to legal protections that flow from that status. As discussed above, while problems still exist, increasing the rate of formal contracting was particularly targeted in the Labour Contract Law and has been a focus of enforcement activity since then.

As independent contractors, agricultural workers, domestic workers, civil servants (unless employed under a labour contract) and armed forces personnel are not legally considered to be engaged in labour within the meaning of Labour Law, article 2; they are excluded from the scope of labour laws. A particularly controversial exclusion is certain classes of construction workers. In many cases the subcontracting arrangement is either illegal or the subcontractor is an individual (and so lacks the legal status to employ workers under a labour contract). Initially MoHRSS issued an interpretation, Notice on Matters Relating to Establishment of Labour Relations 2005, which at article 4 imposed the responsibilities of an "employing unit" on the employer in these types of construction employment relationships. However, this interpretation was specifically rejected by the Supreme People's Court in its Summary of the National Meeting on Civil Trials in 2011 at article 59. That exclusion does not extend to liability for workplace injury, where the provisions of Labour

---

[78] Park and Cai (note 17 above) at 28.

Contract Law, article 94 would apply to impose liability on both the illegal subcontractor and the head contractor.[79]

Another excluded category is retirees. In China, women retire at 50 years old and men at 60. It is not uncommon for many of those people to retire, apply for their retirement pension and be re-employed by the same employer as an independent contractor. The Labour Contract Law, article 44 explicitly excludes this category of person from the scope of labour law by providing that a labour relationship will be terminated inter alia if a person has commenced receiving pension entitlements. Workplaces are thus under no obligation to make contributions to social security funds, to provide paid leave and other entitlements. An increasing number of people are employed in this manner, particularly women. In some cities such as Shanghai (with an ageing population and one million people retiring each year) trials to push back the retirement age have not been very successful, mainly because it is less costly for employers to re-employ workers as independent contractors.[80]

VI. LAW ENFORCEMENT: AVAILABILITY OF A REMEDY

Lack of detailed provisions, gaps and exclusions in the law contribute substantially to problems of wage insecurity, but a much greater problem has been the failure to enforce legal provisions vigorously, or at all.[81] Systemic failures in law and enforcement are implicated in the massive and ongoing problems of wage insecurity.[82]

A. State-led Enforcement Model

In relation to wages, the local labour administration has responsibility to supervise and enforce provisions of the Labour Contract Law in respect of the labour contracting system (article 74), including entering into written labour contracts (articles 81 and 82), probationary periods (article

[79] Many thanks to Li Kungang and Shen Tongxian for their insights on this issue.

[80] Wenting Zhou, "Delayed-retirement plan has trouble finding takers", *China Daily Europe* (10 February 2014).

[81] Gallagher and Dong (note 10 above); Cooney, Biddulph and Zhu (note 7 above) at 144.

[82] Gallagher and Dong (note 10 above); Cooney, Biddulph and Zhu (note 7 above).

83), compliance with labour remuneration, overtime, penalty rates and minimum wage prescriptions (article 85), the prohibition on taking bonds and guarantees (article 84) and breaches of labour hire provisions (article 92). It is empowered to order rectification of breaches and to impose fines in respect of those breaches. It is also responsible for administering local wage guarantee funds. The labour administration thus bears significant supervision and enforcement responsibilities. However, the labour administration itself suffers from being under-staffed and has many disincentives to enforce the law vigorously.[83]

To overcome weak enforcement by state agencies, there has been heavy reliance on periodic enforcement campaigns. Campaigns have the advantage of overcoming administrative silos and providing the incentives necessary to ensure a concerted and more punitive approach to enforcement in targeted areas. Campaigns involve a period of centrally coordinated enforcement by relevant agencies including the labour administration, local government, courts, police and unions and Party organs such as the Political-legal Committee, and Party Stability Preservation Offices, setting of enforcement targets and imposition of harsh punishment on offenders.[84] In the construction industry, where the problem of wage arrears is endemic, an annual campaign is waged shortly before the Lunar New Year holiday. This is a period of heightened political sensitivity as it is a time when the massive numbers of migrant workers who are away from their homes seek to return home (with gifts) and when all sectors, including labour, transport, public security, civil administration and trade unions, are on full alert to ensure that this movement of people takes place as smoothly as possible. It is also a time of year when construction workers expect to be paid for the previous year's work. Failure to pay wages around this time is a much more significant omission than at other times of the year. It is no coincidence that there is a noticeable rise in strikes in the period immediately before Lunar New Year, most of which are in the construction industry and relate to wage arrears.[85]

But involvement of state and Party agencies as well as unions in coordinated enforcement has blurred the line between law and policy and between legal enforcement and extra-legal enforcement (neither legal nor illegal) measures. The fact that an annual campaign is required evidences

---

83 Ho (note 7 above).

84 Sarah Biddulph, Sean Cooney and Ying Zhu, "Rule of Law with Chinese Characteristics: the Role of Campaigns in Lawmaking" (2012) 34:4 Law & Pol'y 373.

85 China Labour Bulletin (note 21 above).

a fundamental failure of the regulatory system to resolve migrant workers' wage payment problems. More importantly, it normalizes the need to adopt special, concerted measures as a regular part of governance.

B. Private Enforcement

Although the model of law enforcement is primarily state-led, legislative reforms have lowered some of the barriers to private enforcement. Where a legal right is infringed, a worker may either approach the labour administration to seek redress, or commence dispute-resolution procedures in respect of that breach her or himself (Labour Contract Law, article 77). For breach of contract or infringement of a legal right, institutionalized channels of dispute resolution are mediation, labour arbitration and litigation. While retaining this basic structure of dispute resolution, the Labour Disputes Mediation and Arbitration Law (LDMA) did lower some barriers to private enforcement of rights. A worker is now given a choice of mediation in either the enterprise mediation committee or in a local government mediation committee. The LDMA removes the fee for labour arbitration (article 52) and streamlines resolution of rights disputes through arbitration and litigation.[86] There are also now some circumstances when an employee can bypass labour arbitration and go directly to court. In respect of wages, an employee may approach the court directly if seeking to recover unpaid wages in the form of a simple liquidated debt (article 30).[87] However, expediting wages claims through direct recourse to litigation has not had a significant impact, as it is only available where the amount of the claim is uncontested, and so is seldom available.[88]

While the number of cases dealt with through labour arbitration and litigation has increased, the total number of disputes is very small compared to the size of China's labour market. For example, in 2014 the total number of labour arbitration cases resolved was 1 362 000 (compared to 1 264 000 in 2010). In 2013 the total number of first instance labour litigation cases accepted was 387 000. It is significant to note that there was also a comparatively large (compared to labour litigation cases) number of

---

86 Cooney, Biddulph and Zhu (note 7above) at 109–11.

87 Ibid. at 110–11.

88 Ibid. at 116; Lin Zhang and Jinke Tan, "Reflection on and Perfection of the System of Payment Orders" (2010) 3 Econ Perspectives 74. Civil Procedure Law, article 216 permits the respondent to object to the application. Once an objection is filed, the applicant bears the cost of the application but must then go back to the normal labour dispute procedures of mediation, arbitration and then litigation: ibid. at 75.

first instance labour service relationship disputes in 2013 (the last year for which statistics are publicly available) at 108 000.[89] Part of the problem with private dispute settlement is that arbitration agencies struggled to cope with the dramatic expansion of the number of cases brought after the passage of the LDMA.[90] Another part of the problem is that adjudication has not proven to be an entirely satisfactory way to obtain a final resolution to disputes.[91] Yet another part of the problem is that individual autonomy to exercise legal rights is seen as a useful strategy for the Party-state to pursue when it can be harnessed as a way of alerting the state to social problems requiring its attention, but which is not intended to go too far in decentralizing and privatizing law enforcement.[92]

C. Industrial Relations System

The main channels for enforcing wage protection provisions continue to be state enforcement and, to a lesser extent, private enforcement. Individualization of labour rights through reliance on individual labour contracts has systematically undermined the possibilities for strong protection of wages through the exercise of union-led collective power.[93] While unions have played some role in legislative drafting and expanding collective contracting, these activities have had little impact on either the minimum wage or on wage protection.

In terms of negotiating improvements in wages and working conditions, China has established a tripartite system for negotiation and coordination of the interests of state, business and workers and resolution of disputes. China ratified the Tripartite Consultation Convention (No. 144) in November 1990. China established a National Tripartite Consultative Committee in 2001, with one of its primary aims being to reduce industrial instability and labour protest.[94] This committee has a mandate to develop policy and frameworks for industrial relations, labour and social welfare

---

[89] Statistics compiled from the *China Statistical Yearbook* (Beijing: China Statistics Press, 2010–15).

[90] Ibid. at 130.

[91] Hualing Fu and Richard Cullen, "From Mediatory to Adjudicatory Justice: The Limits of Civil Justice Reform in China" in Margaret Woo and Mary Gallagher, eds, *Chinese Justice: Civil Dispute Resolution in Contemporary China* (Cambridge, New York: Cambridge University Press, 2011) 25.

[92] Gallagher (note 12 above) at 89.

[93] Friedman and Lee (note 11 above).

[94] Simon Clarke and Chang-Hee Lee, "The Significance of Tripartite Consultation in China" in Malcolm Warner, ed., *The Future of Chinese Management* (London; Portland: Frank Cass Publishers, 2003) 57 at 69.

policies. However, its capacity to perform any of these functions is limited, both by the preference for using administrative mechanisms to regulate wages and by the weakness of employer and employee representatives. As "mass organizations" in the Leninist political structure, both are primarily responsive to the Party rather than their constituencies – a state corporatist model of organization.[95] The primary role of both the union and the China Enterprise Confederation is to give effect to policies developed by central authorities, rather than to participate in developing labour policies based on inputs from their own constituencies.[96] Attempts to establish independent unions have been crushed decisively. As a result, the form of social, regulatory and policy coordination imagined by the Tripartite Consultation Convention does not take place in China. It certainly does not displace the leadership role of the Party in setting labour market policy, or of government in giving it effect. Even in the area of minimum wage setting, the Committee has no input, as this function is carried out by the labour administrative department.[97]

One area where the union has been particularly active has been in legislative drafting, and it was particularly active in drafting the 2007 Labour Contract Law.[98] Unions have also been active in promoting collective negotiation and expansion of collective contracts throughout the labour market. However, collective negotiation, for the same reasons as tripartite consultation, has struggled to produce significant results in terms of improved wages and conditions.[99] The role of the union in negotiating collective contracts remains far removed from an adversarial model of industrial relations that locates the union firmly on the side of the worker. Without any significant change in the role and capacity of unions in the Chinese polity, the prospects for fundamental change to embrace collective bargaining as a tool of interest representation are remote. In fact, as unions have responsibility for implementing Party programs, they are called into action during enforcement campaigns to cooperate with government and party organs to achieve targeted goals (which may result in suppressing worker claims).

---

[95] Anita Chan, "Revolution or Corporatism: Workers and Trade Unions in Post-Mao China" (1993) 29:1 Austl J Chinese Affairs 31.

[96] Clarke and Lee (note 94 above).

[97] Ibid. at 70.

[98] Gallagher and Dong (note 10 above).

[99] Biddulph (note 8 above).

D. Non-institutionalized Forms of Complaint Making

Despite the gradual increase in the number of labour disputes dealt with through institutionalized dispute-resolution mechanisms (mediation, arbitration and litigation), comparatively these numbers are low. A very high number of complaints are pursued through non-institutionalized channels. Aggrieved workers have incentives to use disruptive protest as a way to progress their claims because of the perception that disruption will get the attention of the local government. Not only do workers bypass formal channels to pursue their grievances; local authorities are also mobilized in these circumstances to fragment and dissipate labour-related protests through negotiation, bargaining and paying off protesters.[100] Local government agencies have both the incentive and the finances to defuse protests extra-legally in order to preserve stability, both through accommodation and repression. The willingness to use extra-legal channels to pursue and dissipate protests both encourages further disruptive behaviour and creates contempt for legal rules and forms.[101] Indeed, the concern for stability also impacts on the handling of cases dealt with through formal dispute-resolution channels. Liebman notes that courts often decide cases "in the shadow of protest" and that this concern can override the strict application of law in adjudication.[102]

VII. CONCLUSION: REGULATORY FORM AND FUNCTION

If we return now to the themes of this book – local performance and its relationship to international standards – we see that a proper appreciation of local performance requires a careful analysis of both the substantive law and institutional structures that shape (and limit) enforcement of the law. This chapter has documented the quite extensive legal reforms

---

100 Su and He (note 8 above); Lee and Zhang (note 8 above).

101 Xi Chen, "China at the Tipping Point? The Rising Cost of Stability" (2013) 24:1 J Democracy 57 at 63; Lee and Zhang (note 8 above); Cooney, Biddulph and Zhu (note 7 above).

102 Benjamin Liebman, "A Return to Populist Legality? Historical Legacies and Legal Reform" in Sebastian Heilmann and Elizabeth Perry, eds, *Mao's Invisible Hand: The Political Foundations of Adaptive Governance in China* (Cambridge; London: Harvard University Asia Centre, 2011) 165; Benjamin Liebman, "Malpractice Mobs: Medical Dispute Resolution in China" (2013) 113 Colum L Rev 181.

designed to improve protections for wages and to implement the minimum wage throughout China. It has shown how law now engages with key elements of the ILO wage protection and minimum wage conventions. But this progress has been tempered by the fragmentation of the workforce, which has excluded a large number of workers from these protections, and fragmentation of the legal regulatory regime, which is marked by the periodic, local and sectoral nature of regulatory devices to improve wage security. The gap between law and practice itself also becomes a feature of local performance because of the disjunction between the promise of the law and the reality of lived experience. Additionally, the ready resort to administrative (in the form of campaigns) and extra-legal mechanisms both to address weaknesses in enforcement and to resolve socially disruptive protests must also be seen as a regular feature of governance, rather than as a response to exceptional circumstances.

The analysis of China's wage protection law and practice in this chapter has sought to move beyond approaches to judging local performance against international law and norms that are based either on an evaluation of domestic law against the international norm or domestic practice against the international norm. As this chapter has demonstrated, the shape of domestic law defines the scope and nature of protections, inclusions and exclusions, and establishes the institutional infrastructure for enforcement. Law and practice are thus inextricably linked. As this chapter has also shown, local performance requires a consideration of the interaction between the legal and the extra-legal, as the increasingly ready resort to extra-legal mechanisms to address the social instability arising from wage insecurity both limits the scope and undermines the legitimacy of legal rules and remedies. All of these factors comprise the domestic environment which constitutes local performance.

How might these domestic approaches to wage protection be influential in international fora? It is well known that China (as with other states) seeks to ensure that substantive issues of political importance to it are reflected in international rules and that it rebuffs those that are not – such as establishing independent unions. But this chapter suggests another area where domestic approaches might prove influential internationally – that is in the role of law in regulating difficult problems. This chapter has canvassed the ready leap to strategies and techniques to resolve (perceived and actual) threats to social order that systematically undermine development of regularized forms of governance, interest negotiation and private dispute resolution in favour of Party-state-led policy formation and dissemination and Party-state centric governance techniques that include legal and extra-legal (neither legal nor illegal) regulatory techniques. In terms of both regulation and dispute resolution, these extra-legal enforcement techniques undermine the legitimacy of the formal legal system.[103] Such an approach encourages development of a particularistic and state-led regulatory style which inevitably poses a challenge to a model of international law imagined as rule-based, with (comparatively) predictable modes of private and public enforcement.

103 Biddulph, Cooney and Zhu (note 84 above).

Index